SOCIOLOGICAL APPROACH TO RELIGION

SOCIOLOGICAL APPROACH TO RELIGION

Louis Schneider

JOHN WILEY & SONS, INC.

NEW YORK · LONDON · SYDNEY · TORONTO

10 9 8 7 6 5 4 3 2 1

Library of Congress Catalogue Card Number: 78-94915

SBN 471 76206 7

Printed in the United States of America

Preface

This short volume is designed to do two things: (1) to give a more comprehensive account of structural-functional analysis of religion than is usual in books of its size devoted to the sociology of religion; and (2) to suggest to the student the importance of historical and comparative materials in the study of the sociology of religion.

Part I (Chapters 1 and 2) introduces the subject and reviews the limitations of an older social-science view of religion (the "intellectualist" view) which, in my opinion, it is still most helpful to understand. Part II (Chapters 3–5) examines structural-functional analysis (also often referred to here as functionalism). The presentation of functionalism is followed by a brief assessment of that approach at the end of Chapter 5. I hope that Part II will be as useful to those who are opposed to functionalism as to those who are sympathetic with it. This part is designed to have a certain completeness of its own but, in a number of significant ways, it is also firmly fixed in the structure of the book. It will be evident that the part draws much upon the work of Talcott Parsons.

Part III (Chapter 6) reviews inquiry about the Protestant ethic, with strong emphasis on historical outlooks. But a great deal of Chapter 6 focuses on the relations of religion and nonreligious sociocultural phenomena—an obviously unavoidable matter in a sociology of religion. Weber's work is made the occasion for the brief setting out of a "dialectical" view of relations between the religious and the nonreligious.

Part III picks up a "thread" that may be found in the references to interchange in Chapter 4. Also Part IV (Chapter 7) picks up a "thread" —in this case, one that may be found in Chapter 5 where, at the end of the section on aspects of change, Merton's distinction of manifest and latent functions is reviewed. The distinction is used to motivate a discussion of instrumentalization in Chapter 7. But this chapter is also designed to present some features of religion as culture, which it is important to discuss and which could not be fitted into the crowded "schedules" of earlier chapters. In fact, the discussion of instrumentalization is afforded only after other material has been set out.

"Religion and society" will of course, have been touched on before the final Part V, which deals with that subject, is reached. But, again, much was inevitably omitted, and Part V is designed to fill some gaps that will still be apparent when that part is reached.

There is much here that is presented in a spirit of tentativeness. Two things, in particular, may be noted in this connection. There are many places in the following pages where I point out that there are uncertainties about various matters. Indeed, I may seem to insist that they exist. This does not result from excessive timidity. It simply results from a conviction that, in the interest of accuracy and the proper conveying of information, it is well to report uncertainty where it prevails. I presume that the reader is mature enough to sustain it. Also the theme that "more work is needed" recurs: it is impossible to avoid it. But, despite much tentativeness in the sociology of religion, there is no need to be extremely modest about it. There is enough substance in the field to warrant its serious consideration by anyone.

I should add that there is virtually nothing here that was influenced by matter appearing after about the middle of 1968.

A very considerable debt is owed to Harry M. Johnson, with whom I do not always agree but who is as stimulating as a sociologist as he is reliable and engaging as a friend. My colleague, Louis Zurcher, was kind enough to read and comment on a portion of the manuscript. Tom Mendina, while performing the offices of a research assistant, made several suggestions that have been incorporated. Barbara Pickett and Josephine Schneider performed heroically in the line of typing.

Louis Schneider

Contents

SOCIOLOGICAL APPROACH TO RELIGION

PART I

The Sociology of Religion and the Limitations of Intellectualism

CHAPTER 1

Religion and the Sociology of Religion

It repeatedly has been observed that men are constrained to ask questions that involve the ultimate meaning of life and living. What is human life, in particular, all about? Does it have any reference to any other realm than the realm of nature? Why are we here for thirty, or forty, or seventy or more years, or less? (This, of course, is to be understood in a "metaphysical" sense, going beyond the answers that biology or medicine can give.) Why are the poor oppressed and judgment and justice violently perverted in a province, in the language of Ecclesiastes? It has been observed immemorially that the good die young and the wicked prosper. And human efforts to gain a variety of what appear to humans to be highly commendable ends are often apparently senselessly frustrated. There is a powerful and very ancient impulse to find answers to these questions (which many men persistently refuse to regard as "meaningless") and to work out transcendental "compensations" for the circumstances pointed to. The term "religion" is one about which there is dispute, but the "concerns" we point to are nevertheless clearly concerns that fall within the sphere of religion if the term is to be assigned anything but quite arbitrary meaning.

In answer to questions of the kind indicated and in resolution of problems of the kind noted, religions or religious men have postulated the existence of another order than the one we know—a realm "beyond" that of nature. A contemporary student of comparative religion writes of "a fundamental assumption which religion always either implies or definitely affirms" and proceeds to describe this concisely as "the assumption or belief that the world of our ordinary sense-experience is not the whole of reality but that there exists also a super-sense world which is equally real if not the deepest aspect of reality."[1] There have been numerous statements of this sort, attesting the centrality, for religion, of the

[1] August K. Reischauer, *The Nature and Truth of the Great Religions,* Rutland: C. E. Tuttle Co., 1966, p. 2.

idea that the world as we see it is not all of reality but only a part thereof and that this part is not necessarily the most significant. Thus, we may attend also to William James, who writes:

"Religion has meant many things in human history; but when from now onward I use the word I mean to use it in the supernaturalist sense, as declaring that the so-called order of nature, which constitutes this world's experience, is only one portion of the total universe, and that there stretches beyond this visible world an unseen world of which we now know nothing positive, but in its relation to which the true significance of our present mundane life consists. A man's religious faith . . . means for me essentially his faith in the existence of an unseen order of some kind in which the riddles of the natural order may be found explained. In the more developed religions the natural world has always been regarded as the mere scaffolding or vestibule of a truer, more eternal world, and affirmed to be a sphere of education, trial, or redemption."[2]

James asks us to consider the case of a dog being vivisected in a laboratory. The operations performed on the dog are excruciating to the animal and yet they are designed to help alleviate the sufferings of other beasts and of men. The dog has no glimmering of this "redemptive" aspect of the whole painful situation. This aspect has its being in a world unseen by the dog but not unseen by man. "In the dog's life," James writes, "we see the world invisible to him because we live in both worlds," and James suggests that for humans, too, there may exist not only that world which is humanly seen but also a larger world not seen by the human eye.[3]

Other analogies on lines more or less like these have been suggested. The Scottish philosopher, Adam Ferguson, noted that if the human fetus could reason in the womb (without foreknowledge of postfetal existence) it might well anticipate in the separation from the womb nothing but "a total extinction of life." Yet there are features of the fetal organism that appear to have no relation to the actual status of the fetus, which, however (could the fetus but know it), are pointers to a future world still unseen and destined to be useful therein. So too, Ferguson thought, "prognostics of a destination still future may be collected from present appearances in the life and condition of man."[4] Whatever one may think of this argument for immortality by way of analogy, it again suggests

[2] William James, *The Will to Believe*, New York: Dover Publications, 1956, pp. 51–52. Reprinted through permission of the publisher.

[3] *Ibid.*, p. 58.

[4] Adam Ferguson, *Principles of Moral and Political Science*, Edinburgh, 1792, Vol. I, pp. 327–328.

with entire clarity the significance in the total religious phenomenon of the supposition of the reality of the unseen and even of the "higher" reality of the latter.

Perhaps Adam Ferguson and even William James will now seem to many rather naïve. Problems of ultimate meaning and of faith have hardly been settled forever. On the contrary: they are constantly reopening. We live, it has become nearly banal to say, in a time of marked searching for new ultimate meanings. William James's dog under vivisection, for all the compassion it may arouse in us, is one thing. The Nazi slaughter of millions of Jews is another. It is not so easy to believe, let us say, that that slaughter was all part of a divine redemptive plan, in the end "somehow" redounding to the benefit of the Jews and of all mankind. Indeed, there are many, Jews and others, who find such a notion completely, utterly incredible.

But, whether we approve or not, this does not necessarily mean that men will relinquish the idea of a beyond or a sacred realm (apprehension of which is often referred to as apprehension of the ultimate). Nor must it mean that they will give up the associated idea that the beyond will somehow serve to make better sense of that which is not beyond. To say that the phenomenon of Hitler constitutes a "challenge" to theology is to put matters mildly. This does not prevent continued theological wrestling with various problems that the phenomenon presents. Nor, again, does it mean that theologians, any more than other men, will necessarily give up the notion of the beyond or sacred. Some, as is well known, have spoken in terms of "the death of God." It is outside our scope to ascertain the precise position in regard to *transcendence* of the so-called death-of-God theologians, although we observe in passing that a significant core of these theologians do not actually appear to deny a transcendent reality or are at least somewhat ambiguous on the matter.[5] The element of men's presumption of the existence of the beyond or sacred has, in

---

[5] See, for example, Bernard Murchland, ed., *The Meaning of the Death of God,* New York: Vintage Books, 1967; Harvey Cox, *The Secular City,* New York: Macmillan, 1965, pp. 260–261; Gabriel Vahanian, *The Death of God,* New York: George Braziller, 1961, p. 231. In the volume edited by Murchland, an interesting critical essay by John W. Montgomery affords a description of the work of five death-of-God theologians, in which Vahanian and Cox are represented as relatively conservative death-of-God thinkers or "theothanatologists," while Thomas Altizer, William Hamilton, and Paul van Buren are taken as more extreme. Murchland, *op. cit., pp.* 25–69. The word *transcendence* is used at this particular juncture to suggest a view of the sacred as outside the world, in contrast with an immanentist view, for which the sacred pervades the world. This contrast is not explored here, nor is the vocabulary of our text specially accommodated to it, but it certainly deserves mention.

any case, been so central in what has usually been called religion that we take it as indispensable for any definition or specification of the phenomenon itself.

The realm beyond the natural, beyond appearance, apprehension of which is an apprehension of the ultimate—for brevity, let us now refer to it as the sacred realm or simply the sacred—serves men to make sense of the important values and goals of a society, especially where these seem to work hardship and pain. (Of course, it may come to lose the ability to do this. And it can also work to challenge existing moral codes. Religious legitimation of values such as justice, mercy, and love is compatible with powerful challenge to a society that seems to the religious to realize these values but inadequately.) The sacred has power imputed to it, as in the sense of the phrase, "the power of the living God." The religious attitude toward the sacred is one of awe or near to awe. Religion involves practice as well as belief. It is shot through with symbolism.[6] It is "carried" by men who have some feeling that, in virtue of their participation in the belief-practice scheme it involves, they are members of a distinctive group or community. (Which is not to assert anything so foolish as the view that there cannot be "conflict" in and about religion. Also, it should be observed that private religious emotions interest the sociologist insofar as they have social effects.)

An apprehension of a sacred imbued with power, a conceiving of the sacred in such a way that it makes human life and values meaningful, beliefs and practices relating man to the sacred—to these "bare bones" we may add mediation of the sacred through symbols and the feeling of belonging to a distinctive group on the part of those sharing the beliefs and practices, to give us the elements of a rough definition. In the presence of the elements indicated, then, we have "religion." We shall see in Chapter 3 that the feeling of belonging certainly need not make us exaggerate the services of religion in "integrating" men. Association *about* the sacred need not be confined to a formal church.[7]

The components of the view and definition of religion presented have been suggested by a variety of sources and, especially, by Durkheim, Weber, and Talcott Parsons among sociologists.[8] But if there are distin-

[6] Belief and practice and symbol will concern us in the next chapter.

[7] I leave open the possibility that various phenomena not ordinarily regarded as "religious" might profitably be taken to be such. See below, Ch. 3. This is one reason why the above specification of what religion is should be regarded as somewhat tentative, even if one must insist on the indispensability of the apprehension of the sacred. Further knowledge uncovering the religious character of the only *ostensibly* nonreligious might help the task of definition greatly.

[8] See the statement afforded by Parsons on religious perspectives in sociology and social psychology, in Hoxie N. Fairchild, *Religious Perspectives in College*

guished precedents for the kind of definition that has been proposed, no excessive claims need be made for it. A great deal remains to be learned about the phenomenon itself. Max Weber's very first words in his general sociological analysis of religion were these: "To define 'religion,' to say what it *is,* is not possible at the start of a presentation such as this. Definition can be attempted, if at all, only at the conclusion of the study."[9] It is reasonable to think that a really shrewd, penetrating definition of something would come after much is known about it, although some kind of at least implicit notion of what it consists of is present from the "beginning."

Without doubt, there are very striking variations among so-called religions—and this has caused misgivings about the general term among a number of conscientious students. A distinction often encountered in one form or another essentially contrasts Eastern religions of "eternal world law" (for which the world is indeed eternal or at least without any clear beginning or end, although it is subject to renewal and decay) with Western religions of "historical revelation of God" (for which the world was created at a definite time—and will end definitely—and according to a definite plan of a personal god entirely separate from that world and who also rules it.)[10] Much the same distinction is made by the editor of a recent "concise encyclopedia of living faiths," who sets off "Indian" and "Judaic" religious conceptions, understanding these terms broadly to cover, respectively, such religions as Hinduism, Buddhism, and Jainism, on the one hand, and Judaism, Christianity and Islam on the other. It is noted, for example, that "both Jainism and Buddhism are originally atheistical creeds," and that the tradition within which these religions occur involves unreserved belief in reincarnation, which is regarded as a misfortune, an evil thing. "Human life is not God's greatest gift to man," but "a curse which inheres in the very nature of things." There is even a current in the Indian tradition that would identify the soul with the godhead (quite blasphemously, from a "Western" point of view) and claim that the whole phenomenal world is an illusion. Zaehner suggests that the difference between the two types may perhaps best be stated by saying that the "Western" type "starts with God and his dealings with man here and now," while the other type "starts with the human soul

---

Teaching, New York: Ronald Press, 1952, pp. 286–337. Cf. also Thomas F. O'Dea, *The Sociology of Religion,* New York: Prentice-Hall, 1966. Parsons and O'Dea both rely on classic works by Durkheim and Weber (among others) that will be refered to in due course.

[9] *The Sociology of Religion,* Boston: The Beacon Press, 1963, p. 1.

[10] Helmuth von Glasenapp, *Die Fünf Weltreligionen,* Düsseldorf/Köln: E. Diederichs, 1963, pp. 9–10.

and the manner in which its release *from* this world may be achieved," that the deliverance from "the bond that links spirit with matter" may be effected.[11] Zaehner admits that he casts his contrast in terms of "extreme forms of the two types of religions." The contrast remains.

We can obviously go further. Not only do sets or groups of religions, such as those of "Indian" and those of "Judaic" provenance, differ from one another, but individual religions even within the same general tradition may be said (depending on our perspective) to be notably different from one another. Judaism, Christianity, and Islam do agree on many important things, yet also disagree on a number of likewise important ones, including the way in which they respectively perceive the figure of Christ. And again obviously one can push on. A religion that is, for good reasons and purposes, taken as a single or unitary one may, for other good reasons and purposes, be taken as internally variant. Common usage considers Protestantism and Catholicism as forms of the same religion, but there are certainly differences between the two. The term Protestant itself is applied to scores of groups that show appreciable differences from one another and also appear to be appreciably removed in a variety of respects from "historic" Protestantism, as that is represented in such traditions as those of Luther and Calvin.

The most elementary acquaintance with Islam shows much diversity within it. Perhaps the broad division best known to outsiders is that between the orthodox Sunnites, who allow the validity of the succession to Mohammed of his first four actual successors, and the disagreeing Shi'ites who allow the validity only of the fourth successor among these, namely, Ali, who married Mohammed's daughter Fatima. For the Shi'ites there is a very special feeling about the holy family of Mohammed, Ali, Fatima, and Mohammed's two grandsons, Hassan and Hussein, a family that has been the object of peculiar and widespread veneration in Persia, for example, since early in the sixteenth century. But the Sunnite-Shi'ite split is only the beginning of divisions within Islam.[12]

The world of Buddhism is inordinately complex and exhibits a great range of doctrine and attitude. Numbers of intelligent and sensitive Westerners have long found in it much that strikes them as sublime. But Buddhism also constantly exhibits infusions of elements that, by most definitions, hardly could be called sublime. It is true that a religiously inspired

[11] R. C. Zaehner (Ed.), *The Concise Encyclopedia of Living Faiths,* Boston: Beacon Press, 1967, p. 18.

[12] For this basic split and further developments within the Shi'ite fold in particular, see Dwight M. Donaldson, *The Shi'ite Religion,* London: Luzac, 1933 (pp. xxvi and 357–369 for concise indications of divisions among the Shi'ites) and John N. Hollister, *The Shi'a of India,* London: Luzac and Co., 1953. See also Ignaz Goldziher, *Vorlesungen über den Islam,* Heidelberg: Carl Winter Universitätsverlag, 1963, Ch. 5.

poet such as Tagore can represent a Buddhist ascetic as saying to a radiant dancing girl who invites him to her home that the time is not ripe for him to come to her; while the same ascetic comforts the same girl when her health and beauty are dissolved in the sickness of plague and indicates that it is now time to visit her. But it is also true that in some Buddhist temples there exists the practice of tying a piece of cloth (with "proper" markings) more or less tautly over four sticks, while passers-by pour water on the cloth until it tears—and with the tearing a woman who died in childbirth is supposedly "torn" from her bondage, released from a condition of eternal damnation. If Buddhism retains indications of once having been a religion for aristocrats, its full range also exhibits a great deal that appeals to the masses.

Why should all this raise any particular difficulty? We can, indeed, allow for types or subdivisions, just as the biologist, for example, does in his taxonomies. Insects are none the less insects if some are lepidoptera, some hymenoptera, and others still belong to other orders. Or we may say that stars differ from one another while astronomers still find that they have certain significant things in common. Why should not the situation be much the same with respect to religion? Our difficulties here undoubtedly result partly from the uncertainty and vagueness of our purposes in the field of religion. At a sufficiently abstract level, we can always find *some* "things in common" among the most various "religions." But then there will be students who have the feeling that certain differences are far more important than resemblances, even if they cannot be quite sure why the differences actually seem so important. When we know more, our classifications and definitions become better. Our goals or scientific purposes also become clearer with increased knowledge. Indeed, knowledge, definition-classification, and purpose in defining or classifying interact. Considerable divergences of view among competent students are inevitable, and a number of significant issues cannot be settled now and perhaps will not be settled for a long time. I have already indicated that the differences among and within religions have prompted misgivings about the very word "religion." The editor of a recent volume, designed as a reading guide to the great religions, comments that it is apparently "impossible to abstract from the finished volume a clear and satisfying definition that covers all the traditions dealt with."[13] This view has been suggested by Wilfred C. Smith, a learned student of religion in general

---

[13] Charles J. Adams (ed.), *A Reader's Guide to the Great Religions,* New York: The Free Press, 1965, p. xiii. Adams, in his own contribution to the guide, on Islam, indicates or rather reiterates his sympathy for the view that "the concept 'religion' is inadequate and no longer useful." *Ibid.,* p. 289. (The guide covers primitive religion, non-Buddhist Chinese religion, Hinduism, Buddhism, Japanese religion, Judaism, Christianity, and Islam.)

and of Islam in particular. Smith's relevant ideas are developed in a detail that we cannot reproduce or do justice to. One may agree with much that he has to say and yet resist his bias against the use of the term religion and of such terms as Christianity, Buddhism, and so on.

When Smith avers that "what has been called Christianity is so far as history is concerned not one thing but millions of things, and hundreds of millions of things, and hundreds of millions of persons,"[14] there is a sense in which he is obviously right; and he would clearly be the more right for a term like religion, inasmuch as the extension of that term would be far greater than for Christianity. But one must be alert to the possibility that the many "things" and "persons" have had some significant shared or common features in respects relevant to their location within the history of Christianity. Even if we should agree that not all these things and persons are appropriately covered by a term like Christianity, *some* generalizing terms must be employed if we are not to render discourse futile or impossible. Smith would wish to conceive what has been conceived as religion as consisting in historical "cumulative tradition," for one thing, and in "the personal faith of men and women," for another.[15] It is useful for various purposes to think in terms of these two factors. But surely the content of "personal faith," for example, has definite similarities in case after case for at least significant sets of cases within the ranges of humans historically designated as Christians, Muslims, and the like. None of this is to deny that mistakes have been made by way of exaggerating (or perhaps even "inventing") common features in various religious phenomena. Nor is it to deny the numerous insights that Smith associates with his skepticism about the term religion—for instance, the insight, which he sets out with eloquence and power, that presumably religious men may reify their religion, make it into a kind of idol, a thing existent by itself and worthy of adoration, and come, curiously, to venerate *it* rather than, say, the deity who was the ostensible object of their religious activity in the first place. (Thus, Muslims may venerate *Islam* rather than God.) I suggest that it is still helpful to have, even for a combination of "cumulative tradition" and "personal faith," some such term as religion, granted all the ambiguities that have grown up around it.

For the present, the term seems to have a certain rough but undeniable utility rather correspondent to the nature of the state of knowledge in the whole field. I shall retain the term here in the broad sense that has already been indicated above, hoping with numerous others that we shall

[14] Wilfred C. Smith, *The Meaning and End of Religion,* New York: New American Library, 1964, p. 131.
[15] *Ibid.,* p. 175.

one day have a more apt vocabulary for the description and analysis of "religious" phenomena.

Religions vary. Definitions of religion vary. It seems that there is no end to the formulation of definitions of religion. But the different definitions are not always necessarily incompatible. Sometimes, at any rate, ostensible divergences turn out to be the effects of looking at different aspects of the same thing. And students of religion look at different aspects of it as their interests and purposes differ. In this connection it should be evident that it is entirely legitimate to make a variety of abstractions from the total complex labeled religion. Certain kinds of abstractions are likely to be made by certain kinds of specialists. The famous French sociologist, Emile Durkheim, wrote: "A religion is a unified system of beliefs and practices relative to sacred things, that is to say, things set apart and forbidden—beliefs and practices which unite into one single moral community called a Church all those who adhere to them."[16] Whatever its merits or shortcomings, this is plausibly a sociologist's definition. Durkheim was interested in "integration," the integration of men in society, as indicated by his concern with the operation of religion as uniting men into "one single moral community"—and integration is one of the great historic concerns of the discipline of sociology. Unavoidably, Durkheim stresses the sacred. And, in this brief definiton, he refers to beliefs and practices. This reference, again, must inevitably suggest itself to anyone seeking to define religion. But it is quite plain that Durkheim has a sociological "bias."

Theologians are likely to have "theological" biases; psychologists, "psychological" ones; and so on. We must not oversimplify matters or understand them in a wooden way, but different disciplines will characteristically make their own proper abstractions. A generation or two of American scholars, working late in the nineteenth century and into the early decades of the twentieth, made some notable contributions to the psychology of religion. Their concern was, quite expectably, with the individual as a religious agent, with his emotions in religious context, with what William James called the varieties of religious experience of men and women; with mysticism, for example, as something found in an individual possessed of an organism and senses and capable of states such as raptures and trances. It should be evident that to study religion in this fashion was (and is) to engage in a scientifically legitimate abstraction of features of special interest for a special approach and that various modes of abstraction need not conflict with or deny one another. While a psychologist ponders the amount and kind of food consumed over some period of

[16] *The Elementary Forms of the Religious Life,* London: Allen and Unwin, 1926, p. 47; (New York Free Press, 1954); italicized in original.

time by a mystic, or his hours of sleep, or the history of his relations with his father and mother, a sociologist may inquire whether prestige for the mystical mode of apprehension for the divine tends to promote tolerance for deviant religious opinions in a society, and a theologian can go a way independent of these two in concentrating on the clearest possible specification of the doctrinal components of a mystical outlook; and the work of none need inhibit that of the others.

The matter of legitimate abstraction deserves more comment. Given a particular approach—psychological, sociological, theological, philosophical—one may seem in some sense to be doing violence to, or denaturing, the phenomena approached. Thus it may appear rather misguided to some to study the influence of Catholic dogma on certain human associations while failing to penetrate to the deepest possible comprehension of the dogma itself. After all, shouldn't one's goal be to "understand" religion? An investigator of primitive Australian religion observes that "the study of rites, myths and all the 'languages of the mind' " is simply an aid to grasping "the metaphysic of life" that invests precisely such things as rites, myths, and the like—*"if one's purpose is to understand the religion."*[17] The italics are in the original and one may have a certain sympathy with their use. The writer, Stanner, is an anthropologist, and anthropologists are always likely to exhibit a strong interest in culture. And "the metaphysic of life," to which Stanner refers, is eminently cultural "stuff," a complex of values, symbols, and concepts. It is important to comprehend these things. But some value, symbol, or idea components may be more important *for a social system,* a system of human interactions, than others, and the sociologist may accordingly decide to rest short of a thorough grasp of "all" the components of a religious culture in favor of studying intensively those that have distinctive social consequences or correlates. There is a measure of ambiguity about the word "understanding" or the phrase "understanding the religion," in the present context. One "understands" as surely when one "sees" or adequately analyzes aspects of the social operation or functioning of religion as when one comprehends subtle components of culture whose relation to a social system is somewhat attenuated or remote.

Religion is not "denatured" by being analyzed. Those concerned for a synthetic outlook may at least be assured that some of the materials for an appropriate synthesis are available from specialized analytical endeavors. It is evident by now that the sociology of religion is concerned with an eminently cultural phenomenon that "gets into" men's social life. Culture is, in any case, inseparably involved with human social life, which

[17] W. E. H. Stanner in *Aboriginal Man in Australia* (edited by Ronald M. Berndt and Catherine H. Berndt), Sydney: Angus and Robertson, Ltd., 1965, p. 234.

would not be "human" without it. It is present and at work even in the fleeting contact of two men, one of whom gives another a light for cigarette, cigar, or pipe at a street corner. Rudimentary etiquettes or norms of courtesy (which are clearly of the stuff of culture) are operative in such contacts. The sociology of religion must deal with particularly rich cultural components, even if, as already suggested, it will incline toward selecting and stressing peculiar components that strike close to human interaction. The "totality" of the components of religious culture (ultimate-meaning culture, if one fancies so awkward a phrase), in their relations to one another, in the forms they exhibit, might in various ways interest the anthropologist or the philosopher or the theologian, and the sociologist may find that the work of these is indispensable for his own purposes.[18] We can understand much of what is involved in those purposes if we analyze what is called social structure. We shall do this in Chapter 3, in which structure and function will be considered together. Now, however, it will be helpful to examine some points that arise in the consideration of belief, practice, ritual (a particular form of practice) and symbol.

[18] This should not be understood as a bias in favor of strict demarcations in the fields touched upon. There is too much danger of verbalism and aridity in such things. Our concern is rather to be appropriately suggestive at this point with regard to what the general tasks of a sociology of religion are.

CHAPTER 2

Belief, Practice, and Symbol

It will help our understanding of modern sociological approaches to religion to consider certain aspects of belief, practice, and symbolism. The contrast between belief and practice (which we shall begin with and remain with for much of this chapter) both appeals to common sense and is constantly utilized in sociological and anthropological discourse about religion. We retain the contrast, but later we shall observe that it must not be allowed to conceal subtleties that its utilization in an un-imaginative way might too easily induce one to conceal. The relatively elaborate fashion in which the relations of belief and practice will be scrutinized here will justify itself precisely to the extent that it releases us from certain historic errors that the unwary might well repeat today. We turn to a highly relevant strain in nineteenth-century thought.

An influential group of English thinkers, represented by men like the anthropologist Edward Burnett Tylor (1832–1917) and the philosopher Herbert Spencer (1820–1903), set out a conception of the relations between religious belief and practice that gave clear primacy to the first. Belief was "original." "In the beginning" was the thought. Then came action or practice—the deed—following upon the thought. This is somewhat of an oversimplification, to be sure. Thinkers like Tylor and Spencer are unlikely to be utterly foolish or wholly naïve in their notions of the working of the human psyche and human society. Yet our statement is not very much oversimplified. In the intellectualist tradition in which Tylor, Spencer, and others worked, men essentially "doped out," thought out, certain notions, came to certain conclusions, and instituted practices based on what they had thought out. The central "thinking out" aspect of this line of theorizing is nicely conveyed in Pareto's remark that Spencer's "primitive man" is "like a modern scientist working in a laboratory to frame a theory."[1]

Tylor made famous the concept of animism or belief in spiritual beings

[1] Vilfredo Pareto, *The Mind and Society,* New York: Harcourt, Brace, 1935, Vol. 1, p. 192. It should be quite clear that we do not pretend here to say anything about Spencer's social theory in its entirety but confine ourselves to certain particular lines of thought on his part.

14

and, in a passage often referred to and quoted, he gave a succinct indication of what he considered to be the genesis of the animistic outlook:

"It seems as though thinking men, as yet at a low level of culture, were deeply impressed by two groups of biological problems. In the first place, what is it that makes the difference between a living body and a dead one; what causes waking, sleep, trance, disease, death? In the second place, what are those human shapes which appear in dreams and visions? Looking at these two groups of phenomena, the ancient savage philosophers probably made their first step by the obvious inference that every man has two things belonging to him, namely a life and a phantom. These two are evidently in close connection with the body, the life as enabling it to feel and think and act, the phantom as being its image or second self; both, also, are perceived to be things separable from the body, the life as able to go away and leave it insensible or dead, the phantom as appearing to people at a distance from it. The second step would seem also easy for savages to make, seeing how extremely difficult civilized men have found it to unmake. It is merely to combine the life and the phantom. As both belong to the body, why should they not also belong to one another and be manifestations of one and the same soul?"[2]

Spencer, with an interest of his own in the dreams of primitives, averred that primitives tended to take their dreams as realities. He wrote:

"What then is the resulting notion? The sleeper on awaking recalls various occurrences, and repeats them to others. He thinks he has been elsewhere; witnesses say he has not; and their testimony is verified by finding himself where he was when he went to sleep. The simple course is to believe both that he has remained and that he has been away—that he has two individualities, one of which leaves the other and presently comes back. He, too, has a double existence, like many other things."[3]

These statements, then, will serve as indications of Tylor's and Spencer's derivations of animistic belief. Once animistic belief is in existence, men (as already noted) draw consequences from it and institute practices suggested by the belief and by developments of the belief. The idea of an afterlife emerges among primitives, and "carrying out consistently this conception of the second life," Spencer writes, "uncivilized peoples infer that, not only his inanimate possessions, but also his animate possessions, will be needed by the deceased. Hence the slaughter of his livestock."

[2] Edward B. Tylor, *Primitive Culture,* New York: Brentano's, 1924, Vol. 1, pp. 428–429.
[3] Herbert Spencer, *Principles of Sociology,* New York: D. Appleton & Company, 1896, Vol. 1, p. 135.

And, Spencer continues, "logically developed, the primitive belief implies something more—it implies that the deceased will need not only his weapons and implements, his clothing, ornaments, and other movables, together with his domestic animals; but also that he will want human companionship and services." Accordingly, the attendance that the deceased had before death "must be renewed after death."[4] Developments may be as simple as this and may occur in this fashion of building a system of inferences that induces practices in accord with the inferences. (Even here, however, one may already wonder whether the pathway of some inferences toward realization in practice is reinforced by interests and sentiments while the pathway of others is inhibited by them.) But we know that something that seems a plausible inference from a belief and suggests a certain kind of practice may be motivated by quite different considerations, while the seemingly plausible inference is a rationalization. The slaughter of a dead man's livestock might conceivably be sustained or reinforced by an inarticulate feeling of the *ceremonial appropriateness* that something so close to the dead as his livestock should simply "participate" in the state of death with him. Men unable to express the feeling suggested might (if some belief in an afterlife already exists) represent the matter on the line Spencer indicates, thus rendering a plausible "reason" or justification rather than an operative motive.

Tylor's and Spencer's kind of representation too confidently and easily derived practice from thought or belief. Moreover, since in this view religious belief was regarded as essentially erroneous (as rendering a notion of the world that was quite unfounded in fact), the practices supposedly inferentially instituted on the basis of the beliefs became suspect and either could not be investigated very seriously in their own right, because they were merely pale products of incorrect ideas, or tended to be of interest solely *as* reflections of (incorrect) ideas. In a recent study of mortuary customs among a West African people, Goody remarks of a belief in a future life that it may serve to adjust "differences between the ideal and the actual" and particularly "to compensate for the deprived positions of special categories of persons, such as the poor or the aged"; that it may serve "to reinforce the system of social control and place it past human questioning"; and that it may "assist the readjustment of the bereaved and thus reduce the sense of loss." Goody states that the belief in a future life does perform each of these several functions among the Lo Dagaa people he studied. Yet he suggests that "it would be wrong to place too much stress upon the part played by this notion in social life as a whole" and makes the interesting remark among others that "the Hawthorne effect produced by ceremonial has perhaps as great a

[4] *Ibid.,* p. 186.

consequence for the adjustment of the bereaved."[5] Goody apparently intends by this remark to point to the effect of "improved mental outlook." His remark is of special interest in the present context of discussion of intellectualist views of religion.

Goody evidently makes a convenient separation between belief (in a future life, in this case) and practice or ritual[6] or ceremony (say, at funerals). Belief in a future life can have "adjustment" functions for survivors of the deceased and participants in funeral activities. But the ceremonies can have functions on the same lines and can be just as "important." We must try to avoid confusion here. What we call the "ceremonies" can themselves incorporate explicit or implicit assurances of survival of the dead in another life and can thereby exhibit a "belief" component. (*Some* component on such lines, we think indeed on theoretical grounds, they must involve). This is freely granted and even insistently urged, although it is still convenient and, in many ways, useful to distinguish between belief and practice. A formal creedal or dogmatically grounded reassurance to the bereaved person that the deceased lives may be no more effective in "adjustment" on the part of the former than his witnessing of or participation in relevant ceremonial practices (for instance, on the occasion of a funeral). Such practices might perhaps be merely "allusive" as regards belief in a future life.

Practice may be as illuminating with respect to belief as belief with respect to practice. When Spencer asserted that "until we can figure to ourselves with approximate truth the primitive system of thought, we cannot understand primitive conduct,"[7] he had some justification for the statement. But he would have had some justification also if he had reversed his statement to assert that a primitive system of thought cannot be understood until we have some understanding of primitive conduct. ("Conduct," here again, should not be taken to be unqualifiedly "thought-free" or "belief-free." We do not have here an "absolute" distinction.)

The sociologist, Emile Durkheim, was one of the outstanding critics of men like Tylor and Spencer. It is interesting and relevant to observe how large a role Durkheim could attribute to ritual and ceremony (forms of practice), to the point even where we can mark in him a strain toward regarding elements of belief as distinctly secondary or derivative. Thus, he discussed the primitive Australian conception of the spirit of a newly dead man as being filled with ill will toward survivors. He remarks that

[5] Jack Goody, *Death, Property and the Ancestors.* Stanford: Stanford University Press, 1962, pp. 377–378.

[6] On ritual, see below, pp. 31–32. Cf. the convenient summary of the characteristics of ritual in Harry M. Johnson, *Sociology*, New York: Harcourt, Brace, 1960, pp. 409–410.

[7] *Ibid.,* p. 122.

this conception changes after the performance of certain mourning rituals. Confronted with the problem of explaining this change, he writes as follows:

"The foundation of mourning is the impression of a loss which the group feels when it loses one of its members. But this very impression results in bringing individuals together, in putting them into closer relations with one another, in associating them all in the same mental state, and therefore in disengaging a sensation of comfort which compensates the original loss. Since they weep together, they hold to one another and the group is not weakened, in spite of the blow which has fallen upon it. Of course they have only sad emotions in common, but communicating in sorrow is still communicating. . . . The exceptional violence of the manifestations by which the common pain is necessarily and obligatorily expressed even testifies to the fact that at this moment the society is more alive and active than ever. In fact, whenever the social sentiment is painfully wounded, it reacts with greater force than ordinarily: one never holds so closely to his family as when it has just suffered. This surplus energy . . . dissipates the feeling of coldness which death always brings with it. The group feels its strength gradually returning to it; it begins to hope and to live again. Presently one stops mourning, and he does so owing to the mourning itself. But as the idea formed of the soul reflects the moral state of the society, this idea should change as this state changes. When one is in the period of dejection and agony, he represents the soul with the traits of an evil being, whose sole occupation is to persecute men. But when he feels himself confident and secure once more, he must admit that it has retaken its former nature and its former sentiments of tenderness and solidarity."[8]

	S1	S2
The "Level" of Belief or Formal Creedal Statement	"The spirit of the dead man is ill-disposed." ↑	"The spirit of the dead man is well-disposed." ↑
	C1	P	C2
The "Level" of Emotion and Ritual	Feelings of Dejection and → Apathy	Intervening Mourning Ceremonial	Feelings of → Confidence and Security

Durkheim's bias in this passage is definitely not intellectualist. The view he sets out may be designated as just above (the relations of belief

[8] Durkheim, *Elementary Forms,* pp. 401–402.

and practice are here complicated by the introduction of elements of feeling or emotion, but that is an inevitable complication and one that should occasion no particular difficulty).

In this designation, S1 and S2 simply stand for Statements 1 and 2; C1 and C2 designate two different "conditions" of the members of the group suffering a loss by death; P indicates "practice" in the form of a mourning ceremonial. The arrows at the lower level are designed to indicate a time flow: C1 is followed in time by P and then by C2. The two upward-pointing arrows are designed to indicate that in Durkheim's conception Statements 1 and 2 are "reflections," secondary manifestations of the psychic states of the members of the group in C1 and C2. There is no direct way from S1 to S2 and nothing is accordingly presented or portrayed in the space between them. To "get" from S1 to S2, an indirect path must be traced (for instance, from Cl to P to C2), C2 finally being reflected or projected in S2. It is clear that Durkheim is arguing here that the "ideas" entertained of the soul are symbolic renderings of the state of the society or of the feelings of its members. The assertion, "The spirit of the dead man is ill-disposed," means something on the order of "We feel saddened and lessened," as the assertion, "The spirit of the dead man is well disposed," means something on the order of "We feel reorganized and strengthened anew." Perhaps this is not too farfetched an analogy: when one gets up on a miserable, rainy morning, after a refreshing sleep and with the prospects for a pleasant, productive day, his statement, "It's a great day outside," stands in need of translation. It tells nothing that is true about "the day outside" but much that is true about the person facing the day. In everyday parlance, the statement "It's a great day" should be taken to "mean" that the person uttering it feels "great."

In Durkheim's representation it is, of course, the case that practice plays a crucial role in effecting the change from C1 to C2. Intervening mourning ceremonials—clearly intervening between C1 and C2—effect a transformation of sentiment that is then registered at another (belief) level.[9] And it is plainly Durkheim's intention to feature "ideas" or formal beliefs as secondary, reflective or symbolic indicators of other phenomena. Insofar as we grant his point and concede that religious "ideas" *can,* in certain contexts, be secondary—and this whole matter requires most delicate handling—we should still be careful to note that the level of formal creedal statement must not be hastily taken as necessarily "pro-

---

[9] We write in simplified terms. Thus, we take the intervening mourning ceremonial as "practice," which indeed it is. But it is well to remember once again the nonabsolute character of the practice-belief dichotomy: it is *not* implied that all belief or cognitive elements are washed out of practice.

duced" by the level of emotion and practice. To the extent that Durkheim is right, rather, we would ordinarily expect a reinforcement, a support, a "charging" from emotion and ritual that would motivate belief, while belief itself would have a history of its own and not be a simple, direct emergent from emotion and practice.

It must also be observed that there are only quite limited possibilities in the kind of "translation" that Durkheim has, in effect, done. There are cases in which he is very probably justified in his translation endeavors —cases in which "The spirit of the dead man is ill-disposed" is substantially correctly translated as "We feel saddened and lessened." But there is no question that there are cases in which ideas simply *cannot* be translated in any such fashion, where this kind of reduction simply cannot be effected. Durkheim's outlook, as above indicated, represents an important strain in his thought. He commented that "the theorists who have undertaken to explain religion in rational terms" have seen it before everything else as a scheme of ideas and have accordingly taken its conceptions and beliefs as its "essential elements." "As for the rites," adds Durkheim most appropriately, from the intellectualist point of view "they appear to be only an external translation" of the inner states of belief which command primary attention. Durkheim seeks to correct this intellectualist bias. He intimates his sympathy with the outlook that "the real function of religion is not to make us think, to enrich our knowledge . . . but rather, it is to make us act, to aid us to live."[10] The context in which this is said suggests that Durkheim affords somewhat too rigid a contrast. Ideas and beliefs are certainly not without their own influence in making us "act" and "live"; yet it is clearly Durkheim's intention to make us strongly aware of ritual, which, if it is intertwined with elements of belief, is not exhausted by them.

It is noteworthy that Durkheim was not alone among outstanding figures of modern sociology in casting doubt on intellectualist or excessively rationalist outlooks. Vilfredo Pareto was another considerable figure whose rather similar doubts and reservations are worth recalling. In the course of a discussion of conduct, hypothetical psychic states, and "theories," Pareto affords the following well known representation of his own:

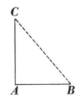

[10] *Op. cit.,* p. 416.

C stands for "expressions of sentiment," but what we must stress above all is that these expressions of sentiment, in Pareto's words, "often develop moral, religious, and other similar theories." We take such "theories" as a primary matter in the present context. *B* stands for "conduct," a set of performances. *A*, finally, represents a "hypothetical psychic state." Pareto writes: "The very marked tendency in human beings to transform non-logical into logical conduct leads them to imagine that *B* is an effect of the cause *C*." This may, for present purposes, be rendered as an assertion that, by virtue of commonly favored intellectualist or excessively rationalist tendencies, men are prone to the notion that, where conduct and "theory" (such as religious belief or credo) are in some way evidently connected, the conduct must be the result or outcome of the theory. Accordingly, a direct relation, *CB,* is assumed. Pareto adds, interestingly, that "sometimes the relation *CB* in fact obtains, but not as often as people think." Clearly, "theory" *may* initiate or bring about conduct (or, at any rate, this is a good enough way to put things for our present purposes), but Pareto is more inclined to the notion that a certain psychic disposition is likely to lead to an act—relation *AB*—(or inhibit it) and simultaneously evoke a theory—relation *AC*—(or, we can add, merely sustain a theory already existent). "A man, for example, has a horror of murder, *B*, and he will not commit murder; but he will say that the gods punish murderers, and that constitutes a theory, *C*."[11]

Again Pareto writes: "The proposition so often met with, 'This or that people acts as it does because of a certain belief' is rarely true; in fact, it is almost always erroneous"; and he comments that "the inverse proposition, 'People believe as they do because of this or that conduct,' as a rule contains a larger amount of truth," although it is "too absolute." The words, "too absolute," in this context, gain force from what we have already noted with regard to a belief (or cognitive) component in conduct. Pareto then remarks that belief and conduct are, as it were, two branches of the same tree.[12] It has already been noted that the psychic state *A* may produce the theory or belief *C;* that *C* may even produce *B*. Not only are there for Pareto cases wherein *A* produces *C* and *B* but also cases wherein *A* produces *B* and then *A* and *B* produce *C,* and wherein *A* produces *C* and then *C* produces *B*.[13] Pareto would have been the last of men not to seek to find empirical exemplifications of his outlook. Thus, he will contend that "before the invasion of Italy by the gods of

[11] *The Mind and Society,* Vol. 1, p. 88.

[12] *Ibid.,* p. 90.

[13] *Ibid.,* p. 180. We depart here somewhat from Pareto's own terms and scheme of lettering, but this is done for the sake of simplicity and brevity and Pareto's essential argument is not affected.

Greece, the ancient Roman religion did not have a theology, *C*: it was no more than a cult, *B*."[14] (We know by now how to understand this, not in "too absolute" a way, yet appreciating its serious and significant intent.) In principle, at least, this kind of assertion is subject to test.

We need not make a close comparison, on relevant points, of Durkheim and Pareto. But it is clear that both men attained a fundamentally important critical attitude toward the old intellectualism that is now part of the heritage of the modern sociology of religion in particular. Both men are also significant figures for the modern understanding of symbol and ritual, which I shall discuss presently. Now, let us note further the stress on religious practice that various scholars have given. But, as we go on to this, it may be added to what has been said above that the severe limitations of the old intellectualist view of religion do not mean that animism as such lacks all significance as an element in the whole religious complex and its early or primitive forms in particular.

FURTHER ON BELIEF AND PRACTICE

Long ago, the historian Fustel de Coulanges argued with regard to Greek and Roman religion of remote antiquity that "the word *religion* did not signify what it signifies for us," for by this word "we understand a body of dogmas, a doctrine concerning God, a symbol of faith concerning what is in and around us." For the ancients, the case was different in that the same word "signified rites, ceremonies, acts of exterior worship." And Fustel adds: "The doctrine was of small account; the practices were the important part; these were obligatory, and bound man. . . ."[15] William Robertson Smith, a student of Oriental language and religion, observed in an influential book that "our modern habit is to look at religion from the side of belief rather than of practice." Smith added that "the antique religions had for the most part no creed; they consisted entirely of institutions and practices." This last statement, however, could too easily lead to misunderstanding and Smith did observe at once that "no doubt men will not habitually follow certain practices without attaching a meaning to them"; but he also then averred that, in ancient religion, "while the practice was rigorously fixed the meaning attached to it was extremely vague, and the same rite was explained by different people in different ways, without any question of orthodoxy or heterodoxy arising in consequence."[16]

Max Weber observed that "dharma, that is ritualistic duty, is the central

---

[14] *Ibid.*, pp. 90–91.

[15] *The Ancient City,* New York: Doubleday, 1955, p. 167.

[16] *The Religion of the Semites,* New York: Meridian Library, 1956, p. 16. The work of Fustel and of Smith may be usefully compared with that of Jane Ellen Harrison, *Themis,* Cambridge: Cambridge University Press, 1927.

criterion of Hinduism. . . . Hinduism is primarily ritualism. . . . The first question a Hindu asks of a strange religion is not what is its teaching (mata) but its *dharma*."[17] James B. Pratt, in his time a well known psychologist and a student of Buddhism, wrote, in language a bit old fashioned, that "rites, ceremonies and ways of acting" constitute, "in low and primitive races," the "great bulk of the people's religion." He added that "for these tribes beliefs are few, indefinite, and relatively unimportant; you may *think* what you like, for you are not expected to think at all, but you must *act,* in sacred matters, as the group acts." Pratt was inclined to the view that "cult did not arise subsequent to belief but in close connection with it, if indeed it was not the older of the two"; nor did he hesitate to write of "the enormous influence of cult upon belief."[18] Granted that in an absolute sense cult could not be older than belief (since cult would in some minimum measure feature or reflect belief and is not a completely mindless or "instinctive" set of activities), there is still something to be said for Pratt's contentions.

Gustave von Grunebaum, a leading student of Islam, notes that in Islam "affiliation with the community is expressed primarily in action—in the common performance of the prescribed practices and the adoption of a way of life." Grunebaum adds, borrowing a term of Wilfred C. Smith's, that "it is orthopraxy that matters most of all, not orthodoxy";[19] and he refers at a late point to "the dissenter" as one "who in the Muslim environment is often more significantly recognized by his practice than by his creed." Again employing Smith's terminology and in the spirit of the latter's work, Grunebaum writes that "Christianity is concerned with its orthodoxy, Islam with its 'orthopraxy.' " This is of course not to be understood as if there were no significant intellectual components in a religion like Islam. That is flatly untrue. The same Grunebaum can also write: "Islam compelled the Arabs to widen their intellectual range; it unlocked the world of metaphysics and it confronted the faithful with questions regarding the nature of God, the universe and man, the rules governing man's relation to the supernatural and the like. . . ." There is no inconsistency in this. Grunebaum writes these last lines, in any case, to suggest the differences that came to exist between pagans and the Muslim Arab. And these differences could come to be while Islam relatively speaking, as a whole, could retain a powerful "practice"

[17] *The Religion of India,* Glencoe: The Free Press, 1958, p. 24.

[18] *The Religious Consciousness,* New York: Macmillan, 1920, pp. 83, 258, 283, fn. 24.

[19] Smith's usage is indicated in this statement: "As 'orthodoxy' means the officially recognized and established beliefs of a religion; so *orthopraxy* has been used here to denote its officially recognized and established practices. Similarly *orthoprax* is a fairly obvious and useful supplement to 'orthodox.' " Wilfred C. Smith, *Modern Islam in India,* London: Gollancz, 1946, p. 305.

bias.[20] Another writer on Islam notes a certain Muslim indifference to theological questions, remarks that "this indifference poses a most bewildering puzzle for Westerners, who have been taught by their own religious tradition to put theology at the center of religious concern," and observes that "the Muslim's faith does not center in theology."[21] And yet another writer who has been at some pains to inform himself about both Islam and Christianity observes that "the underlying incentive of Islam has always been to *do* what God willed . . . [although] this does not obviate theology."[22]

Again, let me warn that the belief-practice contrast can be pushed to the point of absurdity. Religious ritual, if it does not itself directly incorporate "statements" (as through the chanting of creedal verities), can often be illuminated by statements that in some sense go along with it. Given the "story" of Christ, the ritual of the mass may be said to "make sense"; and many another ritual remote from Christianity makes sense in the light of some story with nothing Christian about it. An authority on ancient Egyptian religion usefully reminds us of the inevitable belief or cognitive component in practice once again when he writes: "The ritual preserved in the reliefs of many temples expresses, no less than the texts, those thoughts of the ancients which we try to understand."[23]

We must, indeed, take the cautions that all of this suggests with entire

[20] See Grunebaum's *Modern Islam*, New York: Vantage Books, 1964, pp. 10, 17, 23, 58.

[21] Charles J. Adams, in *A Reader's Guide to the Great Religions, op. cit.*, 1965, p. 309.

[22] Kenneth Cragg, *The Call of the Minaret*, New York: Oxford University Press, 1956, p. 143. It is nevertheless worthy of note, without exploring the matter, that Islam is sometimes classed with Christianity and Judaism as a "book" religion, by contrast with "cult" religions. Thus, Morenz writes of ancient Egyptian religion that it is "characterized by the dominance of cult and is thereby included within the sphere of the cult religions of pagan antiquity, to which the Jewish, Christian, and Islamic book religion with its God who speaks and makes demands and the central importance of holy scriptures stands opposed." Siegfried Morenz, *Ägyptische Religion*, Stuttgart: W. Kohlhammer Verlag, 1960, p. 4. It may be added that even Frankfort, no man to slight creedal components in a religion, could aver that ancient Egyptian religion "possessed neither a central dogma nor a holy book" and that "it could flourish without postulating one basic truth." Henri Frankfort, *Ancient Egyptian Religion*, New York: Columbia University Press, 1948, p. 3.

[23] Henri Frankfort, *Kingship and the Gods*, Chicago: University of Chicago Press, 1948, p. 79. This, of course, should not be understood to exclude the possibility that religious practices whose actual origins or initial foundations are unknown, forgotten, can be "explained" by way of afterthought, so that the "explanations" are in this sense secondary.

seriousness. But certain differences in regard to belief or creed or dogma and ritual (or practice in a wider sense than ritual) do constantly obtrude themselves. These differences are unlikely to be trivial. They may be resumed as follows. Belief or creed or dogma is more *prominent,* more *fixed* or rigid or invariant in some religions than in others. It is more generally *insisted upon* as something important to profess or adhere to deliberately in some religions than in others. The meaning of such differences has, by no means, been fully explored by scholars. A process of conversion is one thing when it requires unequivocal commitment to a belief system whose content is fixed and definite, and another when the beliefs of the prospective convert are allowed very loose rein. Differences between so-called Oriental and "Occidental" religions (which, interestingly, are firmly grounded in the history of the Near East) and between the modern (and medieval) world and antiquity (perhaps especially the pre-Christian era) still need careful exploration in the light of the points referred to.

But we must be content with these hints. Practice, by now, has surely been given sufficient stress. And once we have rendered it justice, we may give due scope also to the element of belief that we have repeatedly noted as in some fashion involved even in practice. Once more, at the risk of boredom let me say that we deal with delicate matters in these premises. Sometimes one emphasis is justified, sometimes another. *Once we have gotten away* from a superficial intellectualism, we can sympathize with, say, Parsons' bias that "while believing is not, *ipso facto,* doing, what one believes has much to do with what one does," as we can understand Frankfort's reference to "the one-sidedness of the prevalent modern tendency to see all our [mythological] material as reflections of cult and ritual."[24]

We are still far indeed from a "complete" statement on relations of belief and practice. But some additional things can be briefly pointed to. Belief and practice can reinforce one another. Thus, if we turn back to the representation given for Durkheim's views of the relations of "levels" it may be argued that either level will reinforce the other. Once C_2, for example, has come into being and feelings of confidence and security prevail, these feelings can reinforce the belief-item that the spirit of the dead man is benevolent, as that belief-item can reinforce the new feeling-state. Generally, in a going religious system it is to be expected that beliefs will not have such appeal as they do exclusively on their own foundation, as it were. The beliefs will occur in a framework of prac-

[24] Talcott Parsons, *The Structure of Social Action,* New York: McGraw-Hill, 1937, p. 538; used with permission of McGraw Hill Book Co. Frankfort, *op cit.,* p. 410, fn. 44.

tices (in turn charged with emotions) that will give them additional appeal, and we will be dealing with a system of interdependent "parts." Groethuysen argued cogently, in his brilliant book on the rise of the bourgeois outlook in eighteenth-century France, that the Catholic Church came to have certain disadvantages in the modern world when the consideration of belief or dogma or doctrine became "abstract," that is, took place under circumstances in which men were removed from the influence of the environment of traditional Catholic practices and paraphernalia. Belief could not be "seen" in the same way then—nor could the traditional practices.[25]

It should also be observed that the analysis of myths (which is clearly pertinent to the area of belief) can be, and often is, conducted in close relationship to the analysis of ritual, and it is hardly surprising that meaning-congruities often are traceable between the two. Thus, Stanner offers an analysis of the so-called Rainbow Serpent myth among the Australian Murinbata, which goes on the assumption that this myth, now unaccompanied by any ritual, did not develop without significant ritual associations. Stanner exhibits the structure of this myth together with that of the myth of *Punj* (an initiation ceremony or ritual) and together with a delineation of the main features of the ritual of *Punj*. On the evidence of his detailed presentation of the relevant materials, he argues that "there is a significant measure of congruence between the design-plans of the two myths and the rite."

Stanner's argument appeals to what he takes as four fundamental features shared by the two myths and the ritual. These features involve certain sequences of transition, common situations, development by change from within, and a way of regarding principal actors. Thus, in point of sequences of transition, Stanner tries to catch the flow of the two myths and the ritual as follows:

"Someone is sent or withdrawn from a safe, inhabited place to a place of solitude. In the second place . . . wildness or terror, and a sort of corruption, become ascendant. Something—trust, young life, innocence—is destroyed there. Then, after a pause, there is a return to the first place. But it is now not the same as before; there has been a change; the old is not quite annulled and the new not familiar."[26]

This example of theme- or meaning-congruity is sufficient for our purposes. Certain evidences that might have been helpful to Stanner are

[25] Bernhard Groethuysen, *Die Entstehung der bürgerlichen Welt-und Lebensanschauung in Frankreich,* Halle-Saale: Niemeyer, Vol. 1, 1927, Ch. 3.

[26] See W. E. H. Stanner, *On Aboriginal Religion,* Oceania Monograph No. 11, Sydney, Australia, 1964, pp. 103–104.

unfortunately lost. But in view of the resemblances that he presents in detail, it appears reasonable for him to argue, as he does, that the Rainbow Serpent myth could stand in about the same relation to the ritual of *Punj* as the myth that now accompanies *Punj* and that we have referred to simply as the myth of *Punj*. It is quite possible, then, that the Rainbow Serpent myth was once definitely associated with the *Punj* ritual or some similar ritual. Stanner may have "caught" the myth at a point in time when he could still trace some of its presumptive one-time ritual associations and before it either died out for lack of ritual nourishment or was subjected to an elaboration of its own that would have obliterated its initial ritual affiliations. (Whether the latter kind of development would have been likely among Australian oborigines is a question best left to experts.[27]). The important point is the notion of meaningful connection on the basis of which Stanner worked.

Stress on meaning-congruity between belief and practice, however, still plainly does not involve abandoment of the distinction between the two, nor is it meant to suggest that the ascertainment of such congruity is always a simple matter. Variant interpretations (or myths) bearing on the same practices are possible, as Stanner's material begins to suggest and as we found Robertson Smith saying previously. Congruities may conceal interesting histories. Meanings can be forgotten or replaced with new ones to account for established practices, as I have previously indicated. With reference to variant interpretations again, Dore, in a sample of inhabitants of a ward in Tokyo, explicitly noted a certain "unity of ritual behavior" accompanied by "diversity of interpretations." He even added that some of the persons who performed certain rites "had no interpretation."[28] But here, as the reader must surely expect by now, we would say that there must be meaning-elements as long as men are human. We recall Robertson Smith's observation that men will not habitually follow certain practices without attaching a meaning to them. This does not imply that the meaning-elements must be alive and throbbing and to the fore in every individual consciousness; nor even that they need be entirely explicit in the mind of any single member of a group that is under consideration.

---

[27] The reference to autonomous elaboration may be permitted to let us remark in passing that in religion, as elsewhere, such elaboration is a very important process. Myth and ritual, belief and practice can interact indefinitely, but, with the breaking out of delimited "primitive" systems of interaction, new creativity may take myths or beliefs to previously undreamt of aesthetic, philosophical or, indeed, religious levels.

[28] Ronald P. Dore, *City Life in Japan,* Berkeley and Los Angeles: University of California Press, 1958, p. 324.

Perhaps enough has been said to indicate both the shortcomings of intellectualism and some of the interesting complexities that belief-practice can confront us with. In barest summary, intellectualism overstressed the importance of the process of taking thought in the religious sphere, and its tendency to view practice as a mere residue of a set of errors in thought is itself quite erroneous. To try to understand religion on the basis of the pattern given by science is inevitably to make fundamental mistakes about it, as we shall see further in the next section. The matters stressed thus far in this chapter have been occasioned by specific contexts and purposes. The critique of the intellectualist approach, especially, should certainly not induce the view that, generally, ideas and values or men's conceptions of the desirable have been unimportant in religion. Other than in contexts such as those in which we mark the excesses of intellectualism, we would be inclined to allow religious ideas and values very large importance, indeed. It will advance our analysis to examine, next, the matter of symbols.

SYMBOLS

In general terms the notion of symbolism within religion is a familiar thing. It is common knowledge that in the Catholic sacrament of the mass, bread and wine symbolize or "stand for" the body and blood of Christ. According to the book of Genesis, the Lord God formed man out of dust, the dust of the ground, and breathed into his nostrils the breath of life. Theologians have often understood the meaning of this in a symbolic sense. Man is part of the realm of nature, a realm that includes rocks and trees and animals and other phenomena untouched by "spirit." Insofar as this is true, man was formed of the dust of the ground. But the spirit of God was also breathed into him, and thereby he comes to participate also in a realm of supernature. He is accordingly a complex creature, born to trouble, destined for perplexity because of his location, so to put it, at the boundaries of nature and spirit. Interesting theological consequences are often drawn from this view. Theology as such, of course, is not our concern, but the important thing to note here is that the words referred to in Genesis can be, and have been, understood by religious persons in a symbolic sense. Genesis affords in these words a portrayal that, whether it is taken literally or not, *can* be taken symbolically, and thereby, again, man's being made of dust "stands for" his solidarity with the rest of nature while his having breathed into his nostrils the divine breath of life "stands for" his participation in a spiritual realm that paradoxically coexists with the solidarity with nature (paradoxically—at least, if one has a late or "modern" view of nature; and such a view will, in turn, affect the view one holds of spirit).

Much religious controversy centers around whether various things in the religious realm are to be understood in a literal or symbolic sense. The sacrament of the mass was mentioned above. The Catholic doctrine of transubstantiation postulates that in the sacrament the bread and wine are converted into the body and blood of Christ. The Lutheran doctrine of consubstantiation postulates not an actual conversion but the mysterious presence of the body and blood together with the bread and wine. There are other interpretations of "what happens" in the mass, including a purely symbolic one that nothing in any sense supernatural happens but that bread and wine simply "stand for" or are representative of the Christ figure. There are times when symbolism or nonliteralism develops to a point where many believers are disturbed and feel, rightly or wrongly and whether one sympathizes with them or not, that their religion is in danger of getting to be understood as a kind of vague poetry without supernatural substance of any kind. On the other hand, it may be argued that symbolic understandings often enable a significant invigoration of old doctrines now understood in a new way adapted to new circumstances of life. Then there may occur what seem to those partial to the new understandings to be signs of freshness and appeal that mark a genuine "break-through" in thought which recasts old materials and generalizes them in such fashion that they can once more carry an important meaning in a time and situation to which an older, narrower literalism is inadequate.[29] The philosopher, Santayana, comments in his book on *Reason in Religion* that "in every age the most comprehensive thinkers have found in the religion of their time something they could accept, interpreting and illustrating that religion so as to give it depth and universal application."[30] Undoubtedly, the "most comprehensive thinkers" have often been helped in this by allowing themselves rather liberal symbolic interpretations of traditional doctrines.

There are cycles and rhythms in the development of doctrine, and one could preoccupy one's self with something on the order of a notion of alternations of "literalistic ossification" and "symbolistic enthusiasm." This hints at matters well beyond our scope. But the observation may nevertheless be made in passing that a kind of simultaneity or coexistence, within the same very broad society of "believers," of literal and symbolic inter-

[29] Notice the interesting use of the term "fundamentalism" to signify opposition to "the demand for greater generality in evaluative standards" in Talcott Parsons, *Societies: Evolutionary and Comparative Perspectives,* Englewood Cliffs, N.J.: Prentice-Hall, 1966, p. 23.

[30] George Santayana, *Reason in Religion,* New York: Scribner's, 1933, p. 3.

pretations of things is often to be expected and often will prove reasonably "satisfying" to all concerned. A novelist (describing one of his characters in the grip of an impulse to do something which that character feels he should not do, yet would greatly enjoy doing) asserts, "The Devil is a great theologian." In the matter of literal versus symbolic interpretations, the situation is often as if one portion of the novelist's readers were to understand that there actually exists (say, somehow beyond space and time) a malignant red entity that argues with great power and eloquence about things divine and diabolical; while another portion were to understand that when we want very much to do things we know we shouldn't we can develop mighty arguments for doing them; while perhaps a third portion were to hold both a literal and a symbolic interpretation— and all concerned were content with their understandings and the implications of them.

These problems must be relinquished at this point. It is now appropriate to document the view that religious belief and practice are symbolically saturated; and, later, to comment on ritual in relation to symbolism. In the study of the West African Lo Dagaa (to which we have already referred), Goody indicates that these people bury the bodies of young children who have perished before weaning and before they have learned to walk or talk "properly," at the side of a crossroad and with a stake driven through the grave. The children are buried under piles of earth covered with thorns, and evidently the Lo Dagaa say, among other things, that this is done to prevent their spirits from escaping. It is believed that children who have died very young may be reborn to die young again. It is desirable to prevent this kind of return, more particularly if it occurs more than once. Goody makes the following statement about this whole belief-practice complex:

"The burial at the crossroads with a stake driven through the grave bears a striking similarity to the treatment of murderers, and particularly witches, in medieval Europe. Indeed, such a practice continued in England well into the last century. This similarity derives, I believe, from the fact that in the burial both of infants among the Lo Dagaa and of the blood guilty in Europe, the community is concerned to separate completely certain categories of unwanted persons from the living and from the ordinary dead. They are separated, of course, by the mere fact of being distinguished. But more precise images are involved. The stake is driven through the corpse not only to destroy it but to fasten it to one place. At the same time, burial at the crossroads involves an image of dispersal, both because the paths go their different ways and because it is a place where strangers foregather. In addition, the Lo Dagaa say that even if the sprite did break loose, the crossroads would confuse its attempts to return to the mother's womb."[31]

Notice that, according to Goody (as we might guess), these West African people do not assign definite "humanity" or "social personality" to a child at the time of its birth. The time for such assignment, indeed, shows some range in human societies. But it is clear that the burial complex described is rife with symbolism. On this point, Goody's description speaks adequately for itself. It would be interesting to know how much of the symbolic picture rendered constitutes something of which the Lo Dagaa are more than just dimly aware. Goody does tell us that these people wish to prevent the spirits of dead children from escaping and that "they" (just who? how many?) say that if a sprite should break loose the crossroads would confuse it in its efforts to regain its mother's womb in order to be reborn. But there is no indication that there is anything like "full" or "universal" awareness among the Lo Dagaa of the symbolism that Goody describes. It should not be surprising that complexes such as Goody here presents can, and often do, develop with much symbolic richness and with only dim realization, at best, of the symbolic quality. The symbolism is a reality despite the dimness, and the human meanings involved are tremendously important, whatever the limitations of particular humans and their consciousness.

The phenomenon of ritual, in particular, is symbolically saturated. It is even in a sense redundant to speak of such things as "rituals having symbolic significance," since we can justifiably insist that the term ritual has no meaning unless it is allowed at once that a symbolic element is always a component of it. Ritual practices or complexes are both addressed to "another" (or sacred) realm and are symbolic in their character.[32] And the symbolic aspect is particularly characterized by the circumstance that the ritual performance cannot be understood on the model of conduct in the sphere of, say, technology or science, which organizes means to achieve ends on a foundation of essential grasp of cause and effects. Ritual "means" and "ends" are connected by symbolic congruity. Insofar as we can speak of initiative taken and effect desired in ritual, we must say that these are in reality by no means bound by a causal tie. If we were to insist on understanding ritual on the model of the means-end performance characteristic for technological endeavor, we might well end again with the view that ritual was mere "foolishness" and thereby seriously impair our understanding of it and of religion generally.

---

[31] *Death, Property and the Ancestors,* pp. 150–151.
[32] See Parsons, *Structure of Social Action,* pp. 258, 429 ff.

We left Pareto and Durkheim at an earlier point with the assertion that both men are significant figures in the modern understanding of symbol and ritual. This was clearly seen by Talcott Parsons several decades ago. Following Pareto in the latter's treatment of ritual, Parsons remarked that, when an observer "in possession of the best available scientific knowledge" examines the nexus between the "means" used in ritual operations and the "end(s)" they are supposed to compass, such an observer can "discern no reason why the operations in question should serve to bring about the realization of the subjective end," that is, the end aimed at by the ritual actor. Parsons went on to say that Pareto afforded no general characterization of ritual except the negative one that "the means-end relationship is, from the 'logical' point of view, arbitrary, and that hence ritual actions are to be regarded less as means of attaining ends than as 'manifestations of sentiments.' " But this was a good deal, for in this fashion Pareto actually imputed great importance to ritual actions and afforded a treatment of them representing "a great advance on the dominant positivistic tendency to treat ritual as depending solely on a form of error."[33]

In connection with a discussion of Durkheim's work on the same lines, Parsons noted that "in so far as sacred things are involved in action, the means-end relationship is symbolic, not intrinsic." This emphasizes again that "means" and "ends" are related by symbolic congruity or appropriateness, not by a causal nexus.[34] The effect of Durkheim's work was "to widen the means-end scheme to include a fundamental normative component of action systems" which cannot be discarded as being merely "irrational." (We need not, at this point, make too much of Parsons' term, normative. It may simply be understood to mean that actions like those involved in religious ritual are not instrumentalities for attaining something else, insofar as we think of such instrumentalities in a context of authentic technology.) Parsons then further observed—and the cogency of the statement will be evident in the light of what we already know—that ritual actions are neither "simply irrational, or pseudo rational, based on prescientific erroneous knowledge, but are of a different character altogether and as such not to be measured by the standards of intrinsic rationality at all."[35]

[33] *Ibid.,* p. 209. For our present purposes, at least, "positivistic" may be understood as a practical equivalent of "intellectualist." (We do not, incidentally, wish to go here into the special matter of just how Durkheim himself conceived religion to be an "illusion.")

[34] Parsons writes: "The norm involved in logical action may be called that of intrinsic rationality.' The term intrinsic is chosen because it suggests an antithesis, symbolic' " *Ibid.,* p. 210.

[35] It is important to allow the outlook whereby religion becomes a set of activities neither "stupid" nor "smart" nor "rational" nor "irrational"—but rather

The kind of understanding thus shared by Pareto, Durkheim, and Parsons, among others, is not the exclusive property of sociologists. It is at least fair to say that it has long been realized by scholars of varied backgrounds that numerous rites and customs, initially seeming quite senseless to certain Western investigators, could not possibly be " 'mistakes' of practice" and could not "rest on 'erroneous' theories of nature."[36] But these rites and customs could still be analyzed in terms of the consequences they had for societies and for human beings as members of societies. (That kind of analysis of them is inevitably centrally important for sociology.) Suzanne Langer remarks of them that "obviously they serve some natural purpose to which their practical justification or lack of justification is entirely irrelevant."[37] Where Mrs. Langer refers to "natural purpose," sociologists are much more likely to refer to "functions." We may try to advance such understanding of religious phenomena as we have achieved by now examining "functions" and "structures." We are a long way from our beginning with Tylor and Spencer. Religious practice in the widest sense can now be regarded as quite adequately redeemed from that state of trivality or near-trivality as a by-product of erroneous notions to which it was once in effect reduced.[38] The importance

---

*non*rational, outside the sphere of considerations having to do with questions of the kind suggested by the words stupid, smart, rational and irrational. In this view, religious action (in which belief and performance now may be conceived to coalesce) is no more rational or irrational than the sex drive, a handshake, or a baseball game played for its own sake. A handshake is a bit of customary behavior, as undertaken say by old friends who meet again. The reference is to a handshake "as such." If one shakes another's hand with a view to pleasing him for some ulterior purpose, then the category of rationality at once applies and we are no longer considering a handshake "as such." The outlook so stressed, as far as the sociologist is concerned, encourages and directs inquiry strongly toward the social consequences of the action designated as non-rational. (One might consider the action aesthetically or in other cultural dimensions, but these things are sociologically important in connection with human social relations.) The outlook stressed does not encourage inquiry about the possible truth-value of religious statements within the whole action-complex. The sociologist's concern is, as noted, with certain consequences. What men believe, provided only that they do believe it, is likely enough to be socially significant whether it is true or not. (In any case, the statements found in the whole religious complex referred to are very often such that they are not subject to ordinary tests of scientific truth: they are ultra-empirical, in the realm of "faith.")

[36] The language just quoted is that of a philosopher. See Suzanne Langer, *Philosophy in a New Key*, New York: Mentor Books, 1948, p. 38.

[37] *Ibid.*, p. 38.

[38] And this reflects a *sociological* orientation, as should be abundantly clear. It is not our province to "justify" anything whatever in a religious sense. It is a fundamental *sociological* error, if we must suggest this yet again, to see practice through the intellectualist eye.

of symbolism in religion has been suggested and the symbolic character of ritual, in particular, has been indicated. A number of things can be left securely behind with the present chapter. If we can now move ahead and achieve understanding of religion in "functional" terms, it is our bias that much of what sociology has to say about religion will also be fairly comprehended.

PART **II**

Structure, Function, and Religion

CHAPTER 3

Structure, Function, System, and Religion

Structural-functional theory in sociology is a rather complex scheme of thought and one that carries with it a considerable conceptual apparatus. A thorough exposition or evaluation of this scheme of thought is not feasible in this short book. Moreover, we are concerned here with religion and with structural-functional theory insofar as it bears on religion, although a few points must be made that relate to the general theory itself. A fuller exposition would enable a detailed presentation of differences among adherents to structural-functional views. It would allow a systematic confrontation of various criticisms of such views. It would also enable us to discuss in detail some of the interesting, faulty logic that has appeared in the work of insufficiently wary functionalists. In very broad terms, structural-functional analysis has both merits and defects. It is helpful in pointing to significant sociological problems, in organizing critical reflection about them, and in generating hypotheses that are far from trivial. It has already stimulated illuminating work in areas such as kinship, the relations of economy and society, the theory of social evolution—and religion. It is quite true that it is not a powerful theory in the sense of the highly developed sciences and it would be useless to pretend otherwise. But this is no reason for repudiating it outright in a discipline that is still notably immature. Our purpose in the next three chapters is to extract what value we can from structural-functional ideas for the understanding of religion.

In the following we shall borrow heavily from Talcott Parsons' highly elaborated form of functionalism. But the borrowing is done selectively, in the light of particular interests. No full or painstakingly conforming exposition of Parsons' views is remotely intended. We must begin with some fundamental notions about structure, function, and system, and Parsons affords us convenient and influential terms and ideas. Some of the views expressed and the emphases given in these chapters might well be out of accord with those of Parsons.

A threefold procedure is adopted in the present chapter.

1. Some essential notions of structural-functional analysis, particularly on Parsons' lines, are set out. These will serve as background for comprehending matters subsequently to be presented in the remainder of this chapter and the two chapters that follow.[1]

2. We shall briefly reconsider the break with intellectualism that structural-functional analysis presents.

3. This brief reconsideration will lead us easily into a statement about naïve kinds of functionalism and will particularly motivate a discussion of religion as "integrative."

STRUCTURE, FUNCTION, SYSTEM, AND ENVIRONMENTS

If the old intellectualism was highly vulnerable to criticism, as we have sought to show, it does not follow that ideas are generally insignificant in human conduct. The broad importance of ideas and of values in particular[2] is indeed constantly intimated in modern structural-functional analysis. Our contexts are now different. It is no longer necessary, for example, to establish the importance of ritual or of the nonrational in religion. Moreover, ideas need not be conceived to get their effects in a rarefied, ghostly way, out of all relation to such things as men's material or economic interests. We can be prepared to see ideas and values bulk large in conceptions of social structure, although without prejudice to our previous critique of intellectualism and without the foolish presumption that all problems bearing on the relation of ideas and values to the motivation of men's actions in society are now resolved for good.

The particular kind of structure in which we are interested is, of course, social structure. Not all sociologists who regard some form of structural-functional analysis as valuable would define social structure in precisely the same way. Moreover, it is often not difficult to trace more than one meaning of structure in the work of a single theorist. Parsons, for example, uses structure in more than one sense (or with more than one emphasis).

[1] Not everything presented will be utilized at once. The reader should regard the section that follows precisely as a resource that may be helpful from time to time.

[2] Note the definition by Clyde Kluckhohn and others: "A value is a conception, explicit or implicit, distinctive of an individual or characteristic of a group, of the desirable which influences the selection from available modes, means and ends of action" (italicized in original), in Talcott Parsons and E. A. Shils, eds., *Toward a General Theory of Action*, Cambridge, Harvard University Press, 1951, p. 395. (When a value is spoken of as a conception, this surely should not be taken to exclude the notion of its representing an end or something actively desired.)

But the usage of his that most concerns us here—and which we shall now employ—is that by which he conceives social structure as consisting in patterns of institutionalized normative culture.[3] This is less formidable than it sounds, as we may observe by breaking down its components in reverse order, considering first normative culture, then institutionalization, and then patterning.

There is more than one "kind" of culture. Or culture may be said to have various "components." Thus, cognitive culture, knowledge-culture, one component of culture in general, is well represented by science. But *normative culture,* in particular, has to do with men's values and standards (it is not, and plainly could not be, void of all idea and belief elements; values themselves are "conceptions"). It prescribes what men should and should not do and thereby sets out what is "desirable" and what is not. It will "judge" that the terms of contracts should be observed; that husbands should not beat their wives; that priests ought to be shown a certain deference by their parishioners; and the like. Normative culture *could* theoretically exist as, say, an abstract system of morals invented by a philosopher and made an object of contemplation but not featuring anything operative in the social relations of men. But when normative culture is in fact so operative—when men actually feel that norms should be obeyed and expect approval from others when they conform to them (and even register "inner" or self-approval when they conform) and non-conformity is met with disapproval (both from others and "inside" one's self)—then the norms that are involved may be said to be *institutionalized.* (Institutionalization is a matter of degree.) Norms as often understood in sociology may already be taken as setting out *patterns* or *generalized forms* of behavior. Parishioners are to show deference to priests and this normative requirement is general. It does not set out very highly specific modes of behavior to be followed and action in conformity with it is not fleeting or accidental: it is likely to be repeated frequently.[4]

But none of this means that structure does not or should not (!) change. It does not mean that nonrepetitive social phenomena are necessarily unimportant. It does mean that structure refers to *relatively* constant phenomena. (Within the *same* general structural framework, numerous

[3] See, for example, Parsons, "An Outline of the Social System," in Parsons *et al.,* eds., *Theories of Society,* New York: The Free Press, 1961, Vol. 1, pp. 30–79, *passim.* This is a convenient (although not the sole possible) specification of social structure. It is helpful in understanding of a number of important things in structural-functional analysis. In Chapter 5 we shall adduce and utilize a different meaning of structure.

[4] Notice Merton's remark that the basic requirement for structural-functional analysis is that the object to be analyzed represent "a *standardized* (that is, patterned and repetitive) item." *Social Theory and Social Structure,* Glencoe: The Free Press, 1957, p. 50.

minor adjustments and accommodations may occur.) Since, in the usage we are following, structure refers to institutionalized normative culture, it refers to *relatively* constant (normative) "contents" that appear in the systems of interaction among men—" contents" in the sense of cultural matter that is involved in the "forms" of men's interactions.

Let us discuss the correlative term, function. Precisely *what* is it that functions? To be sure, it is social structure that functions. (Ultimately, in asking "what" functions, we reach back to the actions of human beings, meaningful, symbolically significant, oriented to ends, normatively regulated.) Just what *are* functions? In one fundamental sense they are outcomes or resultants in the relations of social systems to their environments that are requisite for the systems to continue—or *if* the systems are to continue. Parsons uses the term function in this sense. But functions need not be outright imperatives. Thus, Merton writes of functions as "those observed consequences which make for the adaptation or adjustment of a given system" and uses the term "dysfunctions" to refer to "those observed consequences which lessen the adaptation or adjustment of the system."[5] The "consequences" he refers to are consequences *of* "standardized and repetitive" items of sociological inquiry. In a third, "weak" usage, a function means merely a consequence that is in some way *relevant* to a social system or system of human interactions. This is noted for the reason that it is encountered with some frequency. Imperative "for," adaptive "for," relevant "for"—these are the broad notions involved in "function" that have just been reviewed. The term should preferably be used in either of the first two senses. The third usage is sometimes convenient,[6] but is very loose.

In connection with functions as "imperatives," it is useful to note that Parsons has set out a number of abstract, general functional imperatives for social systems. These comprise what he calls pattern-maintenance, integration, goal-attainment and adaptation. Pattern-maintenance refers to "the imperative of maintaining the stability of the pattern of institutionalized normative culture defining the structure of the social system."[7] Pattern-maintenance centers on two things: institutionalized normative culture and socialization. With regard to the first of these things, pattern-maintenance is concerned with values, here understood as *the most general* forms of what appears desirable to the members of a society—illustrated by "democracy" or "free enterprise," these being very general desiderata indeed, as we shall have further occasion to note. The essential function in pattern-maintenance, writes Parsons, is "maintenance . . . of the sta-

---

[5] *Social Theory and Social Structure,* p. 51.
[6] Another sense of function is referred to below, p. 67, n.31.
[7] Parsons, in *Theories of Society,* Vol. I, p. 38.

bility of institutionalized values through the processes which articulate values with the belief system, namely, religious beliefs, ideology and the like."[8] The notion involved plays a part in Parsons' theory of the social system "comparable to that of the concept of inertia in mechanics." No bias in favor of the "static" is implied and Parsons' intention, at least, in this matter is made plain when he observes that, 'analytically, specialization in both maintenance *and change* of values" should be placed within the category of pattern-maintenance."[9] Socialization, of course, refers to the individual's own internalization of patterns. There are ongoing problems of adherence and commitment to social standards and desiderata throughout individual lives and, in this sense, the pattern-maintenance function is of constant relevance in individual careers.

The functional imperative of integration involves the working out of the relations among units interacting in a system of social relations in such fashion that their relations are "adjusted" (with consideration for their contributions to the whole) and "break-up" of the system is averted.[10] The units referred to may be persons in roles, organizations, or even social classes. There are minimal integrative requirements for the social system of any society (understood as a collectivity), requirements beyond which the system is endangered. The category of integration should be taken as inclusive of problems of "disintegration." From an ethical point of view it may be highly desirable for some system to disintegrate. That is not in question. Instead, the point is: *if* a particular system is to be sustained, there are minimum requirements for it in the way of integration (just as there are minimum requirements for it in the way of pattern-maintenance).

Late-medieval, pre-Tokugawa Japan was a country riven by strife and contention, almost a stage for the enactment of battle, murder, and suicide. There were violent quarrels about succession to high places among warrior families. Warriors who were small landowners seeking to obtain more land or to reduce their tax payments and ever ready to follow a warlord willing to promise them relief were a constant source of irritation. In the middle of the generally bloody three-century stretch that preceded the Tokugawa shoguns, there occurred the so-called Onin War, described as "the most dreadful conflict in the sanguinary history of the Middle Ages."[11] Presumably the writer of these words refers to Japan's particular

[8] *Ibid.*, p. 38. It will be recalled that reference was made in Chapter 1 to religion as making sense of, making meaningful, ultimate social values. Ideology may perform a similar service. But this does not mean that religion necessarily must be "conservative." See above. p. 6.

[9] *Ibid.*, pp. 38–39, 57; italics supplied.

[10] *Ibid.*, p. 40.

[11] George Sansom, *A History of Japan: 1334–1615*, Stanford: Stanford University Press, 1961, p. 212. The brief description given relies on Sansom.

Middle Ages, but "disintegrative" stress had evidently gone to the point where one could much more seriously envisage a threat just to the sheer biological foundations of society than under any "ordinary" circumstances. The sheer "survival" criterion for a social system is sometimes interesting.[12]

A few words will suffice for Parsons' two remaining functional imperatives, since they will not greatly concern us further. The function of goal-attainment, as its name suggests, has to do with the satisfaction of needs. Goal-attainment becomes a "problem," in Parsons' words, "in so far as there arises some discrepancy between the inertial tendencies of the [social] system and its needs resulting from the situation." Goal-attainment has a "personality" reference as it bears on individuals' motives to perform as they must to make necessary system contributions. As regards adaptation, it need only be noted that this poses functional "issues" because of the emergence of "economic" problems, having to do with the allocation of limited resources among alternative uses or for alternative goals. Goal-attainment is intimately tied to the polity, adaptation to the economy.[13]

These functional imperatives can, in principle, be elaborated or refined and "specialized" for the uses of particular kinds of functional analysis. The general notion of functional imperatives can only perform certain tasks for us. Thus, it sets forth an outer "limit" of sorts and we may be interested in many phenomena well within that limit. The question of the sheer "survival" of a society as an actual, going collectivity or community, although it begins to evoke some interest in a case such as that of late-medieval Japan, is not always concretely very compelling, while questions of how and why a society does as "well" or as "poorly" as it does in various specific respects (always within the bounds imposed by the general limit of "survival") may be most cogent.

The term "social system" has been used above with an implicit appeal to the reader's intuitive understanding. Human actors have "to do" with one another. They interact. Their interaction constitutes a social system. That system has a structure. The structure consists in institutionalized normative culture. Again, this is all Parsons, as is the rest of what now follows. The social system has what we may call crucial immediate environments in the form of the cultural system and the personality system.[14]

[12] A focus of integration that should not be overlooked (it is important for religion) has to do with sickness and health insofar as they bear on an individual's capacity and disposition to engage in his normal, expected associations with others. Parsons writes: "Illness is, from one point of view, the lapse of the sick person from his status as a fully integrated member of . . . relevant collectivities." *Societies*, p. 40.

[13] See Parsons, *ibid.*, pp. 39, 40.

[14] Parsons includes an additional environment of the "behavioral organism" which need not concern us; and there are in his view, technically, two further

In a still useful statement in reference to the function of pattern-maintenance, Parsons and Smelser wrote over a decade ago, in words that should
by now have a wholly familiar ring: "A social system is always characterized by an institutionalized value system. The social system's first functional imperative is to maintain the integrity of that value system and
its institutionalization."[15] We know already that the integrity and institutionalization must be maintained *if* the system is to continue more or
less as it is. A social system is somewhat like a sea creature that should
incorporate some portion of the sea within itself while the sea generally
constitutes an environment for it. The social system "incorporates" crucial
cultural components, but there are always environing cultural phenomena
not institutionalized in the system that can represent threats to its
normative elements, its structure. Cultural phenomena that are radically
external may make an invasion that proves quite disorganizing—as when,
say, Christian values and beliefs abruptly impinge on the social system
of a primitive people from "outside" and "take hold." Not only instability
but a threat to the very existence of the system can ensue in such a
case, as relations among the human participants in the system become
precarious and occasion conflict. Although in analysis we can readily distinguish pattern-maintenance from integration, concretely they are closely
connected.

With respect to the personality as an environment of the social system,
it may be said that although personalities are often profoundly socialized
and their socialized components are indispensable to the working of a
social system, there are still always potentialities of dissatisfaction in the
motivational sphere that for their part may also present a threat of invasion
and impairment of the social system. There is a genuine sense in which
personalities can "stand aside" from a social scheme and be devastatingly
critical of it and alienated from it even though they have played and
even continue to play roles within it. "Motivational 'tension' arising from
'strains' . . . may threaten individual motivation to conformity with institutionalized role expectations," note Parsons and Smelser.[16]

Here, then, are crucial environmental frontiers of a social system—first,
an external cultural world unincorporated within the social system
to much of which that system has to "adapt" and portions of which it
must exclude from itself *if* it is to remain recognizably itself; second,

---

environments of human action taken as a whole—namely, an environment of
"ultimate reality" and a physical-organic environment. The environment of ultimate reality is of course that to which religion addresses itself.

[15] Talcott Parsons and Neil J. Smelser, *Economy and Society,* Glencoe: The
Free Press, 1956, p. 16.

[16] *Ibid.,* p. 17.

a kind of personality-reserve that has not been captured in contented roles. The latter is associated with the capacity to criticize and reject a system featuring roles that critics and rebels may have played or may even still be playing, themselves, and it represents an environment to which there must be "adequate" responses *if* the extant social system is to remain itself. Let me repeat that a functional imperative such as that of pattern-maintenance is an imperative *if* the structure of a social system is to be maintained. It need not be maintained in fact. It may be swamped, in fact, by patterns alien to it. And there is no necessary moral virtue in its maintenance. Moral virtue may all be on the side of nonmaintenance in any number of particular cases.

It is well to remind ourselves how crucially important the idea of system is in structural-functional analysis. In a convenient summary of conditions under which the notion of function applies, Dorothy Emmet adduces three such conditions, of which the first is that "the object of study can be considered as forming a system taken as a unitary whole." A social system can prevail between two persons or among the members of a large collectivity. Relations among the elements of a system are not haphazard. Events in part of a system have repercussions elsewhere in it, although the system may theoretically be divided into subsystems, with more intimate relations of the elements within the subsystems than between those elements and others in the larger system framework. In terms of the same general logic, systems are delimited from one another and have boundaries, although these may shift.

Emmet's second condition is that "the unitary whole must be ordered as a differentiated complex, in which it is possible to talk about 'part-whole' relationships." Thus, we may talk about the norm of clerical celibacy as a distinct item in the complex of Catholicism and inquire about the relation of the part (the norm) to the whole (the complex of Catholicism). Or we may talk about a distinct religious establishment (a part) in the light of what it does in relation to a larger complex of establishments (a whole). Then, Emmet (after referring to purposive constructions that do not interest us) gives it as the third condition that the parts can be shown to maintain the "ordered whole" in a "persisting or enduring state."[17] Here we would prefer to say at once that it is a system which is always in question and there are consequences of the operation of parts that maintain the whole and other consequences that may even "break it down"—or else, in Merton's words previously cited, "lessen the adaptation or adjustment of the system." Dysfunction is certainly as important as function and it is an empirical issue whether some-

[17] Dorothy Emmet, *Function, Purpose and Power,* London: Macmillan, 1958, p. 46. See also Emmet, *Rules, Roles and Relations:* London, Macmillan, 1966, Ch. 6.

thing works to "maintain" or to break down. Breakdown possibilities are further suggested by Parsons' use of the concept of strain.[18] But the importance of the idea of system in all this is evident.

Aside from the three conditions Emmet notes, we should also remark– and this important matter is something of which Emmet and others are perfectly well aware–that where we deal with functions in systems of human interrelations, there is always likely to be *some* awareness of, and interest in, the larger system consequences of actions. This awareness and interest then can work as further elements in the total situation to reinforce or to weaken various actions previously undertaken. (Unintended conse- quences of action are of tremendous significance in human society, but, once such consequences have come about, they may be recognized.)

TOWARD A STRUCTURAL-FUNCTIONAL VIEW OF RELIGION

We may now understand better the efforts in the direction of structural- functional analysis of religion that were made by scholars like W. Robert- son Smith, Durkheim, Malinowski and Radcliffe-Brown, among others, and that continue to be made today, more particularly in sociology, by scholars like Parsons. The impression should not be given that the work of these men is all quietly unitary. (The usage of *"structural*-functional" has become especially self-conscious in recent years.) There are differences among them and they are by no means always unimportant, but there are also significant resemblances and all would repudiate the intellectualism we have criticized.

Now let us review briefly some matters previously noted. Religion ad- dresses itself to what men conceive to be an ultimate or transcendent reality. In so doing it will seek to give meaning to human life and it will tend to legitimate the values of the members of a society, although it may also challenge them in a "prophetic" way. As such, religion may usefully be regarded as a cultural phenomenon, but again as we already know, it "gets into" men's social life. It brings into that life beliefs about ultimate reality[19] and standards relating to men's behavior that become

---

[18] Note: "If the strain becomes great enough, the mechanisms of control will not be able to maintain that conformity to relevant normative expectations neces- sary to avoid the breakdown of the structure." Parsons, *Theories of Society,* I, p. 71.

[19] It was noted parenthetically, above, that normative culture could not be void of all idea and belief elements. Religious beliefs get a normative grounding when, for instance, all members of a society are exhorted to act in certain ways to please the gods and failure to act in those ways is met by disapproval. Items of a religious credo, however, are taken in themselves part of what may be called an "ultimate-reality" culture. As such, they are not normative. But they can and

institutionalized. In none of this is there any emphasis on the "errors" of religion.

We are now back where we were at the very end of Chapter 2 and may expand some notions there offered. A certain willingness not to be especially concerned with error can be very helpful for some purposes. A primitive man of religion or practitioner of magic—and whether we turn to religion or magic is for the moment unimportant[20]—asserts that some activity he performs puts a stop to a most undesirable illness on the part of a "patient." As a proposition in medicine, pathology or physiology, the assertion may be entirely unfounded. But it would be the poorest possible sociological strategy to infer, therefore, that the entirety of the religious or magical activity is "silly," and then to pay it no attention. We should certainly allow and take seriously a distinction between what the religious or magical actor has "in view," what he seeks to accomplish or believes he accomplishes, on the one hand, and what the actual (social and psychological) effects of his activity are, on the other hand. This distinction is indeed crucial. Another way to state it is to assert that subjective intentions constitute one order of things and objective consequences or "functions"[21] another—and the two kinds of things need not coincide. If any "medical" sort of effect is in fact impossible, purely an illusion on the religious or magical actor's part, the outcome of his practice can still be significantly curative. If, for example, the patient's illness is a matter of considerable public concern while the "treatment" is reasonably elaborate and is witnessed by kin, neighbors and others, a beneficial effect can be generated as the patients' morale is heightened, as he comes to feel that he is important and an object of authentic solicitude to his fellows, or the like. It is interesting and most pertinent that in cases of

---

of course do get involved in social systems and accordingly in men's relations to one another. There is a tendency in the relevant literature to label them as items of social structure when they are so involved, although, once more, they are not strictly normative. They may also be called "institutionalized" when they become expected or standard beliefs.

[20] One way (although not the only possible one) to define magic is to state that it has to do with the application of ritual means to empirical ends. This view of magic is taken by Parsons, *Structure of Social Action*, pp. 258, 432. In this sense, symbolically significant behavior that is otherwise addressed to transcendental ends or sacred objects can get a deflection to the empirical realm, as ritual is applied to such objects as capturing elusive game or compassing the death of a powerful enemy. For the view of magic we take, see below, p. 152.

[21] See Robert K. Merton, *Social Theory and Social Structure*, p. 24. One might usefully make a *threefold* distinction here. There is what the actor in view or thinks he does or says he does. There is what he does in fact do. There is the social and psychological outcome of what he does.

this kind attempted refutation of the practitioner's "wrong ideas" need not affect the core functions of his activity. (The patient could still be effectively reintegrated with his fellows.) One could try to demonstrate to the practitioner the foolishness of his ideas and indeed demonstrate it at least to one's own entire (and just) satisfaction, while the precise therapeutic way in which his procedures worked would remain an unequivocal reality—even if a reality of which he himself was quite unaware and of which he could give no verbal formulation.

In the light of considerations such as these, scholars such as the anthropologist Radcliffe-Brown turned away from the effort to find the orgins of religion in erroneous ideas. Radcliffe-Brown sought "another way" to analyze religion. He wrote:

"There is another way in which we may approach the study of religion. We may entertain as at least a possibility the theory that any religion is an important or even essential part of the social machinery, as are morality and law, part of the complex system by which human beings are enabled to live together in an orderly arrangement of social relations. From this point of view we deal not with the origins but with the social functions of religions, i.e., the contribution that they make to the formation and maintenance of a social order. There are many persons who would say that it is only *true* religion (i.e., one's own) that can provide the foundation of an orderly social life. The hypothesis we are considering is that the social function of a religion is independent of its truth or falsity, that religions which we think to be erroneous or even absurd and repulsive, such as those of some savage tribes, may be important and effective parts of the social machinery and that without these 'false' religions social evolution and the development of modern civilization would have been impossible."[22]

These sentences say a number of important things. First, to deal with religion in terms of "functions" is at least an alternative to dealing with it in terms of "origins." Then, a significant sense of function is rendered by the notion of "contribution to the formation and maintenance of a social order" or social system. Third, function is in principle independent of presumptive truth or falsity of a religion. Fourth, religion is in any case in some sense tied in with societies, a "part of the social machinery," in Radcliffe-Brown's words. Radcliffe-Brown might have added the point that the functions of religion are typically achieved without human intention: religious actors usually act as they do to relate to the sacred, perhaps

[22] A. R. Radcliffe-Brown, from his Henry Myers Lecture, 1945, "Religion and Society," as reprinted in his *Structure and Function in Primitive Society,* Glencoe: The Free Press, 1952, p. 154.

to appease the gods or celebrate their benevolence, not to enhance social order. But, important as all this is, it is hardly surprising in view of what we already know from our critique of intellectualism and outline of some elements of structural-functional analysis. Yet Radcliffe-Brown's statement is interesting as an extraordinarily succinct summary of a functionalist position at a time when structural-functional analysis was less sophisticated than it is now and at a time when numerous scholars, often attending to primitive religions in particular, were probably readier to take for granted than they should have been that religion does in fact contribute to "the formation and maintenance of social order."

We must make problematic the functions of religion. Those functions must, in other words, be made matter for actual inquiry. The point is simple but fundamental. A theory neglectful of realities is obviously going to be worthless. One of the very important and constant imputations of function to religion has been on the line that religion integrates. We already know very well that if it is true that the provision of integration at a certain level is functionally imperative for a social system it does not follow that that level of integration will necessarily be realized. If religion has been important in fulfilling integrative functions in some system, it does not follow that it will continue to do so. Nor does it follow that religion alone will fulfill integrative functions. (It seems reasonable to contend that in a highly developed society, law, for example, is of major integrative importance.[23]) Nor must religion fulfill integrative functions alone. It has had obvious historical importance in relation to pattern-maintenance, to say no more.

But there has certainly been much functionalist endeavor to show that religion is integrative, as we have just suggested, and we may here concentrate on this point as one on which misunderstanding arises too easily. One major source of difficulty about structural-functional analysis has lain in the notion that it must assume a kind of universal beneficence of functioning. A relatively early functionalist like the anthropologist Malinowski could indeed often give the impression that functionalism made such an assumption. In departing from intellectualism, the functionalists made some great gains. The paragraph we have quoted from Radcliffe-Brown points clearly to what those gains were. But the functionalists were sometimes exuberant or over-enthusiastic in their claims for the beneficent functioning of religion, magic and numerous other phenomena. Everything then seemed to work for "balance," "harmony," "maintenance," "integration" and the profound satisfaction of human desires in remote island paradises. This is perhaps a provocative way to put the matter,

---

[23] Cf. Parsons in *Theories of Society*, I, p. 40.

but it does suggest a significant tendency. It is certainly clear, in any case, that an assumption of universal beneficence of functioning is dubious indeed.[24] The particular assertion that religion "integrates," without qualification, is (to put the matter mildly) suspect. The point deserves documentation in some detail.

THE FUNCTION OF INTEGRATION: INTEGRATION AS PROBLEMATIC

First, it is important to be clear about our precise references. In Matthew it appears that while Christ was speaking to "the people" on an occasion, "his mother and his brethren" wished for their part to speak to him. When told about this, he asked, "Who is my mother and who are my brethren?" and continued, as he pointed toward his disciples, "Behold my mother and my brethren! For whosoever shall do the will of my Father which is in heaven, the same is my brother, and sister, and mother." (Matthew 12:46–50).[25] If our reference is to the family unit, there is plainly a sense in which Christ's religion was hardly integrative, hardly likely to bring solidarity among kin merely because they were kin. Plainly, too, that religion would be likely to create integrative bonds among non-kin, among men who might have nothing to do with one another or be unequivocally hostile to one another were they not touched by a religion making a universal appeal. In a quite different context, Pratt noted in his popular but very thoughtful work on the pilgrimage of Buddhism that a Buddhist monk in Ceylon observed to Mrs. Pratt: "I have mother and father and sister but leave them all to themselves and think of myself only and my salvation. . . . To love your husband or your father very dangerous. If you live pure life without attachments you will be young and good-looking when you will attain eighty or one hundred years."[26] The Buddhist emphasis on the evil of desire and on detachment

---

[24] We do not, incidentally, imply some simple and happy story of progress in which, as step one, the drawbacks of intellectualism were firmly grasped; as step two, an improved structural-functional view of religion was introduced, although this was still vitiated by some errors; as step three, the errors were removed and a very powerful structural-functional theory of society supervened. This is too romantic a view. The functionalist social theory has not attained staggering scientific heights, although it has had noteworthy development in the hands of a pre-eminent functionalist like Parsons.

[25] Cf. also Luke 14:26: "If any man come to me, and hate not his father, and mother, and wife, and children, and brethren, and sister, yea, and his own life also, he cannot be my disciple."

[26] James B. Pratt, The Pilgrimage of Buddhism, New York: Macmillan, 1928, p. 137.

can occasion this sort of attitude, which is hardly integrative, again with reference to familial or kinship units.

It is not at all difficult to show that if we refer to "religion" in a way that, in common sense terms, is thoroughly legitimate, it frequently does not operate integratively. This has long been known by functionalists. Let us turn to some pertinent historical circumstances.

Where divisions obtain within the same general religious framework, as is well known, there are often particularly bitter attitudes on the part of one group toward another. There has been a certain amount of internal conflict within Islam. In Kashmir around the end of the fifth century, "religious disputes" among Muslim nobles reached such a point that the nobles killed each other with their swords in the presence of their king in an audience hall. Persians (with their Shi'ite persuasion) are said to write the names of the first three (in the Shi'ite view, illegitimate) successors to Mohammed "on the walls of latrines, or on the soles of their shoes." It has happened on the other hand that Shi'ites caught on pilgrimage to Mecca have been put to death by Sunnites who regarded them as apostates. Kashmiri history relates violent clashes between Shi'ites and Sunnites. In the month of Muharram, which commemorates Hussein's martyrdom at Kerbala, the Shi'ite holy city in Iraq (in which Shi'ites are likely to exhibit great emotion about their martyrs), there have been frequent conflicts between the two parties. Hollister reports strains and clashes between them in twentieth-century India, strains and clashes at least ostensibly centering on the old conflict about succession and the Shi'ite attitude that Ali's rights were usurped by Mohammed's first three successors.[27] The great Islamic scholar, Ignaz Goldziher, was inclined to trace such clashes back to political causes,[28] but their reality, the absence of "integration" they imply, and the existence of irreducible religious elements in them remain.

It would seem likely that the internal integration of the groups in conflict would be heightened by the conflict itself. Here our group references are quite obvious. Conflict integrates in-group members and virtually by definition decreases solidarity across group lines, and it is even quite plausible that it should the more effectively integrate members of in-groups the more effectively it opposes different groups to one another. Common values and shared beliefs should still bind those who belong in the same general religious framework, but special bitterness does often seem to attend the conflicts of those who differ on a background of some agreement. Those from whom one differs greatly one can perhaps become

[27] John N. Hollister, *The Shi'a of India*, pp. 188–190; cf. also pp. 5, 146, 148–49, 178.

[28] Ignaz Goldziher, *Vorlesungen über den Islam*, Ch. 5.

indifferent to. They are truly "hopeless" and may for some purposes be left quite out of account. But rage can be aroused against essentially more instructed persons, who *should* "know better."[29] Moreover, sectarian differences can reach the point where a truly radical departure from common values or shared beliefs threatens, as in the case of extremists among the Shi'ites whom the latter themselves have called "exaggerators."[30]

Let us remain formally within the framework of the same general religion and turn to the Far East. A famous historical case of intolerance with notable counterintegrative effect is afforded by the brand of Buddhism upheld by the Japanese monk and prophet Nichiren (1222–1282). Nichiren proclaimed the one Buddha, the Eternal Buddha of the Lotus Sutra.[31] Beliefs that diverged from his own doctrine he condemned as lies and deception. This is the more remarkable as the early Buddhist tradition in Japan had been one of harmony among different branches and of regarding different doctrines as variants of a single truth. But Nichiren was "a quarrelsome saint and a master of vituperation," in Sansom's words.[32] Zen teaching, Amida worship, the Shingon sect—such phenomena as these, in Nichiren's view, accounted for Japanese powerlessness. The anger of heaven would come upon the country if the regime did not finally forbid the sects. Without the Lotus Sutra and without a leader to read it, the land would fall into confusion and eternal damnation. Nichiren struck numerous others as being a man of fanaticism, unprecedented effrontery, and radical intolerance. When Kublai Khan in 1268 threatened to attack Japan, Nichiren called for an end to the seduction of the people by the sects and for unity of the country in worship of the Lotus Sutra in order to forestall the disaster the Mongols threatened. On this occasion, his refusal to spare anyone at all from his denunciations and his predictions of destinies in hell led to his imprisonment and a sentence of death. His execution did not take place, but he would not compromise with other religions or desist from his attacks upon them.

Nichiren opened up for Mahayana Buddhism a novel method of salva-

---

[29] Thus, Goldziher observes that Shi'ite traditions show almost a more hostile attitude toward other Muslims than toward non-Muslims and he notes the case of an important Shi'ite writer who recommends that where the religious law does not give ground for taking a definite position the principle to follow is that of doing the opposite of what the Sunnites believe to be right. Goldziher, *op. cit.*. pp. 239–240.

[30] Goldziher, *op. cit.*, p. 208.

[31] A distinction is implied between an individual, historically existent Buddha who lived and died in India five to six centuries before Christ and an eternal, true, universal Buddha, lord of the world. See Masaharu Anesaki, *Nichiren, The Buddhist Prophet,* Cambridge: Harvard University Press, 1916, pp. 25, 150–151.

[32] George Sansom, *A History of Japan, 1334–1615,* p. 295, footnote.

tion, that of "aggressive belief." It has been suggested that his failure to achieve his goal of a Japan internally united by belief in the Lotus Sutra or his goal of a Japan-centered worldwide Buddhism was completed by the circumstance that he has gone down in the history of Buddhism as the founder of still another sect and therefore as one who increased the presumed evil his object it was to fight.[33] The well-known present-day Japanese movement called Sōka Gakkai traces back on the religious side (via Nichiren Shoshu) to Nichiren and has had a history marked by fanaticism and intolerance.

It is of interest that Nichiren's outlook brought him into conflict not only with representatives of other religious groups but with political authorities. Strife between religion and political authorities has, of course, prevailed elsewhere and at other times. Thus, persecution of Buddhism by political authority in the history of China has often been pointed to.[34] Eisenstadt, basing his comment on work by a number of specialists on China, writes with particular reference to the T'ang regime (618–907) that "the religious persecution which often developed in China was usually predominantly a political phenomenon, and much less a cultural-spiritual one," and he adds that "in China, persecution and intolerance usually developed when the state or power groups within the ruling stratum grew apprehensive about the political or economic power accumulated by another group, which happened to belong to a certain religious denomination."[35] However "accidental" religion might be in such circumstances, it could still hardly be said without qualification to work integratively for Chinese society as a whole when one focuses on its involvement in conflict with ruling groups.

To return to Japan for a moment, at the end of the eighth century the Buddhist church threatened governmental stability. Its leaders were politically ambitious and abused fiscal immunities. The state was deprived of much needed revenue by the taking of public lands into ecclesiastical domains. Armed men less pious than brawny, but with certain minor religious offices or affiliations, became attached to the medieval Japanese monasteries. They would get out of control from time to time and create problems of order in the capital. They were apparently no great military threat but they were awkwardly "religious" from the point of view of

[33] This brief statement has followed the vivid account of Nichiren's life and work in Gerhard Rosenkranz, *Der Weg des Buddha,* Stuttgart: Evang. Missionsverlag, 1960, pp. 302–319.

[34] *Cf.,* for example, Kenneth Ch'en, *Buddhism in China,* Princeton: Princeton University Press, 1964, as at pp. 136, 150, 191, 232, for statements on persecution in the fifth, sixth, and ninth centuries.

[35] Shmuel N. Eisenstadt, *The Political Systems of Empires,* New York: The Free Press, 1963, p. 59.

rulers not inclined to risk supernatural sanctions. Oda Nobunaga, the famous warrior and dictator of the sixteenth century, hated the Buddhist churchmen's intrusion in political matters and resented their recourse to military strength.[36]

The tale could be carried on at considerable length. The circumstances adduced are presumably somewhat less familiar to the reader than similar things closer to home. Western history obviously could furnish us with an enormous amount of relevant documentation. It is more than twenty years since Merton noted that the flat, unqualified presumption that religion exercises integrative functions involves "blotting out the entire history of religious wars, of the Inquisition (which drove a wedge into society after society), of internecine conflicts among religious groups."[37] This brief reference will have to suffice as indicator for the relevant history of the West, while it may also serve to reinforce the proposition that it is only the most naïve and undiscriminating kind of functionalism that could conceivably adhere to the notion that "religion," without further specification—without indication of precisely what normative structures, what elements of credo, what groups, one refers to—always and everywhere operates "integratively"—without indication of incidence of presumed functional effect.

In the first chapter of this book we noted that religion is carried by men who have some feeling that they are members of a distinctive group or community in virtue of their shared religious beliefs and actions. This suggests a measure of integration. And Durkheim, it will be remembered, wrote that religious beliefs and practices "unite into one single moral community" that is called a church all who adhere to them. In the light of what we have just been saying at some length, this may appear paradoxical or puzzling. But it need occasion no difficulty. We may suggest that Durkheim was quite right–for certain limited (although most important) aspects of religion or for religion in certain limited references. This leaves unchanged our view that religion in a wide, comprehensive sense does not by any means always "integrate"–and we have been at some pains to support this view. We need to know more about how different "aspects" of religion operate, certainly, and thereby we may be helped toward better "definitions" of religion.

[36] George B. Sansom, *A History of Japan to 1334,* London: Cresset Press, 1958, pp. 270, 273, 399; and Sansom, *A History of Japan, 1334–1615,* p. 295.
[37] *Social Theory and Social Structure,* p. 29.

CHAPTER 4

Hierarchy, System, Control, and Religion

Once overoptimistic or simplistic notions about the functions of religion have been looked at askance, it is still necessary to inquire further how structural-functional approaches to religion in society may help illuminate that phenomenon. It is the object of the present chapter to continue the enterprise undertaken in the previous one, now with reference to hierarchy, system again, and control, and with due regard for how these matters bear on the field of religion. Important contributions, once more, have been made by Parsons, and it is again necessary to draw heavily from his work.

The idea of structure alone does not lead us very far in the analysis of systems at the social level. (Again, structure is used in the sense of institutionalized normative culture.) Structures need to be *discriminated,* if that is possible. When they are discriminated, we may expect to find that different structures perform different functions (although this does not in principle preclude the possibility of some "substitutions," as one structure "substitutes" for another). At the biological level, we would look to the performance of different functions by the structures called heart, liver and kidneys in the bodies of animals possessing these organs. This suggests the possibility of something comparable or analogous at the social level.

STRUCTURE, HIERARCHY, AND CONTROL

The beginnings of discrimination, as well as hierarchical ordering, of social structure are found in Parsons' categories of values, norms, collectivities and roles. Values are in this context once again the most general forms of what appears desirable to members of a society. They are overall or overarching forms of the desirable. They are, as it were, "at the top" of a social system. Just because they are "master" conceptions of a generic kind and set out very general ends, they do not provide certain *specifications*—particularizations, if one will, that are needed in the concrete conduct of affairs in a society. We have previously mentioned "democracy" and "free enterprise." Smelser writes relevantly that the value of democracy provides "only criteria for judging the legitimacy or illegitimacy of whole classes of behavior." He adds: "Various rules must be established which indicate how democracy (or any other system of values) may be realized—rules of election, office-holding, rights and privileges of the state and the citizens." And he observes that these rules "represent, in certain respects, a narrowing of the possible applications of the general values." Or free enterprise (as Smelser again observes), as a general value, "does not define any detailed mutual rights and privileges of actors, or norms for expected behavior," and we must seek such norms more especially in "the legal institutions of contract, property and employment" (as well as in some other more informal phenomena such as "understandings among producers concerning the share of the market which should go to each").[1]

We need to stress the specifying role of norms, *now using the word in a particular, technical sense* to refer, precisely, to (second-level) structural factors that do specify or particularize (first-level) values. (Both values and norms are of course "normative" in a general sense.) In virtue of this specification, values, as master conceptions of the desirable, still form an indispensable component within the norms and thereby exercise control. Norms are necessary in order to "implement" the values and carry them on toward actual performances or actions in human society. "If values only are present, no action is possible."[2] Moreover, it is necessary to go on beyond values and norms in a process of further specification. Smelser, again, notes that "by themselves values and norms do not determine the *form of organization* of human action." In supplying general ends and general rules, values and norms still "do not specify . . . who will be the agents in the pursuit of valued ends" or how the actions of these agents will be shaped in the context of organizations and roles.[3] Collectivities and roles, then, introduce further specifications. It is well to note that Parsons, in setting out the hierarchy of values, norms, collectivities and roles, stresses *the normative-culture component* of collectivities and roles, so that all four elements in the hierarchy are in this way cog-

[1] Neil J. Smelser, *Theory of Collective Behavior,* New York: Free Press, 1963, pp. 26–27. Smelser here sets out notions traceable to Parsons. A recent relevant statement by the latter may be found in *Societies,* p. 23.

[2] *Ibid.,* p. 27.

[3] *Ibid.,* p. 27.

nate.[4] It is well also to emphasize that the control of values is the "deepest," since it extends all the way down to roles, where there occur specifications or particularizations at a "lowest" level.[5]

If values exercise control "downward," it is nevertheless true that in a social system in which this occurs, there may be some back-up or reverse effect. Changes in values are bound to operate downward, as changes in values pertaining to free enterprise may finally effect changes in the roles and concrete business activities of businessmen in various organizations. But some reverse effect is at any rate possible. Changes beginning relatively low in a hierarchy may finally "work up" to the top, although numerous relatively low-level changes will occur while the top "contains" them and remains substantially unchanged.[6]

The attempt Parsons makes to discriminate structures and order them hierarchically is plainly an attempt to move toward refined structural-functional analysis. It may be that the whole effort will have to be recast. We know little about structures in a really systematic way. The sheer *listing, description and ordering* of elements in social structure may have to be worked with for a long time before we have something of high scientific utility. Yet what Parsons has done is already most suggestive. When he discriminates and sets up in hierarchical order the four structural elements referred to, he evidently means to assign them different functions. Roles do not and cannot perform the same functions as values, for instance.

The significance of the term, system, may now be brought out more plainly. Elements of social structure are related to one another in a system context, as we already know, and we may now seek to grasp this point more firmly and extensively. We need not use Parsons' particular terms

---

[4] See, for example, *Theories of Society*, Vol. 1, pp. 43–44.

[5] An analogy may be helpful in all this, *provided* we recognize its limitations. Let us understand the word "anthropomorphism" to mean the ascription of human form and attributes to beings not human (such as dogs or gods). This is a very inclusive ascription and we may understand it to include even human *physical* form. Let us agree to understand the word "anthropophuism" to mean the ascription of human nature, in the broadest psychological sense. This excludes human physical form but includes *all* human psychological traits. Let us understand the word "anthropopathism" to mean the ascription of human emotions or feelings, specifically and alone. The increasing specification is plain; and it is plain that the common word root (meaning "man," to be sure) in the three words goes "downward," "to the end" and exercises control until the series is finished. (So "free enterprise," too, can still prevail in *very particular* business roles in a free enterprise economy.) But, while this is suggestive, it is still defective. Thus, norms in society "implement" values and allow them ultimately to be operative in concrete behavior in a fashion that this analogy fails to suggest.

[6] *Cf.* Parsons, *Theories of Society*, Vol. 1, p. 72, for some appropriate comment.

in what follows, but the general character of his endeavor to illuminate social systems in connection with hierarchy, control and discriminated or differentiated structures is well worth keeping in view. The idea that sociocultural phenomena are involved in a system of more or less determinate relations to one another, in which events do not occur haphazardly but within certain constraints or degrees of freedom—this general idea is a very old one. It is indeed far too old for one to be able to say that structural-functional analysis in a modern sense has created it. But in its taking over of the idea, structural-functional analysis has begun to give it a certain clarity of outline that it did not previously have.[7] What follows in the present section should help to explain why this is said. The argument proceeds by way of consideration of the Catholic Church in Latin America and relies greatly on an analysis by Ivan Vallier.[8] (There are features of the analysis that may now seem to many to be overoptimistic, in the light of recent circumstances pertaining to Catholicism, but the analysis retains value, nevertheless.)

The Catholic Church in Latin America has tended to identify with the powers-that-be in the secular society. Houtart and Pin, writing from a Catholic point of view, and listing various "deficiencies" that stand in the way of a Catholicism more oriented to mass needs, note among other things that church teaching and moral instruction have tended to consist in a code frequently "reduced to a few obligations and a few taboos (principally in sexual matters)." A specifically "social" morality has received relatively little stress, and this, say Houtart and Pin, "partially explains the failure to instill true Christian principles in the traditional elite."[9] Meanwhile, Latin American social systems have been, generally, quite vulnerable to their culture and personality environments in the contemporary world. "Information," cultural matter, comes from abroad to indicate to Latin Americans that certain standards of life are possible for the masses and are being at least in some degree realized or aimed at elsewhere. Persons, more especially if they have had some inkling of "better things" and have received the hint that they are in themselves somehow valuable beings, are likely to become alienated from systems that given them unenviable roles with small economic, health and status rewards.

Vallier indicates that a substantial group in Latin America continues

[7] See also, in this connection, Merton, *Social Theory and Social Structure,* pp. 70–82.

[8] See Ivan Vallier, "Challenge to Catholicism in Latin America," *Trans-action,* June, 1967, pp. 17–26, 60.

[9] François Houtart and Emile Pin, *The Church and the Latin American Revolution,* New York: Sheed and Ward, 1965, p. 230.

to uphold the views of the "traditional elite." The members of this elite, whom Vallier calls politicians, "ignore the laity, carry out rituals pro forma, make the sacraments available to those who can pay the fee, and define social evils as implicit in the human situation."[10] The politicians are also markedly antagonistic to recent church innovations in regard to liturgy and the involvement of the laity in religion.

However, aside from these traditionalists, three new elites have emerged, and to these Vallier assigns the names of papists (the word is used with no pejorative connotation), pastors and pluralists. The papists stand for "a militant, modern Catholicism oriented toward re-Christianizing the world." They rely on the sacraments and on social action and represent an "apostolic conception" of the relation of modern Catholicism to society which is based on recent European experience. (We shall return to the papists in a moment.) By contrast with the papists, the pastors are primarily oriented toward the development of worship and toward the welding into a single spiritual body of priest and laity. The pluralists are strongly concerned with social justice and are willing to work with other faiths in order to help the poor and disadvantaged. They see a role for the church in Latin American social change. (But their attitude toward papists, traditionalists—politicians—and pastors, in that order, is suggested in these summarizing observations about them: "They refer to the conforming, clerical Catholic Action elite as 'sacristans' or 'goon squads.' They talk with bitterness about the traditional 'politicos' and their maneuverings. The pastors' exclusive concern with the church's inner life is criticized as 'escapism,' 'retreatism,' and 'withdrawal.' ")[11] It is vital to note that, as Vallier puts the matter, "the papists appear to play a key facilitating role in the development of the other two new elites, pastors and pluralists." The papists *legitimize the general bias toward change* of which a Latin America that hopes to modernize has obvious and tremendous need. Vallier observes:

"Institutional change in Roman Catholicism requires the imprimatur of the hierarchy, and the papists provide for a structural reorganization which makes the granting of this imprimatur to the efforts of the pluralists and pastors much more likely. Once the church has undergone a series of structural and ideological changes, including a "liberalization" of the hierarchy, the pluralist and pastoral strategies become a fully integrated part of a total mission and thus may add strength to the church and aid in the positive development of society."[12]

[10] "Challenge. . . .," p. 21.
[11] Vallier, *op. cit.,* p. 21.
[12] *Ibid.,* p. 22.

Vallier proceeds to sketch stages of Latin American development which are clearly tied in with the activities of papists, pluralists and pastors, respectively. The stages involve, first, making change rather than mere maintenance of tradition a central value; second, translating social acceptance of the notion that change is desirable into "actual mobilization patterns," into concrete transforming activities; third, "developing new modes of integration to replace traditional bonds and sustain full modernization."[13] Change-legitimating, mobilizing, and integrative functions are thus marked. The (particular) integrative function of the pastoral group (or, let us say, of its normative culture) is indicated when Vallier writes that this group provides for "the critical modicum of integration needed at the grass roots level to overcome individual and communal disorientations which might otherwise erupt in social conflict."[14] It would appear that there is indeed some foundation for asserting that different structures perform different functions within the framework of the same over-all society. Each of the three main groups—papists, pluralists, pastors—is the carrier of distinctive cultural components. The papists, for example, at least aspire toward the institutionalization at strategic social loci, or indeed on a large scale, of the normative culture of liberal social action Catholic ideology. The following representation of the role of the elites, given by Vallier, suggests much of the latter's argument:[15]

ROLE OF NEW ELITES-CHRONOLOGICAL DEVELOPMENT

		Legitimating Change	Mobilizing Resources	Reintegrating Society
Levels of the Sociocultural System	Culture	PAPISTS		
	Intergroup		PLURALISTS	
	Person-Group			PASTORS

But this representation may also help us to see that we actually have to do here with more than the circumstance that different structures perform different functions. Structures and functions articulate with one another, combine, conflict, interpenetrate, and do so within a framework of system, not randomly. Vallier writes of the cases of Colombia, Argentina and Chile against the background of the analysis he affords. The case of Colombia is most pertinent at this point.

[13] *Ibid.,* p. 23.
[14] *Ibid.,* p. 24.
[15] *Ibid.,* p. 24.

Colombia is evidently still a strongly traditionalist country, "not yet fully committed to the necessity for social change." Numerous Colombian power groups both resist the idea of change and "manage to obstruct even minor social reforms." It is not that pluralists, for example, are lacking on the Colombian scene. Vallier in fact notes that there is "a solid core" of the pluralist group involved in action having directly to do with resolving social problems but that there is also "a growing, volatile group of pluralists who want to make a direct frontal attack on changing the social order, through revolution if necessary."[16] Most significantly, it is observed that the latter category of radical pluralists would seem to be "a concrete manifestation of a 'missed stage' in the evolution of the church." It is well to quote Vallier rather amply here:

"Because the crucial contribution of the papists has not been made, the new elites are turning directly to secular change without the support of a Catholic social ideology which legitimates development and modernization. This is a tragic situation for both the church and Colombian society. For the traditional hierarchy to legitimate the more radical pluralist strategies at this time would be too destructive of their own authority; at the same time, the conservative secular groups are not prepared to confront the problems pointed up and attacked by the pluralist priests and laity. If both of these tradition-oriented sectors had been prepared for these developments by contact with a modern Catholic ideology, the pluralists might have won their support in building an effective social action movement. Theoretically, if the more radical pluralists were to retrench and concentrate their energies on the development of such an ideology, the stabilization and reintegration of the church would be accomplished and the context set for the pluralists to move out into direct social action again."[17]

The reference to a missed stage in the evolution of the church should now be clear. In the course of his analysis Vallier also refers to "absence of functional integration between levels of social structure." In the Colombian case an entire level has been effectively absent. It is the strategic (top-level) normative contribution of the papists, specifically, that has been lacking, and there can hardly be a "functional integration between levels of social structure" if relevant structures with which other structures might make contact and "integrate" are simply not there. Again we are dealing with a system. Structures can and do often "integrate" and interchange with one another, and their functions are of course vital in this. Or structures fail to "integrate" or make effective and coordinated contact.

[16] *Ibid.,* p. 25.
[17] *Ibid.,* p. 25.

Or structures are missing at the levels where they "should" be—or, without the quotation marks, where they should be *if* certain functions are to be fulfilled or certain results are to come about. Biological organisms are systems in the very general sense suggested, too, and, within limits, it is not useless to think in terms of organismic analogies. But once we work with the notion of system and take seriously the ideas of structure and function within a system framework, we are likely to be especially alert to avoid a kind of magical thinking by which (when it is at its worst) we might assume that "anything at all" can happen in sociocultural premises, or that structures and functions have no determinate relations therein; or that the structure of the social system in particular lacks features of hierarchy and differentiation (as in the sense of differentiation or discrimination of values, norms, and so on).

The above is also suggestive with regard to the notion of hierarchy of control, specifically. One could well conceive a Latin American social system with a strong, modernized, socially conscious Catholicism legitimating "progressive" social measures. A pervasive legitimating influence from such a Catholicism would work "downward" and be a significant root element in a variety of specialized, particularized activities at "lower" levels. To say this is merely to make quite explicit what has already been strongly intimated above.

It will be recalled that we previously followed a useful summary of Dorothy Emmet's of conditions under which the notion of function can be applied. *First condition*: the object studied is susceptible of approach as "a system taken as a unitary whole." By now we need say no more than that a diagrammatic representation such as that reproduced from Vallier, with the background argument that accompanies it, points plainly to "objects" that can be studied as systems (both "old" and "new" Latin American systems). *Second condition:* the unitary whole is a differentiated complex, and one can refer to part-whole relationships in it. We have clearly encountered differentiated "parts." The principles and goals of the papists (a "part") would have a distinctive role to play in a modernized Latin American social system ("whole"). We may state the *third condition* as that by which the parts or elements in a system contribute to the system's maintenance or breakdown (or "nonadaptation" or the like). Again the papists' principles and goals could well contribute to the maintenance of a changed system in which there would be at least a certain minimum meeting of the needs of the masses for decent nourishment, lodging, and so on. The material Vallier affords might allow us further play with these conditions, but what has been noted will suffice us. In summary of other points covered: First, different structures within systems perform different functions. Second, structures make contact, articulate, "mesh," "integrate" with one another—or fail to do so when there are structural gaps or omissions. Third, we have again been dealing with a control hierarchy. And it may be added that it should not be difficult to see how the modernized Latin American system, say, which Vallier sketches might present interesting problems in the "downgoing" of papist values and in the possible "upgoing" of lower-level phenomena as grass-roots normative changes might manage to reach toward the top in a kind of reverse or back-up action. Religion as implicated in society is evidently susceptible of analysis in social system terms. (This is what is important here, no matter what the particular lines on which Latin American societies may ultimately seek to solve their problems.) We need not forget in all this that some actor awareness of the functioning of relevant structures can be important in maintaining or weakening those structures.

The idea of control will be considered in the next section. A final brief section of the present chapter will address itself to the notion of system once more.

FURTHER ON CONTROL

Religion may be conceived to cover huge areas of social life and personal conduct, as virtually "everything" is judged in religious terms. The details of a man's dress may come in for criticism couched in religious terms, as may the details of a woman's use of cosmetics or her manner of doing her hair. Where religion is conceived in this way or operates on these lines, then, as Smelser, for one, suggests, "specific dissatisfactions with any social arrangements eventually become religious protests. . . ." Thus, "if interest on loans is defined as sinful rather than merely economically unsound, controversy over interest becomes a religious conflict rather than a matter of economic policy." Smelser further observes that "in a theocratic setting objections against artistic and architectural styles become moral and theological matters," instead of simple matters of taste, and accordingly "aesthetic criticism is not differentiated from moral outrage."[18]

Bellah makes the same point as Smelser and goes on to suggest a crucial contrast:

"Traditional societies . . . tend to have a normative system, in which a comprehensive, but uncodified set of relatively specific norms governs concrete behavior. But in a modern society an area of flexibility must be gained in economic, political, and social life in which specific norms may be determined in considerable part by short-term exigencies. . . . Ultimate or religious values lay down the basic principles of social ac-

[18] *Theory of Collective Behavior*, p. 320.

tion . . . . but the religious system does not attempt to regulate economic, political and social life in great detail. . . . In traditional . . . societies . . . . the social innovator necessarily becomes a religious heretic."[19]

The reference to "an area of flexibility" in a modern society is significant. The freedom to act *variably* in numerous areas of social life and personal conduct is no trivial thing, precisely from the point of view of its social importance. In the "modern" situation, insofar as a religious orientation in fact prevails, it might be said to operate on some such motto as, "Believe in God and, for the rest, do as you please." The individual in this situation can be powerfully exhorted to be just in his dealings with others, to be honest in those dealings, to be cognizant of and compassionate about the whole matter of the well-being of others. But the detail of how these values are to be realized is left to the individual himself. In the ideal case, "top-level" values such as those of justice, honesty and compassion will exercise a "downward" effect and penetrate even into the intimate details of the individual's dealings with others. The individual's generic religious commitment is "enough" and he can be allowed considerable freedom beyond it on the ground that he is not likely to do anything terribly reprehensible in any case, precisely because of the commitment itself. We are again dealing with a matter of control. We are also dealing with a matter of social structure. Structures differ in the relevant respects when we deal with modern societies on the one hand and traditional societies on the other. On the modern side, we witness institutionalization of the normative standard that the individual shall be "let alone," allowed to proceed as he will, although it is to be expected that he will proceed within the limits set by the institutionalization of additional normative standards that lay down general prescriptions for his behavior. A different kind of structure would evidently emerge as we move toward traditional societies,[20] where lower-level, *specific* prescriptions would be set out, without reliance merely on *general* control from "above."

This is all connected with the coming together within the same general society of more and more different subgroups with differing moral outlooks. On various moral *particulars* there will be a good deal of disagreement among the different groups. But a measure of agreement on more *general* points may not be hard to discern. Rules relating to the conduct of family life are appreciably different among Americans coming from

[19] Robert N. Bellah, "Religious Aspects of Modernization in Turkey and Japan," *American Journal of Sociology*, **64**, July, 1958, pp. 1–2.

[20] In the relevant literature it is sometimes said that values and norms are fused in a traditional, but differentiated in a modern society. This language has been avoided (and reference has just been made to "normative standards") in order to prevent possible confusion.

different countries. The requirements of obedience to parents set out in one subgroup could easily appear to the members of other subgroups to be too exacting and rigid, while all can still agree on the general view that it is well to "honor thy father and thy mother." If some kind of overarching normative component is useful in integrating a society containing many different subgroups, the code embodying *that* agreement is indeed bound to be of a generalized kind.[21]

Different groups have, of course, come to live together in the United States. Protestantism, Catholicism, and Judaism live side by side. They have not always done so in entire harmony, but they coexist with a certain mutual tolerance, nevertheless. The country has no established church. The United States is not, for instance, "Catholic," although various subgroups, taking in a good percentage of the whole population, are Catholic. Parsons argues that "values derived from common religious orientations are still institutionalized."[22] There are, as it were, common denominators in the three religions and they represent something much more general than did, say medieval Catholicism, to which Parsons particularly refers. Such things as the notion of the infinite worth of every individual life or soul or a bias toward the religious or moral equality of all (the equality of all "in the sight of God") might represent the common denominators referred to. But, then, with reference once more to medieval Catholicism Parsons further observes that "*such a narrow and detailed religious consensus* [as medieval Catholicism represented] *is not a necessary condition of stable value-consensus at the societal level.*"[23] A "narrow and detailed" consensus—and the intent of these words is clearly descriptive rather than pejorative—prevails or is to be found, if anywhere, at the "lower" levels, where Catholics, Protestants, and Jews live their particular religious lives conducted with the particularity and detail that are peculiar to them.

Two observations are in order. (1) The matter of the institutionalization of values "derived from common religious orientations" points to empirical questions. Are such values effectively "incorporated" in the social intercourse of Americans? That, of course, is what the word "institutionalization" at once suggests. The question asked is clearly very "general" and would be susceptible of considerable refinement. In the very

---

[21] Dissatisfaction with such a generalized code that expresses itself on the line that nothing is morally adequate but a full-scale commitment to one of the particularized codes from which the generalized form emerges and from which it abstracts is called, by Parsons, "fundamentalism." See, on this, his *Societies,* p. 23, and also, and particularly, his paper, "Religion in a Modern Pluralistic Society," *Review of Religious Research,* 7, Spring, 1966, pp. 125–146, at pp. 137–145.

[22] *Theories of Society,* Vol. 1, p. 57.

[23] *Ibid.,* p. 57; italics supplied.

general form in which I have stated it, however, my inclination would be to answer it in the affirmative.[24] But it should be plain that it is a question on which there must be openness to evidence and inferential argument based on evidence. (2) All that has been said about top-level normative elements points up the great significance of questions relating to them, perhaps especially in a pluralistic society. The significance of top-level beliefs, *as such* (apart from, abstracted from normative elements), is also suggested. Beliefs, as such, deserve comment in the present context.

It is profitable to consider belief complexes or systems with an eye to the matter of control. In a report on Protestants and Catholics in the United States, Stark and Glock state that "although only a minority of church members so far reject or doubt the existence of some kind of personal God or the divinity of Jesus," yet it is true that "a near majority reject such traditional articles of faith as Christ's miracles, life after death, the promise of the second coming, and the virgin birth."[25] Top-level belief, at least according to this research, thus maintains some hold, although Stark and Glock's "so far" should not be neglected.[26] Belief in "some kind of personal God" would presumably be sufficiently top-level to encompass believing Jews as well as Christians. Top-level belief can certainly travel "downward" to make what appears to the believer to be good sense of various lower-level beliefs and strengthen them, although these latter inevitably involve points not encompassed by top-level items. Destruction or lapse of top-level belief (on the line, perhaps, even of credence in "some kind of transcendent realm") should, then, make lower-level items senseless, pointless, meaningless. What about reverse or back-up effect? It could well be that belief-obliteration at lower-levels would have some top-level effect. Our positive knowledge here, however, as distinguished from our intuitions about such matters, is slight indeed.

Yet the importance of positive knowledge in these matters need hardly be argued. A good part of what is involved in today's so-called Catholic

[24] Of the numerous evidences that explain this inclination, some of the most important are still to be found in Gunnar Myrdal, *An American Dilemma,* New York: Harper, 1944. Of course, Myrdal was thoroughly aware of conflict about values centering on what he called the American Creed, and to claim, as he did, that the creed was important and effective in the lives of Americans is definitely not to claim that it prevails without opposition—which would be a ridiculous claim.

[25] Rodney Stark and Charles Y. Glock, "Will Ethics Be the Death of Christianity?" *Trans-Action,* June, 1968, pp. 7–14, at p. 8.

[26] The intention of this qualification is not to suggest that religious belief is due to decline into the indefinite future. See Chapter 9. The possibility that top-level belief may sometimes represent a rather empty "general" residue of belief should not be overlooked.

crisis[27] relates to increasing uncertainty or doubt about lower-level items in the Catholic structure of faith. This much seems clear enough. But it is not easy to establish and order a scientifically valid and useful belief-hierarchy. Thus, Catholic priests may be queried about matters of ecclesiastical organization, some of which appear rather close to belief and others of which seem rather far apart from it. There is a distinct difference between being asked, on the one hand, whether, if there were a married priesthood, promotion to the pastorate and the episcopacy should be reserved for celibates and being asked, on the other hand, whether a married clergy would be more, or less, effective than a celibate clergy in parish ministry.[28] The latter question, whatever one may decide about the former, clearly is not within the realm of religious belief. But the question of what items specifically should be entered into a belief hierarchy structure is not invariably so easily answered. The problem of getting the hierarchy properly organized or ordered for analytical purposes, with various beliefs fitted in at the "right" points, as we have also just suggested, could well present its difficulties. The technical issues thus intimated are also of evident theoretical interest. Understanding of the architecture of a belief hierarchy as such could well prove useful in understanding the architecture of a normative hierarchy.[29]

INTERCHANGE AND SYSTEM

We revert to the idea of system, which has been so pervasive in contemporary structural-functional analysis that it is encountered at virtually every turn. Thus, it comes up unavoidably in connection with the treatment of interchange, as that has in fact been afforded by Parsons and his collaborators.[30] We refer briefly to interchange in order to note how the

[27] See the cogent treatment by Thomas F. O'Dea, *The Catholic Crisis,* Boston: Beacon Press, 1968.

[28] See Joseph H. Fichter, *America's Forgotten Priests—What They Are Saying.* New York: Harper and Row, 1968, p. 218, questions 37 and 39–40.

[29] A tentative impression from interviewing of a number of priests in San Antonio, Texas and its environs which the writer has been conducting may be mentioned here. The impression is simply that there is something of a bimodal tendency in the effect that lapse of, or uncertainty about, various lower-level beliefs has on the top-level belief items. One set of men tends to believe more strongly than ever in top-level items after weakening of lower-level ones. For another set of men, lower-level weakening, on the contrary, threatens top-level items.

[30] Two of the more important treatments are: Parsons and Smelser, *Economy and Society;* Parsons, "An Approach to Psychological Theory in Terms of the Theory of Action," in Sigmund Koch, ed., *Psychology: A Study of a Science,* Vol. 3, New York: McGraw-Hill, 1959, pp. 612–711. Parsons' interest in interchange continues and can be traced, for example, in Part 3 of his *Sociological Theory and Modern Society,* New York: The Free Press, 1967.

idea of system is once again touched upon and also in order to observe that we shall not attempt to analyze religion, in this volume, in technical Parsonian interchange terms.

Interchange takes place between systems or between the subsystems of a larger system. Where Parsons writes of the subsystems of the social system we may say that he has in view subsystems functionally discriminated on the basis of whether they effect pattern-maintenance or integration or goal attainment or adaptation. Functions are somewhat loosely allocated to a variety of structures even in a highly developed society, such as that of the United States today. It is accordingly well to note that the notion of a functional subsystem "pulls together" or abstracts functions as such, as the subsystem of the economy abstracts adaptive functions or that of the polity goal-attainment functions. Interchange takes place not only among the subsystems of the social system but in a larger "action" context, in which a cultural system and a personality system, for instance, are thought of as involved in interchange along with the social system.

The elements of a system stand in a certain closeness of relationship to one another and the system has margins or frontiers or boundaries, where its distinctive character fades out and a different system may be said to begin. The concept of interchange is inevitably related to that of boundary. Systems effect interchanges across their boundaries.[31] The

---

[31] In a specialized sense of the term, a function is an output of one system (of action) into another. The reader interested in this may wish to consult Charles Ackerman and Talcott Parsons, "The Concept of 'Social System' as a Theoretical Device," in G. J. Di Renzo, ed., *Concepts, Theory, and Explanation in the Behavioral Sciences,* New York: Random House, 1966, p. 31. The article by Ackerman and Parsons is a generally useful résumé of Parsonian theory and contains a helpful exposition of hierarchy of control along with an exposition of hierarchy of conditioning, which we have not previously mentioned by name in order to bypass certain complexities not strictly necessary for pursuit of the themes that have interested us. Very briefly indeed, hierarchy of conditioning refers to reverse effect, but it also has a significance that "reverse effect" does not sufficiently convey. The hierarchy of conditioning involves influences going "upward" from below in a hierarchical system, and thereby it goes in the opposite direction from that of a hierarchy of control. Limits on what can happen "high up" are imposed by elements "low down," which are nevertheless indispensable. The limits may be broad but they are still real. The circumstance that man lives in a physical world and must obey its laws imposes constraints on him. At the same time man can control much in that physical world, once he knows its laws and can apply them. His cultural achievements give him considerable control of elements "below" culture, but he cannot do just "anything at all"—for conditions *are* imposed from below. Conditions, however, may also be allowed to suggest "preconditions." Higher developments are dependent on the elements below. Were there no physical world and no organisms there would be no human personality or society or culture.

concepts of input and output, utilized in this framework, have been particularly stressed in concern with the economy and the polity. In elementary but typical interchange propositions, for example, it will be contended that the economy gets labor services from the household, while it gives wage income as a return output to the latter, or that the polity gets generalized support from the public and returns effective leadership.

These Parsonian notions all serve to make sharper the sense of system. Much needs to be done with them still. It is not always easy to ascertain what is the best way—or a "good" way—to conceive the actual input and output elements or units to be; that is to say, the best or a good way to conceive precisely what it is that is "put in" or "put out." Yet the whole interchange approach, whatever the value of its details at present, makes generally good sense in the light of what structural-functional analysis is concerned with. To repeat: structures and functions should affect one another within a more or less determinate system. Failure of a certain kind of output from one subsystem to another should have distinctive consequences, as changes in the structure and functioning of the heart in the case of the biological organism should have consequences for the structure and functioning of the kidneys. Parsons' definition of strain as "a tendency to disequilibrium in the input-output balance between two or more units" of a system[32] is interesting in this connection. Analysis of interchanges might prove most useful for the study of social change, and that is not the least important aspect of such analysis.

With regard to analysis of religion and our brief rehearsal of Parsons on interchange and system, three things are to be noted.

1. Interchange analysis in the terms that have been set out is new and a distinctively Parsonian development for the field of sociology. Much in this mode of analysis remains to be worked out (as we have already observed) and, in particular, much has not been worked out for the "sphere" of religion in relation to others.

2. In the broadest sense, the problems of analysis presented by the relation of religion and other "spheres" or systems (religion and polity, religion and economy, and so on) are in any case unavoidable for the sociologist, and they were unavoidable before Parsons' formulations relating to system and interchange were ever made, as they will be unavoidable whether Parsons' often brilliant notions prove durable or not. They cannot be completely overlooked even in a relatively brief treatment of the sociology of religion. We do not overlook them. They are touched upon in Chapter 6 (Part 3).

3. As might be expected in a problem area that has been to the fore

[32] In *Theories of Society*, Vol. I, p. 71.

for a long time, there are other ideas—on the line, for example, of dialectical relationship—which have been applied to the relations of religion
and nonreligious sociocultural phenomena. We shall touch upon these
ideas and develop them in our own way. The task we shall be seeking
to accomplish, however, is not incompatible with tasks that Parsons' mode
of interchange analysis could well set for itself. . . . But, at this juncture,
let us consider the whole matter of structure in a sense not previously
given.

CHAPTER 5

Structure, Differentiation, Change—Assessment

The term "social structure" has been used to mean patterns of institutionalized normative culture, although it has been intimated that this is not the only sense in which functionalists have used it. But it is a sense of some importance. Also important is that sense of social structure whereby it refers to what for lack of a better term we shall label distribution. It is convenient to speak of social structure in a *normative* and in a *distributive* sense.

A frequently cited social development which points to the meaning of distributive structure is the development from a kinship-grounded household which serves both as "unit of residence" and as "primary unit of agricultural production," in a peasant society, to a two-unit situation in a nonpeasant society where there is separation of household from productive work in factories, offices and the like,[1] There are now, in the latter case, two "boxes," as it were. In one, there are household and kin activities. Or one might say there are two "houses," one for kin-familial, and the other for productive, activities. Webster's dictionary defines the word, monoecious, as "having both male and female reproductive organs in the same individual;" while the word, dioecious, it defines as "having the male reproductive organs in one individual, the female in another." The common Greek root in the two words is *oikos,* meaning "house." When there have come to be two separate "houses" for the reproductive organs of the two different sexes, a process of differentiation has occurred. At the social level, differentiation occurs also, as in the example given, in which economic activity separates from a household-kin matrix and takes up a "box" or "residence" of its own.

Just as the two sexes maintain contact after the organs pertaining to the two have become separately "housed," so at the social level in

[1] See Parsons, *Societies,* p. 22.

70

the case noted there are problems of maintaining contact for the separated "houses." Workers are also members of families and are ordinarily constrained to maintain some kind of active relation to them. Somehow, too, "sense" has to be made of the new arrangements in broader terms. Thus, it must appear legitimate that a man should, say, both have a certain authority over his son and *not* supervise the work or economic production of that son.[2] But all this is said incidentally. The point that needs emphasis is that in virtue of just such things as the rise of separate "houses"—that is, the *distribution to different units* (household on the one hand, factory or office on the other) of different roles and sets of activities which were originally amalgamated—the form or structure of a society changes in a special sense. This is a change that does not *in itself* feature normative elements. The norms (in the general sense) that shape conduct in the household will undoubtedly change, given the differentiation indicated, and new norms will regulate the intercourse of workers in factory and office (differing from the norms regulating workers in the pre-factory, preoffice situation). But that is a normative concomitant of a distributive transformation. A highly differentiated society will "look different" from one that is but slightly differentiated and the reference here is to the distributive physiognomies of the two societies.[3]

The distinction of structure in normative and distributive senses merely, in our view, makes explicit what is already implicit in the relevant literature. (Parsons, for one, uses structure in both the normative and distributive senses.) But the term structural differentiation has not been lacking. It has been in heavy use by Parsons, who has made it virtually his own. It will here be understood as referring just to that process whereby there is a shift of a set of distinctive roles and activities from a situation in which they are amalgamated or fused with another set to a situation in which they achieve separate "housing." The distributive sense of structure is prominent in references to structural differentiation. And to turn to structural differentiation is to turn to areas where significant structural-functional interests lie. Structural differentiation may refer to relatively small, relatively unimportant changes, to be sure, but it may also refer to large-scale and important ones involving major social transformations. It has been suggested that it is a crucial aspect of large-scale, evolutionary social changes.[4]

[2] This involves some interpretation on our part of Parsons, *ibid.,* pp. 22–23.

[3] At the same time there is always some normative structure, no matter what distributive structure may be, and that normative structure can always be considered in the light of functions or of questions about functions. (Also, in the sense that structure generally refers to *relatively* stable phenomena, *both* the "normative" and the "distributive could be labeled "structural.")

[4] Parsons, *ibid.,* p. 22.

We turn to a very significant case of structural differentiation in the next section of this chapter. The case could be argued to exemplify an "evolutionary" step in the development of religion, but we concentrate on its structural-differentiation side, as it were. The case is presented at some length for two reasons. It is of a *kind* that has become a typical concern of present-day functionalism as represented more particularly by Parsons. It seems desirable to reinforce the suggestions that the reader will have gotten that structural-functional analysis is now often ambitiously applied to large-scale social phenomena. It is by no means exclusively concentrated on such things as the nature and functions of religion in primitive society. First, then, we wish to stress that functionalism has long since gone beyond such constricted frameworks and concerns itself with large problems indeed.[5] The case chosen for this purpose, it is true, has been treated especially by Gustav Mensching, whom we shall draw upon, in terms of a contrast between folk and universal religion,[6] and Mensching has had no interest, discernible from his main writings, in functionalism. But, without the label and without the particular elaboration of the basic contrast by Mensching, the case is well enough known.[7] It could easily be made a major concrete problem for structural-functional analysis, and that is what is important.[8] A second reason for presenting the folk-universal contrast at some length is that it illustrates some very important changes and it is well to emphasize at this point that structural-functional analysis has become most alert to problems of change.[9]

It should be noted, however, that as regards the folk-universal contrast itself, we do not seek to go much beyond a descriptive statement. Our main task as we conceive it at this particular point is to *portray* a problem

[5] The sources of the structural-functional theory, in any case, have not been in an older anthropology alone. They can be found in the sociological heritage as such and they have obviously been influenced by biological models.

[6] See Gustav Mensching, *Die Religion,* Stuttgart: C. E. Schwab, 1959, esp. pp. 65–77 (a translation of these pages is afforded in Louis Schneider, ed., *Religion, Culture and Society,* pp. 254–261) or the statement in the same author's *Toleranz und Wahrheit in der Religion,* Heidelberg: Quelle and Meyer, 1955, pp. 18 ff.

[7] See the treatment of Judaism in relation to Christianity in Parsons, "Christianity and Modern Industrial Society," reprinted as Chapter 12 in *Sociological Theory and Modern Society.*

[8] Of course, the convergence of functionalism and nonfunctionalist approaches to social data on the same problems has an interest of its own.

[9] We deem it justified to continue to speak of structural-functional analysis even when we deal with top-level normative (value) pattern change. Notably in the case of Parsons we do not get elimination of functionalist terms of analysis in the face of such major change. Changed systems can still be analyzed in functional terms and structural-functional analysis should theoretically be helpful in probing such phenomena as, say, "breakdowns" that herald or precede or introduce value change.

area of a type to which structural-functional analysis has been turning increasingly and to suggest its importance.

Since the contrast that follows illustrates important changes, as said, it may be allowed to motivate a consideration of change on other fronts. Such consideration will be afforded in the next section of this chapter. Then an assessment of structural-functional analysis with special reference to religion will be presented.

STRUCTURAL DIFFERENTIATION: FOLK AND UNIVERSAL RELIGION

There has been awareness of the distinction of folk and universal religion, in principle, in structural-functional premises, and the distinction, further, itself in a sense rests upon a point that has been made particularly well by Parsons. The point referred to is not novel, but it is stimulating to have it presented in terms of a differentiation of culture and society.[10] It is a familiar circumstance that cultural phenomena can come loose from their initial social anchorings and get exported or diffused well beyond them. When cultural constructions, such as myths and stories, are made, they frequently feature and elaborate an experience significant in merely local terms, interesting or exciting or generally affecting only to the members of a single society. They have no power of spread or transmission to other societies. They are "fused" with a particular society. But when cultural constructions "make sense" and appear meaningful far beyond an original social matrix and potentially convey a message that "speaks to the condition" of all men, then society and culture need no longer be fused. The cultural constructions can, as it were, go abroad and travel. They are differentiated from a social matrix of origin, autonomized, no longer bound to it. (A universal religion is so released.) So much for Parsons' well stated point.

A folk religion, as the name suggests, is bound to a particular people, folk or tribe, just as the particular people, folk or tribe is bound to the particular religion. Who says either says the other. Mensching notes that there is a peculiar tolerance about folk religions. Their adherents expect that those who are members of other "tribes" will have different religious outlooks. This divergence is "natural." What seems unnatural and may even be regarded as heinous is the failure of someone born into, or in any case unequivocally affiliated with, a tribe or folk or people to follow its particular religion. Universal religions are detached from a folk base. They address themselves to individual men anywhere and everywhere.

[10] See Parsons, *Societies, passim,* including that volume's important Chapter 6, on "seed-bed societies."

They speak to man as a being who universally has a problem in relating himself to his cosmos and whose particular tribal affiliation is in principle totally accidental or irrelevant. There is a plain sociological meaning attaching to statements of the type that say that in Christ there is neither Jew nor Greek.

In the emergence of universal religion a process of structural differentiation is clearly at work. Religion in the folk case has as it were one house, one dwelling, one box from which it is inseparable. In the universal case, it comes out of the folk matrix and may theoretically "strike" anywhere—in any folk or tribal or national locus. It may then be said to have a house of its own—a distinctively religious house. Another way of putting this is to say that when universal religion has supervened, religion is no longer "distributed" to the folk base. A very significant structural-distributive change has occurred. And it is to be expected that it should bring with it structural-normative change, although it is not identical with that.

Folk and universal vary on a continuum. Judaism, the religion of a particular folk, for a long time had the potential of becoming a universal religion. The conception of a God of all mankind developed in it long before Christianity arose; and certain political experiences of the Jews, in connection with exile, centuries before Christ, had made it easier than it might otherwise have been for them to conceive of their religion as at least apart from the organization of political power. But what we might call detribalization in a special sense, "de-folking," if so queer a word may be allowed, did not take place effectively and fully until the Christian gospel began to be systematically propagated among persons who were not of the circumcised and therefore not of the Jewish folk or tribe. Then the Jewish religious culture, to be sure with modifications introduced by new, distinctively Christian components, did become thoroughly detached from a tribal base and the core Judaeo-Christian religious phenomenon was on its way to developing into a universal religion. In separating itself from Jewish tribal bonds Christianity achieved a certain freedom, a freedom which, in Max Weber's words, "Paul celebrated triumphantly again and again; for this freedom meant the universalism of Paul's mission, which cut across nations and status groups."[11]

If Judaism was for a long time "intermediate," the same thing, with necessary qualifications, is true for example of Hinduism. Being a Hindu in the religious sense is bound up with belonging to a Hindu caste, an affiliation that is supposed to come only with birth. "Hindu belief" cannot make one a Hindu. Conversion from another religion is thus out of the question. To the extent that this is true, Hinduism has been said to be

[11] Weber, *The Religion of India*, p. 37.

a national folk religion of the Hindus and not a world religion. But despite these things, Hinduism has always carried on extensive missionary activity. This could be justified on the ground that it restored to entire tribal groups or peoples "the eternal religion" of all mankind—and the tribal groups or peoples were incorporated as castes once they were ceremonially purified. Although not an authentic "missionizing" religion, Hinduism has nevertheless had considerable missionizing success via the work of its priests, the Brahmins, in spreading its rites and doctrines over all India. (There have actually also been instances of individual going over to Hinduism or "conversion," whose legitimacy might indeed be questioned by orthodox Hindus but whose reality remains.) In this context, one can see the aptness of a description of that more truly universal religion, Buddhism, by Sir Charles Eliot, to the effect that Buddhism is the "export form of Hinduism," in which the notions (for home use only) of caste, precedence of the Brahmins, and recognition of the Vedas as divine revelation are excluded.[12]

In other religious forms, also, "arrests" have taken place, and intermediate, compromising solutions have been worked out, so that fully universal religion has not been attained. Islam is most interesting in this light. A leading student of Islam writes:

"Muhammad made Mecca the seat of the foremost sanctuary of Islam, the Ka'ba, toward which the believer turns when praying, and he imposed the obligation on every Muslim to perform at least once in his life the pilgrimage to this hallowed place and to participate in the ceremonies which the Prophet had adapted from age-old heathen ritual. It is still a moot question whether the Prophet conceived of his mission as universal or as confined to the Arabs (which, in his day, meant: to the Arab Peninsula). In any event Islam, in this respect resembling Judaism, remained at bottom a national religion, despite its universal claim and its international expansion. In the early days conversion to Islam was not complete for a non-Arab unless he also had found for himself a place in Arab society by becoming affiliated as a client to one of the Arab tribes. At the same time the rulers, while rather indifferent to the beliefs of their subjects outside of Arabia, rigorously pursued a policy of making Arabia entirely Muslim. The same tendency found expression in the particular aversion there shown by some circles to Christians of Arab blood—an aversion stirred less by their religious dissent than by the dissociation from national unity that seemed implied. Thus, although frequently in-

[12] Helmuth von Glasenapp, *Die Fünf Weltreligionen*, pp. 27–39. Note that Sir Charles Eliot's statement easily prompts the notion that Christianity is the export form of Judaism.

debted to non-Arabs for the higher development of Islam and although fighting under the banner of non-Arab princes for the greater glory and the wider dissemination of his faith, the Arab most fully realized the integration of religion and what we now call nationality."[13]

Another student of Islam remarks that even today "the Muslim in the Arab world thinks of the Christian Church as a separate millet perhaps with a different language, certainly with a different 'ethos' and different cohesion."[14] Let us particularly note the significant word, *millet.* In modern Turkish, this evidently means a "nation," while in classical Arabic it appears to have meant a "community of faith." In nineteenth-century diplomacy it had the sense of "a non-Muslim community in the Ottoman empire."[15] The meanings suggest well enough the strong nondifferentiation of the ideas of "nation" (or folk or people) and "religion." Cragg, who has just been quoted, is interested in making out a case for Christianity to Muslims. This is no part whatever of our interest as sociologists, but a significant sociological point is involved when Cragg asks: "Is it possible to familiarize the Muslim with the truth that to become a Christian is not a mere shift of communities, that it does not rob Muslim society, as such, of a potential servant and the local community, as such, of a loving son?"[16] Cragg is obviously seeking to get away from the idea-complex of the millet, fusing religion with things "nonreligious." In Christ there is neither Jew nor Greek—and neither Arab nor Englishman nor American. In his book on modern Turkey, published in 1961, Bernard Lewis noted that even at the time he wrote, after three and a half decades of the Turkish secular republic, a non-Muslim in Turkey might be called a Turkish citizen, but not a Turk.[17] There is a persistent memory here that once more suggests a peculiar amalgamation of folk and religion,[18] one that is the more interesting because Turkey has been in the very forefront of so-called Islamic nations in disentangling nation from religion and generally "modernizing."

[13] G. E. Von Grunebaum, *Islam: Essays in the Nature and Growth of a Cultural Tradition.* Reproduced by permission of the American Anthropological Association, from *Memoirs of the American Anthropological Association,* No. 81, vol. 57, No. 2, Pt. 2, April 1955, pp. 59–60.

[14] Kenneth Cragg, *The Call of the Minaret,* New York: Oxford University Press, 1956, p. 347.

[15] Niyazi Berkes, *The Development of Secularism in Turkey,* Montreal: McGill University Press, 1964, p. 514.

[16] Cragg, *op. cit.,* p. 348.

[17] Bernard Lewis, *The Emergence of Modern Turkey,* London: Oxford University Press, 1961, p. 15.

[18] In Islam, to complicate matters further, there is the circumstance that Islam itself has tended to be conceived as a kind of nation.

It is not implied that a tendency to fuse folk (or people or nation) and religion is something from which the Western world has been exempt. If, traditionally, Turkish meant Muslim, Polish meant Roman Catholic. Religion constantly is found associated with phenomena not themselves religious. But this does not reduce the cogency of the folk-universal distinction, and differences of *degree* in fusion of folk and religion are important. We obviously live in a world in which the scope of tribal religions has been greatly reduced. The universal *impulse* of the universal religions is evident, even if it does not work without significant inhibitions.[19]

With the structural-distributive change brought by the transition from folk to universal religion there is associated or involved, as the most obvious normative change, the shift to the outlook that one acts as a "brother" in religion, not necessarily to a blood-brother or fellow-tribesman, but to one, no matter who he be, who shares the same beliefs and adheres to the same ritual practices. The universal religion is thereby equipped to take in an indefinite number of members—an important circumstance. Religion clearly no longer functions to integrate the members of a tribal group. The focus of integration has changed. The terms of salvation have become different. In particular, in folk religion the individual is "saved" in virtue of his membership of, and good standing in, the corporate tribal or folk group. Removed from that group or in a condition wherein his relationship to it is seriously threatened (as when he faces ostracism) he tends to be in a peculiarly hazardous, isolated position, or else insignificant and in any case without prospects for salvation. Folk religion, in Durkheim's terminology, is powerfully altruistic—the individual is so related to the group that he depends on it greatly and is extremely sensitive to any break in his solidarity with it. Universal religion is not without its bonds of integration for its adherents, but they appear to be less unreservedly altruistic.

[19] Adherence to the norms of a universal religion may of course be motivated by extrareligious, "folk" considerations. Thus, Dutch Catholics seem on available evidence to be "obedient" to church norms but to lack "religious motivation" for their obedience. This is to say that the obedience looks very much as if it is often prompted, not by religious outlook but by an extrareligious set of social circumstances with their historical foundations in the group relations of Dutch Catholics and Dutch Protestants in the seventeenth and eighteenth centuries. This is ably discussed by Joseph Poeisz, in his article, "Gruppenisolierung, Kirchlichkeit und Religiosität: das Niederländische Beispiel," in *International Yearbook for the Sociology of Religion,* Vol. 1, Westdeutscher Verlag, Cologne and Opladen, 1965, pp. 113–148. It may also be observed that the bonds of a universal religion would distribute men on one axis, but inevitably other than "purely religious" bonds must unite men at the same time, and these other bonds distribute them on different axes. Ideally, one might contend the different bonds should not conflict. Often, however, to be sure, religion has been employed to express and reinforce nonreligious identifications, in ways detrimental to religious claims of the brotherhood of all.

An interesting problem arises here. We are bound to expect generally that as structural differentiation occurs, with its concomitant of normative change, there will also be functional changes. Without doubt, the transition from the type of the folk religion to the type of the universal religion brought functional changes in religion with it. Folk and universal sustain different patterns. The incidence of integration in the two is different. Of this there is no question. Yet difficulties do arise here of which it is well to be cognizant. The very statement of what one *means* by folk and universal readily involves or suggests the assertion that men are differently integrated by these two types of religions. It is accordingly necessary to be wary of the possible tautological character of assertions about differences in integration in the two types of religion that *purport* to point to things independent of the original description of the two types themselves. One of the hazards of present-day functional analysis is that description or analysis of structure sometimes gives the impression of being "loaded," and the functional theorist then sounds presumptuous when he asserts that certain structures have certain functions, as if he were as far as possible from pulling out of a hat what had previously been put into it.

As structural-functional analysis has shifted from being a certain kind of outlook on very limited phenomena–such as the phenomena of primitive religion and magic–to seeking to attain the status of a comprehensive theory of society, it has in fact taken in more and more areas of analysis such as those that have been indicated in the present section and has been constrained to do so.[20] More refined analysis than is now available of folk and universal and intermediate types would be desirable. The relations of structure in the distributive sense and structure in the normative sense call for further work that may help illumine the entire concept of structure itself. The factors that operate in major transformations, as in that from folk to universal religion, are hardly unknown but are obviously susceptible of additional investigation. But resources for the kinds of work suggested have been developing for some time in modern sociology and, recently, Parsons in particular among functionalists has been contributing to the development of such resources.

ASPECTS OF CHANGE

A mode of sociological analysis not seriously concerned with social and cultural change would be vulnerable indeed. The observation is sometimes made that structural-functional analysis is "static." This could mean

[20] See the two items by Parsons previously referred to, his *Societies* and his essay on "Christianity and Modern Industrial Society;" Robert N. Bellah, "Religious Evolution," in *American Sociological Review*, **29**, June 1964, pp. 358–374.

a number of things. If it be taken to mean that such analysis does not have the resources for analysis of change that might be at its disposal if it could apply a high-powered mathematics to its problems, then the observation is true, although in a sense it is trivial since it would have such wide application in sociology at large. But if the observation is taken to mean that those seeking to develop structural-functional analysis have neglected change or quite failed to develop any kind of apparatus for dealing with it, then the observation becomes more dubious, in the light of recent theoretical developments. It was noted in Chapter 3 that (normative) structure refers to *relatively* constant phenomena. There are ongoing changes in a system that come *within* the compass of equilibrating processes, such that structure finally remains intact. But *structure itself* can certainly change. Modes of change can be and have been distinguished, going all the way to change of a system's overall, most general structural patterns.[21]

An acknowledgment of the reality of change and a distinction of types or levels of change do not, it is true, carry one very far. Parsons, in particular, has gone beyond these matters, in his working out of an ingenious "paradigm" of evolutionary change.[22] (Interest in the evolution of religion, specifically, comes to the fore again, in new terms and without intellectualist presuppositions that would lead religion—sometimes with a supposed precedent "stage" of magic—from a primitive pathway of error and illusion at length on to the high road of science, where religion would finally be done away with.)

Despite an authentic functionalist sensitivity to change that is thus indicated, there is a great deal about change that remains to be understood, and it is indeed nearly banal to say so. It has already been suggested that the concepts of strain and dysfunction need stress. They clearly imply human discomforts in social experience and strongly suggest motivation to change. They need further development. In the interim, it is impossible

[21] See, for example, Parsons, in *Theories of Society*, Vol. I, p. 37. We overlook numerous niceties, such as the distinction between change *to* or *in* a pattern and that type of more radical value-transformation in which there occurs change *of* a pattern.

[22] *Societies*, pp. 21–24. The paradigm involves structural differentiation; coordination or integration of newly differentiated units; adaptive upgrading (as when a newly structurally differentiated unit such as a factory performs the task of economic production better than it was performed when production was amalgamated with the household); inclusion or taking into community membership of groups once excluded (as outcastes might be "taken in" if caste were abolished in a society with a caste system); emergence of a generalized type of value pattern to accommodate the enlarged range of normative biases appearing in a complex social system. (This last point may be referred back to the discussion of common denominators in Chapter 4.)

to disagree with O'Dea when he argues that religion can, and with some frequency does, work in such fashion that it reconciles to an order of society most vulnerable to moral criticism; that it casts an aura of the sacred about, and rigidifies, limited, provincial intellectual conceptions, as well as values and norms that become of dubious merit or social utility outside restricted circumstances of time or condition; that on its "prophetic" side it can encourage an intransigence that exacerbates human conflicts; that it fixes men's loyalties to the prejudice of development of new identifications that may have much to be said for them in altered situations; that it leads individuals to excessive emotional dependence instead of emotional maturity.[23]

These are important points that intimate vast human dissatisfactions that must make the sociologist of religion constantly sensitive to the possibility and actuality of a variety of changes within and about the religious sphere. Also, these points of course suggest the utter inadequacy of the type of functionalism that would be inanely optimistic and find "everything" functioning "for the best." It is clearly true at the same time that not "everything" invariably functions "for the worst." A sophisticated structural-functional model should alert us to possibilities and probabilities *both* on the lines of the "best" and of the "worst." If we could begin to get moderately rigorous answers to question about "how much" of the "best" and the "worst" one might have under various circumstances, we would be on the way to an improved form of structural-functional analysis which would yield better accounts of change than are now available. Such an improved form would also plainly be of aid to structural-functional analysts who have been irritated by presumptions that their mode of work commits them ideologically to a status quo.

In consideration of change, it is sometimes a source of uneasiness among sociologists that certain modes of analysis do not appear to them to allow sufficient attention to material interests and thereby slight important sources of change. The whole sociological tradition stresses precisely such things as culturally molded beliefs, ideas, ends, standards, and it is no accident that the conception of institutionalized normative culture plays so large a role in Parsons' sociology. Material interests are different things from these (although one could hardly presume that interests are unaccompanied by idea-components). But interests need not be (and are not) neglected by sociologists in general or by functionalists in particular, although it is true that there remain problems of how to handle them. It is helpful to recall that Max Weber's views about the relations between the social, economic, and psychological situations of various strata that have been historically salient and the religious outlooks and values enter-

[23] O'Dea, *The Sociology of Religion*, pp. 100–101.

tained by those strata are at any rate not incompatible with a functionalist point of view. Weber proposed, for example, that notions such as those of sin, redemption and humility do not sit well upon the members of politically dominant strata and particularly not upon the members of a military nobility. To be humble before priest or prophet scarcely suits the distinctive pride of such a nobility (although the situation does change when religious conceptions give scope to the idea of the *warrior* against unbelief, to whom religious promises or rewards are held out). This is not only plausible but simple. But Weber was well aware that relations between stratum and religious outlook are by no means always utterly simple or immediately evident. This is well brought out in a few striking lines of the large section on sociology of religion in his major work. Fischoff, who has translated this section, renders these lines as follows:

"If one wishes to characterize succinctly, in a formula so to speak, the types representative of the various classes that were the primary carriers or propagators of the so-called world religions they would be the following: In Confucianism, the world-organizing bureaucrat; in Hinduism, the world-ordering magician; in Buddhism, the mendicant monk wandering through the world; in Islam, the warrior seeking to conquer the world; in Judaism, the wandering trader, and in Christianity, the itinerant journeyman. To be sure, all these types must not be taken as exponents of their own occupational or material class interests, but rather as the ideological carriers of the kind of ethical or salvation doctrine which most readily conformed to their social position."[24]

The lines that Fischoff translates in his last sentence are evidently crucial, and we would prefer to give the following translation of them: "These are all to be looked upon not as exponents of their callings or of material 'class interests,' but as ideological carriers of an ethic or doctrine of redemption *such as had an especially easy affinity with their social situation.*"[25] This suggests well Weber's somewhat "light" or flexible rendering of connections between class or material interests and religious outlook or values. One might well want to know much more than this about these connections. The statement might ideally be considerably refined, but at least it does not suggest a totally "pure" state of values out of all connection with or radically unconditioned by material interests. At

[24] Max Weber, *The Sociology of Religion,* copyright 1922, 1956 by J. C. B. Mohr (Paul Siebeck) English translation (from 4th ed.) copyright 1963 by Beacon Press, pp. 131–132. (British publisher: Methuen and Co., London). This translation is reproduced in Max Weber, *Economy and Society* (eds., Guenther Roth and Claus Wittich), New York: Bedminster Press, 1968, Vol. 2, p. 512.

[25] The translation given is based on Weber, *Wirtschaft und Gesellschaft,* Tübingen: J. C. B. Mohr, 1922, p. 293; italics supplied.

the conclusion of his recent analysis of evolution in a number of pre-modern societies, Parsons has afforded a general statement of what he regards as the significance of material interests within the framework of his overall approach. He appeals to the notion of hierarchy of control and indicates that in the sense of emphasizing the "highest" elements in what he calls action systems, he would be "a cultural determinist, rather than a social determinist." (Culture as such is here plainly conceived as standing "above" the social system.) He continues:

"Similarly, I believe that, within the social system, the normative elements are more important for social change than the 'material interests' of constitutive units. The longer the time perspective, and the broader the system involved, the greater is the *relative* importance of higher, rather than lower, factors in the control hierarchy, regardless of whether it is pattern maintenance or pattern change that requires explanation."[26]

This is obviously intended as a very broad statement. Parsons has been frank enough to write that he "believes" in the relatively great importance of normative elements within the social system. His statement, broad as it is, may conceivably be wrong or slanted in the wrong direction. It is not easy to say. It may be that this kind of statement does not have much utility for theoretical or empirical purposes and that the issues it suggests may have to be restated in considerably different form before they can be approached profitably (although we do not doubt the *general* usefulness of Parsons' notions of hierarchy). But, at any rate, it is evident that material interests have not been forgotten in this statement by an outstanding theorist, nor is it presumed that they are trivial even if highest significance is not allotted them. This is not to say that the role in social change of material interests is now generally understood in a theoretically impressive and empirically very helpful way. (We do not mean to slight perception of constant interaction of "real" and "ideal" factors.)

A final matter that may be usefully fitted under the rubric of change has to do with Merton's distinction between manifest and latent functions. The distinction is one between objective consequences of structures that contribute to the "adjustment" or "adaptation" of a given system and at the same time are "intended and recognized by participants in the system" (and therefore are manifest), on the one hand, and objective consequences of structures that make the same kind of contribution as in the first case but at the same time are "neither intended nor recognized" by participants (and therefore are latent), on the other hand. Merton himself poses the "basic query"—"What are the effects of the transformation of a previously latent function into a manifest function (involving the problem of the role of knowledge in human behavior and the problems

[26] *Societies,* p. 113.

of 'manipulation' of human behavior)?"[27] Religion has often had functions (regarded by some as desirable) of which awareness has come to exist, and thereby a new motivation has been given (to some) for "religious" activities that are presumed to have just those functions. In cases of this kind, as Dorothy Emmet observes, "function becomes causally efficacious through reinforcing *motives*."[28] Awareness of consequences works back to the activity that produced the consequences initially and has, precisely, a reinforcing effect as previously unavailable "information" becomes available. Let me stress (before the resumption of this matter in Chapter 7) that Merton's query is a query about change, about a kind of change whose significance in religion it will not be hard to demonstrate.

TOWARD ASSESSMENT OF STRUCTURAL-FUNCTIONAL ANALYSIS IN RELATION TO RELIGION

Structural-functional analysis has been understood by us as involving a mode of approach to social phenomena to be found in the work of Robertson Smith and Durkheim and present in such anthropologists as Malinowski and Radcliffe-Brown. It gets a certain sophisticated development and elaboration in the writings particularly of Parsons among sociologists. It is granted that, as we have suggested, there are differences among these men; and these men are not the only ones to whom one may refer as representatives of the functionalism we have had in view.) A fuller discussion would attend to work by Marion Levy and many others. The core of functional analysis was initially a rather loose set of notions about the self-maintenance of a system and its ability to re-equilibrate itself. (This early functional analysis of course was not so methodologically full and self-conscious as later discussion, pro and con, of functionalism has become.) Important also in the general development have been the ideas previously mentioned more than once about susceptibility of phenomena studied to being approached as a system in which one can validly speak of part-whole relationships and in which the parts operate to maintain or break down the system or reduce its "adaptation." We have included the ideas of discriminated structures (values, norms, and so on) and structural hierarchy within the scope of functionalism. We have even suggested that it can be appropriate to speak of structural-functional analysis when we deal with large-scale, evolutionary changes that mark notable advances in "adaptation" and enhanced inclusion and that proceed by way of important structural-normative and structural-distributive mutations. Here, especially, there might be concern about the width of our interpretation of structural-functional analysis.

[27] *Social Theory and Social Structure*, p. 51.
[28] See Emmet's *Rules, Roles and Relations*, p. 129.

But there is no doubt that the work of that outstanding functionalist, Parsons, retains a very important underpinning of functionalism in discussion of evolutionary change. In that discussion Parsons continues his reliance on the function-categories of pattern-maintenance, integration, goal attainment and adaptation. It is of course granted that his views have changed and his concerns developed and shifted. And functionalism generally has not stood still to allow us an easy description and explication of a frozen form of thought, as it were. Moreover, it is not invariably a simple matter to decide whether some particular approach to social phenomena is unequivocally "structural-functional." There is after all a very broad concern with "structure" (somewhat differently conceived in different cases) on the part of sociologists generally. When investigative interest does indeed extend to large-scale structural differentiation and to major historical and evolutionary changes, then we have at least one frontier on which the lines between what is structual-functional and what is not begin to be less plain. Our review of folk and universal religion should have indicated amply–has been intended, in part, to indicate–that approaches that are certainly not formally labelled "functionalist" have effected accomplishments in areas in which it might at least be contended that functionalism has legitimate interests.

Nevertheless, there is a developing structure of sociological thought that it is appropriate to call functionalist. We hold with those who contend that there is no special scientific *method* to be called structural-functional analysis. Such analysis simply consists or aspires to consist in scientific analysis in a broad sense. But functionalist have not been without their special concerns and points of view. Even if lines of difference are not invariably clear and there is much effective overlap between the work of functionalists and those who are differently labeled, a Parsonian sociologist, say, is certainly not the same as a Marxian sociologist. The most committed functionalists might well contend that the best portions of work that is ostensibly non-functionalist are really functionalist. Functionalism then has *historically* constituted a fairly discriminable, fairly distinctive approach and we have allowed this approach broad scope, not considering it arbitrary to see it as extending from roots in the anti-intellectualist orientation of Durkheim to important elements retained in the Parsons who has become interested in evolutionary transformations.[29]

---

[29] A fuller statement on functionalism would, as was suggested at the very beginning of the present Part, enable a refined presentation of difference among functionalists. Controversies in and about functionalism have been most interesting. Something of the flavor of these comes through, for example, in Emmet's *Rules, Roles and Relations,* Ch. 6, in brief reference to Kingsley Davis. An effort to present issues in dispute is afforded by Nicholas J. Demerath and Richard A. Peterson, eds., *System, Change, and Conflict,* New York: The Free Press, 1967.

But functionalist concerns and points of view also continue into the present day, as is obviously implied when we refer to "a developing structure of thought." Parsons' social theory has expanded to become a general "theory of action" and it is now often thus referred to, but its foundation remains functionalist. And sociology with a functionalist bias has had profound influence on the field as a whole and may very well continue to have considerable influence. This, however, has hardly inhibited criticism of functionalism. There are those who would even deny it the name of theory and question whether it is indeed "analytical." Such a stance is challengeable. Our position, in saying this, rests ultimately on a view of theory that cannot be elaborated here. It may be noted, briefly, that one could argue for the applicability of the term, theory, to efforts to clarify fundamental problems at any stage of scientific development and to construct subtle conceptual apparatus, more especially when these are taken as part of a strategy aiming at a richer "theory" (now in a more rigorous sense) than would otherwise be available.

Yet, by certain standards, much criticism of functionalism is justified. Crucial terms, such as "adaptive" and "integrative," are hardly always crystal-clear (although the quality and level of functionalist writing and the merits of functionalist definitions vary). It is possible to talk a kind of poetry of science without getting to the work of science itself. A fair amount of structural-functional analysis is of this sort. It is adumbrative, that is, it shadows forth, sometimes in a very talented way, what a science conducted in structual-functional terms might be like, but then it stops, without going on to the actual building of the science, which would involve systematic development of a body of well tested empirical propositions as well as a theory related to those propositions. This is an extremely easy criticism to make (and functionalism has not been built without *reference* to considerable evidence). But the criticism is not to be simply thrust aside. In these several chapters we have done a certain amount of labeling and describing in structural-functional terms which we believe to be most instructive. They help the scientific imagination and may one day afford a rich yield. The idea of system has been given considerable emphasis because of a desire to do justice to the scientific bias of functionalism (although that idea is certainly not functionalism's exclusive property). Yet if one wishes at this time to apply rigorous standards of science to functionalism, it is not difficult to see that functionalism has its very marked limitations. (It remains a question what standards it may be most "useful" to apply at present.)

Numerous criticisms that have some force for functionalism in sociology as a whole will also have force for the functionalist sociology of religion. But it has surely already been strongly suggested that functionalism has achievements to its credit. In the field of religion, the demonstration of the inadequacies of intellectualism, to which we have so often alluded, was a towering achievement.[30] (We have no hesitation whatever in asserting that this was a basic *theoretical* achievement.) And it has its positive sides. With it there came penetrating insights into the detailed functions of rites and ceremonies. Some of the best work in modern anthropology and sociology rests upon those insights. With functionalism there has also come heightened realization that religion comes into play (as magic may do also) at points where human resources for attaining cherished goals fail and at points where ordinary, everyday explanations of tribulations and injustices seem wanting and suffering appears unjustified.

In recent years there have been additional achievements. Parsons' discrimination of structural elements, his incorporation of so-called cybernetic notions, his portrayal of hierarchies of control and conditioning are most suggestive on the line that religion, too, can be analyzed in social-system and cybernetic terms. We noted indications in the work of Vallier of the susceptibility of religious phenomena to a structural-functional approach in effect stressing control and also exploiting the idea of system. It seems to us a defensible position to regard this whole development as integral to the development of structural-functional analysis. And if there is still a certain amount of "poetry" in all this, it at least looks like poetry that may have a scientific future.

The movement of concern into areas of large-scale differentiation and the taking up of that process within the broader conception of social evolution mark a kind of maturation of structural-functional analysis. We already know that it is now far removed from narrow or small-scale, primitive-tribal preoccupations, that it had been moving away from such preoccupations for some time, that it is concerned with important types of change. The conceptions of generalization of values in pluralist societies and the correlative conception of fundamentalism are illuminating and suggestive both generally and for the religious field. True, there are uncertainties in these premises. Able functionalists are well aware that in analyzing structure in process of change one needs a firm hold of the "what" that changes and should have good reason to think that it is the same "what" after, and although, it has changed. Just how much of a contribution functionalism can make in these matters is not entirely

---

[30] This does not mean that there were no pre-functionalist intuitions of the defects of intellectualism. Functionalism might conceivably profit from a close consideration of historical anticipations of itself in modern thought. Cf. the treatment of the "problem-history" of the sociology of religion by Joachim Matthes, *Religion und Gesellschaft* (vol. 1 of his *Einführung in die Religionssoziologie*), Hamburg: Rowohlt, 1967, pp. 32–88. (We cite this interesting volume despite our disagreement with some of its fundamental outlooks, including its author's negative view of sociological notions of the "sacred" in a general sense and of the present prospects of a comparative sociology of religion.)

clear. (And the matter is even less clear than it might otherwise be since it is always possible that a contrast between "functionalist" and "non-functionalist" approaches too easily assumes simple opposition where there is in fact an appreciable measure of overlap, even where that is not immediately apparent.) In view of long-standing "non-functionalist" contributions to these problems that functionalism now considers, the possibility suggests itself that there may be an element of self-liquidation in functionalism as it matures and expands; or it may be that functionalist treatment of a variety of problems touched also by various other "approaches" will prove so outstandingly meritorious that it will gain a kind of unchallenged sway in many areas of the sociological field of inquiry. But meanwhile functionalism obviously has numerous particular jobs to which it would presumably do well to attend. In the crucial field of development or evolution of religion, specifically, there are even factual difficulties that, if they are hardly disastrous, yet complicate the task of forging a good theory with some sort of structural-functional base or bias.[31] The idea of reexamining the evolution of religion is itself a stimulating one and at least—no trivial thing, this—will recall the sociologist of religion to a sense of his larger tasks.

There are other contributions of functionalism which are important for the sociology of religion.[32] But it is now relevant to recall that it has been a long time since the basic victory over intellectualism was won,

[31] Frankfort's remarkable book on *Kingship and the Gods* powerfully suggests that whereas kingship and divinity were fused in the person of the monarch in ancient Egypt, so that the king was unequivocally a god, in the Hebrew case the king was not divine and stood under divine judgment himself. With this "differentiation," a prophet could, in the name of the divine and of righteousness, inform a king of his moral deficiencies, as Nathan informed David of David's deficiencies after the king had had Uriah the Hittite killed because of his desire for the latter's wife. The contrast is important for a theory of the evolution of religion. Stark, for one, makes us aware that it involves rather complex issues and that there is not complete scholarly unanimity on it. See Werner Stark, *The Sociology of Religion,* London: Routledge and Kegan Paul, 1967, vol. 3, p. 39 *ff.* (Stark himself does argue—convincingly, to us, for that matter—that even if "quasi-religious ruler exaltation" made inroads into the thought of Hebrew court circles, nevertheless such exaltation was never seen as legitimate by the Jewish people as a whole.) When Frankfort makes a contrast of Egypt, Mesopotamia and Israel which suggests an increasingly moralized or ethical conception of the divine as we go from the first to the third (*Kingship and the Gods,* pp. 278–279), one may indeed suspect that Frankfort has a point but be made uneasy by the title of a section of a work by a contemporary student of Mesopotamia who writes of "why a 'Mesopotamian religion' should not be written." See A. L. Oppenheim, *Ancient Mesopotamia,* Chicago: The University of Chicago Press, pp. 171–183. Here, too, we deal with matters that may be argued to have a significant bearing on religious evolution. But relevant historical materials do not always easily, "simply" fall into "place."

[32] Mention should here be made again of Merton's distinction of manifest and latent functions, taken up below in ch. 7.

even if we date it as late as 1912, the year of the initial appearance
of Durkheim's *Elementary Forms of the Religious Life*. It is, even, more
than three decades since the initial appearance of Parsons' *The Structure
of Social Action* (in 1937) which further ensured the basic victory by
its brilliant grasp of the importance of the non-rational in social life.[33]
There have been able functionalist works on religion since then. There
have been the achievements already alluded to. But fundamentally, we
would argue, the functionalist view of religion has not greatly advanced
in a long time, despite all impressive refinements. What might constitute
a really considerable advance? What follows may be taken as a possible
answer to this question.

In 1951, Parsons offered a characteristic statement "locating" religion
sociologically:

"From what we know of the psychology of expectations and the consequences of frustration, it is clear that there are difficult problems of adjustment in these areas. Just as it is not possible to be indifferent to the
death of an object of intense attachment, so it is not possible simply
to take the frustration of one's fundamental expectations with respect
to values, as to what, for example, is fair, 'in one's stride,' as it were
saying 'what the hell.' It is therefore imperative that there be some sort
of socially structured orientation to these problems of discrepancy precisely
between events and *institutionalized* expectations. This problem of the
Ausgleich, the ultimate balancing of the motivational and moral economy,
is the core of the significance of religion in a sociological context."[34]

At a later point in the same volume from which this statement is taken
Parsons resumes the problem of religion in relation to "tension manage-
ment" which he thus opens up. He points to two possibilities of reaction
to "discrepancies between expectations in terms of the institutionalized
value-system and the actual course of events."[35] The severe disappointments and frustrations that arise in connection with such events can, again,
be handled in terms of a transcendental *Ausgleich,* a smoothing out, a
compensation in another realm. But there is also a worldly way of reacting,
on the line of somehow seeking to "improve" society, so that future
states of the social order will be considerably less frustrating. Parsons
mentions the scientific claims of revolutionary utopianism and asserts with
respect to this utopianism: "It seems . . . legitimate to suggest that in
fact a supernatural order . . . plays a central role in this type of orienta-

---

[33] In connection with the non-rational see also the able and significant work by
W. Lloyd Warner, *The Living and the Dead,* New Haven: Yale University Press,
1959.

[34] *The Social System,* Glencoe: The Free Press, 1951, p. 164.

[35] *Ibid.,* p. 372.

tion, that the 'dialectic' and other such entities are more like 'providence' than the proponents of 'scientific socialism' are wont to admit. Certainly by the criterion [of] the attitude of respect, they qualify as sacred entities."[36]

This line of argument is by no means unfamiliar and has been forthcoming from numerous sources other than Parsons or functionalism. But it has not been carried forward in any substantial way by structural-functional analysis.[37] The notion of alternatives—other forms or structures than those involved in what is conventionally recognized as religious—that can perform religious functions still stands in great need of development. At times assertions are encountered to the effect that nationalism is a substitute for religion or more generally that religious orientations that once flowed in conventional religious channels now flow in new, disguised ones. The discussion of these issues still has to proceed in terms not far removed from common sense. Does a class struggle really siphon off religious impulses? Are the elements that cohere in a structure or complex that we agree to call specifically religious separable? Let us turn to Parsons' "revolutionary utopianism." It is argued with some frequency that the work of Karl Marx suggests the background influence of Old Testament ideas of righteousness and justice, as well as of apocalyptic visions of plainly religious stamp. Although much of Marx's theory of surplus value (thought of by him as value garnered by the capitalist group from the workers over and above that value which is required merely to sustain and maintain them in their work) is couched in the terms of a seemingly dispassionate analysis, it is arguable that Marx betrays a passion of justice formed by a background of religious sentiment when he bursts out in bitter words such as: "Accumulate! Accumulate! That is Moses and the prophets."[38] The rather vague idea that movements like socialism have some religious inspiration has long been commonplace. (This is said despite the obvious "anti-religious" stance to which Marxism in particular has held.) Lines between "ideology" and "religion" can become quite thin.

We may range nationalism along with socialism for present purposes. A famous social scientist has just been referred to in relation to socialism. Another may be referred to in relation to nationalism. We mean Max Weber. No one can read his widow Marianne Weber's biography of the great German sociologist[39] without noting how strongly nationalistic Weber

[36] *Ibid.*, p. 374. Previously, Parsons, *ibid.*, p. 373, had referred in the same general connection to "a belief in the 'supernatural' possibilities of social development itself."

[37] Cf. O'Dea *The Sociology of Religion*, p. 17.

[38] Karl Marx, *Capital*, Vol. 1, New York: Modern Library, 1936, p. 652.

[39] Marianne Weber, *Max Weber: Ein Lebensbild*, Heidelberg: Verlag Lambert Schneider, 1950.

was. The "prestige and power" of his own fatherland constituted for him "an incontrovertible good, putting most other goods in the shade."[40] He could and did temper his nationalism with sagacity and political prudence. But this aside, he could look upon war as a "splendid" expenditure of heroic power and loving preparedness for sacrifice.[41] He could think of the 1914–1918 war as "a great and wonderful war," despite all.[42] He held the view that "he who carries on earthly political activity must be free of illusion and recognize the fact of the eternal war of men among themselves."[43] There was no question whatever of Weber's allegiance to Germany in that "eternal war." He could wax poetic about the fatherland and about the insuperable merit of dying for it. A great nation might overlook damage to its interests but never to its "honor." National honor was indeed a thing Weber took very seriously. Marianne Weber refers to her husband's lasting self-confrontation with men's religions as the form in which the genuine religiousness of his maternal family lived on in him.[44] But whatever the intimate significance for Weber of his notable studies in the sociology of religion, the reader of his life might well incline to the view that idolatry of the German nation was for him at least a significant aspect of a personal religion.

Ideas of the general type that socialism and nationalism can have religious significance now need to be examined with the greatest care—and not only nationalism and socialism but a variety of other things extending to some phenomena of drug use and perhaps to much less "exceptional" and "dramatic" things.[45] The search for the "religious," *wherever* it may manifest itself, as long as it can be shown that it is in some scientifically defensible sense the religious (and has consequences for society), is indispensable to the sociology of religion. In this connection, a book like Thomas Luckmann's *The Invisible Religion,*[46] which looks for religion outside conventionally recognized (churchly) religious forms,[47] has considerable significance. (But it is also well not to confuse merely non-

[40] *Ibid.,* p. 104.

[41] *Ibid.,* p. 595.

[42] See, for example, *ibid.,* pp. 568, 571, 579.

[43] *Ibid.,* p. 256.

[44] *Ibid.,* p. 383.

[45] Plainly, aesthetic experiences of no unusual sort may intimate the sacred. The effect of, say, El Greco's pictures upon those who observe them might be interesting to study in this connection, although of course this case is so plain because of El Greco's closeness to "usual" religious themes.

[46] New York: Macmillan, 1967.

[47] Note Lloyd Warner's explanation of his use of the word, sacred, in *The Living and the Dead,* p. 5, where Warner writes that he applies that word "not only to Divine Being and the central experience and sacraments of Christian faith" but also "to objects and phases of life to which the special reverence arising from religions in general has been extended."

institutionalized religion with religion in "unconventional" or "new" areas—such as that of politics.)

In terms of a structural-functional orientation, one might start with a crude initial notion to the effect that religion performs certain functions and reason that those functions would have to be performed even when religion in the conventional (churchly) forms was, let us say, threatened or seriously mitigated. Therefore, one might go on to argue, there must be substitutes and religion must crop up elsewhere if the conventional forms greatly lose ground. This, however crude, is a *heuristically* sensible approach. It may indeed help us to probe and "find out." But there is some danger that it can become a *proreligious ideology* which insists that man is and must be "religious," no matter how evidence on the matter turns out (and if "church" lapses, then "nation" or something else will come to substitute for it). One might well entertain the view, in fact held by numerous sociologists, that religion, in some form that authentically justifies the use of the term, is probably "here to stay" and yet be flexible and open to all pertinent evidence on the matter.

Pro-religious ideology aside, the sociology of religion can only profit from well conceived efforts to probe for the presence of religion even in what appear to be most unlikely places. In the present religious situation, also, it would not be at all surprising to find the most subtle mingling of the conventionally religious, the nonconventionally religious, and anti-religious, "desacralizing" trends and sentiments. None of this suggests easy tasks for inquiry. It is not especially difficult merely to allude to ostensibly nonreligious phenomena that may yet be called religious in "a scientifically defensible sense," but this points to a work of investigation that might be very difficult indeed.

Nor is this all. It has to be added that we can be deceived about the religious character of a variety of things whose "religiousness" it may not readily occur to us to challenge. A pious gentleman of an earlier day might have referred to sweetheart or wife as "a handmaiden of the Lord." The style or form of language could change and the same sort of woman be referred to later as "a very fine girl;" and, with further stylistic shift, as "quite a kid." The language of the first phrase would certainly be influenced by religious atmosphere but could have *relatively* little religious significance, being essentially cognate with and fairly close in "meaning" to the other two phrasings. In a "religious" environment, "a handmaiden of the Lord" may simply be the way in which one says, "a very fine girl," or the like. We could assign overmuch *religious* meaning to the first phrase merely because of a peculiar style or language convention, just as we might underestimate the religious character of, say, certain political movements because of their self-presentation in nonreligious style or language.

There are dangers in all this. It might seem to invite to disastrous confusions. But that is certainly not intended and, whatever the hazards involved, it would appear that they must be faced. No sociology of religion worth the name can in the end avoid finally raising in very serious form the question whether much that is not conventionally or ostensibly religious might be religious in an important sense after all. It cannot afford to look away from any potentially socially significant experiences that intimate the sacred to those who have them. It cannot avoid the effort to penetrate beneath the surface of relevant cultural forms. If structural-functional analysis does not face up to the various problems thus suggested and make a distinctive contribution to their solution, its utility for the sociology of religion in the future will be very considerably less than it has been in the past. It does not give us adequate guides for gathering up or aggregating the elements of "religion" so that they can be analyzed appropriately in relation to the social system at large. The observations by Parsons last quoted above merely lead, as it were, to the threshold of a large room that awaits intensive search. But crossing the threshold might conceivably bring a notable and fundamental advance.[48]

The three preceding chapters have been intended to give an account of structural-functional analysis that should stand by itself to some extent but also be built into the framework of our whole presentation. In particular, it may be recalled that two matters that have been touched upon will be taken up again. The subject of interchange will occupy us in the next chapter. Manifest and latent functions will require attention once more in Chapter 7. And even apart from these matters, we shall never wholly lose sight in the sequel of what has been gone over in the chapters of the present part. In the next chapter we shall be concerned with religion and "extra-religious" spheres. We shall understand extra-religious in more or less usual, more or less common sense terms. We must proceed, now, in this fashion but need not relinquish hope that the future may bring us a more penetrating understanding of what is "religious" and what is not. (Nor need we lose sight of the circumstance–even if we cannot exploit it in our terminal chapter–that discussion of "secularization" would in the end be bound to be affected by the issues that have just been presented.)

---

[48] Imaginative preludes to at least some small part of the work that needs to be done are to be found in Warner, *The Living and the Dead*. Cf. also Robert N. Bellah, "Civil Religion in America," *Daedalus,* Winter, 1967, pp. 1–21.

PART III

Religion and Extra-religious Spheres: The Case of the Protestant Ethic

CHAPTER 6

The Case of the Protestant Ethic

It was noted in Chapter 5 that the problems Parsons touches upon in discussing interchanges cannot be bypassed even in a relatively brief work on our general subject. The relations of religion and other cultural and social spheres—for instance, the sphere of the economy—make a vast area of inquiry. Aside from religion and the economy, religion and the polity might alone occupy one indefinitely, as might religion and science or religion and literature or religion and the arts generally or religion and kinship, and so on. Some attention is given to a number of these various matters in the pages that follow. The attention is afforded within the framework of consideration of controversy about the Protestant ethic. Two objects rather than one may thereby be achieved simultaneously. We may obtain some useful hints about problems that arise in the relations of religious and nonreligious spheres but also learn something of the present standing of a famous and disputed area of study that no one concerned with the sociology of religion should neglect.

Max Weber's work on *The Protestant Ethic and the Spirit of Capitalism,* which originally appeared early in the present century, is much acclaimed and much criticized. It. has certainly been a higly influential study of the relation of a religious ethic to "nonreligious" phenomena. In view of Weber's particular concern with Calvinism, it has been remarked with considerable justification that "virtually all the modern world has been read into Calvinism."[1] One might also say, not that "virtually all" of modern social science stems from Weber's work—which would manifestly be a foolish exaggeration—but that a good deal of modern social science does derive from or take nourishment from it. We shall address ourselves largely (although not exclusively) in the following to statements on the Protestant ethic and other cultural and social phenomena that have ap-

---

[1] Michael Walzer, *The Revolution of the Saints,* Cambridge: Harvard University Press, 1965, p. 300.

peared in quite recent years.[2] Also, it is well to bear in mind that Weber's study of Protestantism was only part of a larger set of studies in the sociology of religion and that a full understanding even of the study of the Protestant ethic is not possible without paying regard to its place in the larger work.[3] Only incidental reference to the larger work can be made here.

Weber's thesis in the work on the Protestant ethic is so readily available from his own words and has so often been summarized that the barest of summaries will suffice here. The Protestant ethic was, for Weber, an element of major importance in the genesis of modern capitalistic development,[4] although it was not the only element and although, *strictly*, no matter how important the agency in human affairs of religious ideas may be, those ideas do not operate in entire independence of economic and political circumstances. (The Protestant ethic, too, is not "merely" a matter of ideas: it is closely involved with interest in salvation.) The ethic is most centrally represented by Calvinism, but Weber meant to include, under the crucial category of ascetic Protestantism, four principal forms: Calvinism itself ("in the form which it assumed in the main area of its influence in Western Europe, especially in the seventeenth century"); Pietism; Methodism; the sects that grew out of the Baptist movement.[5] The influence of Lutheranism is quite different from that of these forms. Lutheranism does not have the significance in relation to modern capitalism that Calvinism and Puritanism do.

In the strategic development out of Calvinist thought, a transcendent God had decreed from eternity, and without being affected by His foreknowledge of what humans would be and do, that some of those humans should be saved and some condemned to remain in that state of sin and death in which they were "by nature." Nothing a man could do could help him in regard to salvation and he could not know whether he was saved or damned.[6] But, since interest in salvation was very great, pressures arose that led to the notion that there could be signs or indicators, in this world, of salvation in the next. Pastors faced by the practical problems of anxious men desiring a conviction of salvation recommended the combatting of all doubts as coming from Satan and engagement in hard, me-

---

[2] A compact review of some of the important items in the older literature on the Protestant ethic is provided by André Bíeler, *La Pensée Economique et Sociale de Calvin*, Ch. 6, pp. 477–514.

[3] Cf. Weber, *The Religion of China*, Glencoe: The Free Press, 1951, esp. ch. 8; Weber, *The Religion of India;* Weber, *The Sociology of Religion*, Boston: Beacon Press, 1963. Cf. also Parsons, *The Structure of Social Action*, pp. 500–578.

[4] Cf., however, Weber's cautions stated in *The Protestant Ethic*, London: Allen and Unwin, 1930, pp. 91–92.

[5] *The Protestant Ethic*, p. 95.

[6] See Chapter 7.

thodical work within the world.[7] The world was, in any case, "for God," and man must labor in it for His glory. Willingness to work came to be construed as showing forth a state of grace.

The spirit of capitalism—the complement of the ethic, in Weber's title—involves an orientation to which waste of time is utterly reprehensible. That spirit is antitraditionalist: it desires to conduct enterprise with high work-discipline, with maximum rationality by way of relating means to ends in the technological-economic context, with no limitation on enterprise imposed by the restricted set of needs to be met in terms of a traditionally "appropriate" standard of living. This perhaps suggests sufficiently that Weber thought there were significant congruities between the Protestant ethic and the spirit of capitalism and that the ethic was a vital element, though not the only one, in the genesis of modern capitalistic development. Modern capitalism itself must be understood in a technical sense. It is not based simply on acquisitive desire, which is very ancient and can hardly "explain" the specific form of occidental capitalism today. Nor is modern capitalism to be equated wth the capitalism of the capitalistic "adventurer," which involves speculation in chances for pecuniary gain, as, typically, in the case of exploiting the financial possibilities of wars. Rather, modern capitalism involves the rational organization of formally free labor[8] together with rational bookkeeping and the separation of business from the household.[9]

On the religious side again, an asceticism once confined to the monastery became "innerworldly." It went into the marketplace and the workshop and expressed itself in hard, disciplined labor, in acquisition willed by

[7] This view has been disputed, as by Knappen, who concedes that relevant theological documents show that good works were thought necessary to obtain assurance of salvation but is disposed to believe that the average Reformed churchman was very little worried about such assurance. See Marshall Knappen, *Tudor Puritanism,* Chicago: University of Chicago Press, 1939, p. 348.

[8] The laborer in the sense of this phrase is formally his own man, theoretically free to dispose of his power to work where he will, as well as "free" of the instrumentalities of production in the sense that he does not own them. Also, under modern capitalism the laborer is relatively "rationally" responsive to monetary incentives to increase or step up work, by contrast with workers under a "traditionalist" system, who will reduce output when more is paid per unit of output, in order to make merely as much as previously. This was a most important matter for Weber. Thus, he remarked in his study of India that Indian factory labor showed "exactly those traditionalist traits" which were also found under early capitalism in the West. Workers responded to wage increases, not with more work but with less, and increase prompted them to take holidays or allow their wives ornaments. See *The Religion of India,* p. 114. Weber's work obviously could not deal with what is going on in India today.

[9] For Weber's fuller notions on capitalism, see Parsons, *op. cit.,* pp. 503–506 and Reinhard Bendix, *Max Weber,* Garden City: Doubleday, 1960, pp. 72–76.

God, in saving and in refraining from expenditure on esthetic and cultural goods. The connection with the economic side is now plain enough. The ascetic Protestant ethic has evident affinities with the spirit of capitalism and thereby with the modern capitalist order, and these affinities are unlikely to be accidental and they are taken by Weber, at least in an "experimental," tentative way, as likely to have come from the influence of the "ethic" upon the "spirit." A new kind of human being, it may also be said, had emerged to work in an economic world that he was helping greatly to transform. Or so Weber believed. The contrast between the types of human beings that Weber saw as somehow "proper to" different religious systems is *suggested* in this distinction between Confucianism and Puritanism: "Confucianism demanded constant and vigilant self-control in order to maintain the dignity of the universally accomplished man of the world; Puritan ethics demanded this self-control in order methodically to concentrate man's attitudes on God's will."[10]

ECONOMY, SCIENCE, LITERATURE, AND POLITY

The relation of Protestantism and the economy continues to be of interest to historians and other social scientists. Indications of this continuing interest during very recent years will be given. Protestantism in relation to science, literature and the polity, in that order, will then be dealt with more briefly. Our overview should enable us to discern at least some of the issues that come out of the heritage of Weber's work and that are vital for the sociology of religion.

Among the indicators of continued controversy about Weber's thesis regarding Protestantism and capitalism is a recent critique which finds Weber's concepts extremely "vague" and regards his method as "unwarrantable."[11] Involved in the argument of the critic himself, Samuelsson, is evidently a failure to understand that those economic effects of the Protestant ethic, which Weber presumed, had nothing in particular to do with the economic "intentions" of the Protestant reformers, as Weber regarded matters. Samuelsson appears to think that something on the order of an unreserved, direct approval of economic worldliness on the part of the reformers would be necessary for Weber's thesis to be supported.[12] There is nothing "mystic" (Samuelsson's word[13]) about the economic effects Weber imputed to the ethic, unless it is arbitrarily decided

[10] *The Religion of China*, p. 240.

[11] Kurt Samuelsson, *Religion and Economic Action*, New York: Harper and Brothers, 1964 (originally, 1957), p. 150.

[12] Our implied disagreement does not mean that wealth could never be construed as a sign of salvation. See below, pp. 103–104, 115–117.

[13] *Ibid.*, pp. 123, 137.

that it is in itself "mystic" to suppose there could be such effects. Samuelsson is an economic historian, and it is interesting that a prominent reviewer of his work took occasion to deplore the tendency of historians and sociologists to talk past one another in matters pertaining to Weber on the subject of the ethic.[14]

We have just touched on a point about which there has apparently been considerable misunderstanding. The point is elementary, but also quite central and therefore worth further attention. Another historian, reviewing the presumed connections of Puritanism with capitalism, democracy and science remarks that his reading of the Puritans convinces him that they were overwhelmingly preoccupied with a godly life. ("Few references were made to economics, or more specifically capitalism, apart from scattered remarks to work hard and avoid idleness.") The same historian quotes Knappen's *Tudor Puritanism* to the effect that the sixteenth-century Puritan might "incidentally or accidentally" have done something in the way of contributing to capitalism (and other modern phenomena) but actually cared nothing for these things, for his concern was to save souls from hell.[15] This kind of statement can indeed argue for the grossest sort of misunderstanding, unless it is very carefully explained and fitted to Weber's argument. For Weber had made it utterly clear that the Protestant reformers themselves were precisely concerned with the salvation of the soul, not with the promotion of a spirit of capitalism, not with the positive evaluation of worldly goods.[16] The point of the sociologists following Weber has been that the representatives of ascetic Protestantism launched changes that they never foresaw, and quite a different historian, for one, argued that Calvin let loose a revolution which *he* did not want or foresee, although it was a revolution which emerged from his "dialectic."[17]

As if to put the point involved beyond all doubt, Weber averred it more than once. Again in the study of the Protestant ethic he wrote that "the cultural consequences of the Reformation were to a great extent, perhaps in the particular aspects with which we are dealing predominantly,

[14] See Talcott Parsons' review in *Jn. for the Scientific Study of Religion*, Vol. 1, Spring, 1962, pp. 226–227.

[15] Leo F. Solt, "Puritanism, Capitalism, Democracy and the New Science," *American Historical Review*, Vol. 73, October, 1967, pp. 28, 29. Cf. Knappen, *op. cit.*, p. 350.

[16] *The Protestant Ethic*, pp. 89–90.

[17] Henri Hauser, *Les Débuts du Capitalisme*, Paris: Alcan, 1931, ch. 2. Another historian who is clear on the point that in Weber's view ascetic Protestantism brought changes in modern society that its representatives neither foresaw nor intended is H. R. Trevor-Roper. See his "Religion, the Reformation, and Social Change," in G. A. Hayes-McCoy (ed.), *Historical Studies* IV, London: Bowes and Bowes, 1963, pp. 18–44, at p. 20.

unforeseen and even unwished-for results of the labors of the reformers."[18] In a related study he wrote that Puritanism created an intermediate link between a religious ethic and "a civic and methodical way of life;" and he added that Puritanism did so "unintentionally," and that we are thereby instructed in "the paradox of unintended consequences," in the discrepancy between what men want and what actually comes out of their action.[19] The sociologist Robert K. Merton, who was stimulated to do an historical-sociological investigation of the emergence of modern science by Weber's work, wrote unequivocally that one of the basic results of his study was that "the most significant influence of Puritanism upon science was largely *unintended* by the Puritan leaders." Merton added: "That Calvin himself deprecated science only enhances the paradox that from him stemmed a vigorous movement which furthered interest in this very field."[20] Still another representative of the social science area, in this case a political scientist, observes succinctly with regard to an important aspect of his findings on the historical relations of Puritanism and the polity: "The saint appeared at a certain moment . . . and is remembered afterward for the effects that he had rather than for his own motives and purposes."[21]

Briefer comment may be made on other recent and germane historical work. Scoville, a very able historian of the Huguenots or French Calvinists in the late seventeenth and early eighteenth centuries, holds that the pertinent evidence regarding trade, industry and finance that he reviews in detail gives strong support to the notion that the Huguenots exercised an influence on the French economy greater than their numbers would lead one to expect. Scoville treats Weber's thesis with respect, but he regards the sheer circumstance that the Huguenots in the seventeenth and eighteenth centuries were a penalized minority as "perhaps more significant" than any of the matters Weber considered central in *The Protestant Ethic*. As a penalized minority, to be sure, the Huguenots suffered social, economic and legal discrimination, and the suggestion is that this challenged them to outstanding economic endeavor.[22] Once more, in their book on English Protestantism from 1570 to 1640, Charles and

[18] *Ibid.*, p. 90.

[19] *The Religion of China*, p. 238.

[20] Merton, *Science, Technology and Society in Seventeenth Century England, in Osiris*, Vol. 4, Bruges: St. Catherine Press, 1938, pp. 360–632, at p. 417, fn. 6.

[21] Michael Walzer, *The Revolution of the Saints*, p. 18.

[22] See Warren C. Scoville, *The Persecution of Huguenots and French Economic Development 1680–1770*, Berkeley: University of California Press, 1960, p. 149, and Weber, *The Protestant Ethic*, pp. 39–40. Scoville cautions (*ibid.*, p. 145) that the impact of Protestantism upon capitalism in France was not necessarily like its impact elsewhere. The Huguenot case is important, but obviously not the only one of relation of Protestantism to economy.

Katherine George express various reservations about Weber's work and aver that religion is merely one among "many conditioning factors" in any social or historical situation—one that in fact is "itself conditioned far more than it conditions." But they also assert—somewhat ambivalently, it would appear—that "the association of Protestantism with capitalism is nevertheless a unique and doubtless important historical fact."[23]

Another historian (Hill) argues that the besetting problem of seventeenth-century society in England was that of a backward economy—an under-use of the country's human resources. He adds that an ideology advocating regular and systematic work was required for the country to achieve economic advancement. Hill comments further that the Soviet government has had its problems of labor discipline, particularly in ensuring *continuity* of labor. (This is of course reminiscent of Weber on traditionalistically oriented workers). Part of the answer in Russia, Hill contends, has been "the education of the population in a new body of ideas which, like Puritanism, stresses the dignity and social value of labor." Hill refers to the Puritan horror of waste of time and argues interestingly that this helped to prepare for the rhythms of an industrial society, alert to alarm clock and factory whistle.[24] Still another historian contends that if Puritanism did indeed work to promote capitalism, then it would seem to him that Anglicanism was equally conducive to it.[25] We note, too, that a historically oriented sociologist who is also a lifelong student of Weber contends that there was "*some kind* of relationship between Protestantism and the development of trade and industry."[26] (The language of this assertion is interesting and we shall return to it.) Trevor-Roper and Luethy are two more recent historian-critics of Weber, who assign

[23] Charles and Katherine George, *The Protestant Mind of the English Reformation,* Princeton: Princeton University Press, 1961, pp. 75, 173.

[24] Christoper Hill, *Society and Puritanism in Pre-Revolutionary England,* New York: Schocken Books, 1964, pp. 125, 129, 130–131. (Secker and Warburg, London).

[25] J. F. H. New, *Anglican and Puritan: The Basis of Their Opposition, 1558–1640,* Stanford: Stanford University Press, 1964, p. 100. See fn. 29, below, where Merton is quoted on Puritanism within the Anglican Church.

[26] Reinhard Bendix, "The Protestant Ethic—Revisited," *Comparative Studies in Society and History,* vol. 9, April, 1967, pp. 266–273, at p. 271. Two other recent opinions on the part of sociologists may here be referred to. Smelser is rather favorable to Weber's views of the relations of the ethic and the economy in a specific historical case. See his *Social Change in the Industrial Revolution,* Chicago: University of Chicago Press, 1959, p. 77. Guy E. Swanson, in *Religion and Regime,* Ann Arbor: University of Michigan Press, 1967, pp. 247–252, is rather more sceptical of Weber on broader grounds. Swanson begins his comments on the relations of Protestantism and capitalism with the observation that he has "no firm answer" to questions about those relations.

considerable significance in capitalist development in Europe north of the Alps to the effects of the reactionary character of the Counter-Reformation rather than to the Protestant ethic.[27]

But enough has been said, perhaps, to give some notion of the controversy still active about this aspect of Weber's work. There are five points that must now be noted with regard to the relations of Protestantism and capitalism. First, then, the matter of *time* is extremely important. Weber himself was apparently interested in Calvinism "especially in the seventeenth century," and it is worth recalling that he used the Westminister Confession of the middle of that century as a primary document. Leading authorities on Calvin and the history of Calvinism have urged that the theology of Calvin is not the theology of later Calvinists and that the connection of Calvinism and capitalism is not the same at different historical periods.[28] Any thoroughly careful examination of Weber's work will have to accord some attention to delimitations of time. Second, definitions of crucial *terms* are important. Numerous critics of Weber have been taken to task by his defenders for carelessness about the character of that modern rational bourgeois capitalism which was his crucial frame of reference on the "economic" side. And on the other side of the terminological situation, as it were, there have been difficulties in particular with such terms as Puritanism.[29] These difficulties are apparently not at

---

[27] See Trevor-Roper, *op. cit.*, and Herbert Luethy, "Once Again: Calvinism and Capitalism," *Encounter*, Vol. 22, January, 1964, pp. 26–38. Luethy and Trevor-Roper are criticized by the historian and sociologist Benjamin Nelson, who thinks that both are overly narrow in their approach to Weber's work. See Nelson's letter in *Encounter*, Vol. 23, August, 1964, pp. 94–95 on Luethy. His paper on "Conscience and the Makings of Early Modern Culture" (unpublished at this writing) is critical of both men.

[28] Cf. Biéler, *op. cit.*, Ch. 6, and John T. McNeill, *The History and Character of Calvinism*, New York: Oxford University Press, 1954, pp. 222, 421.

[29] This is not a historical work, but the sociologist who wishes to take historical material seriously obviously must have the patience to seek to disentangle some complicated things. A notion of the complexities of terminology he would face in connection with Puritanism may be suggested by merely reproducing and juxtaposing three statements by prominent scholars. Hill writes: ". . . I agree with contemporaries in thinking that there was in England in the two or three generations before the civil war a body of opinion which can usefully be labelled Puritan. There was a core of doctrine about religion and church government, aimed at purifying the Church from inside. This doctrine for various reasons won the support of a substantial and growing body of laymen. It is not to be identified with either Presbyterianism or Independency." *Society and Puritanism*, p. 28. Reprinted by permission of Schocken Books. (Associating Puritanism with "purity"—as of worship and discipline—and "purifying" represents an old tradition. Cf. David Hume, *History of England*, New York: Harper and Bros., 1879, Vol. 3, pp. 526–531). Walzer writes that "the term Puritan is used . . . to refer only to those English ministers

an end. Third, the *specific character* of the imputed influence of Protestantism is something that must be closely considered. When Scoville suggests that the relative economic importance of the Huguenots derived mainly from their status as a penalized minority, he is really far removed from Weber's thesis, which has to do most significantly with a complex of values and attitudes, with their inevitable idea-components, intimately connected with interest in salvation—a complex coming out of the religious "sphere" to bear on the economic. That is a very different matter from the theory that the French Calvinists were discriminated against and handicapped and reacted in compensatory fashion by outstanding economic performance. When Bendix avers that there was "some kind" of relationship between Protestantism and trade and industry, he may in a sense be quite justified in the light of present evidence in putting the matter in this indeterminate way, but with our preoccupation with the sociology of religion we must be interested in whether or not there was an influence from the heart of religious doctrines, values and concerns upon particular extrareligious areas.

Two further points out of Weber's own work have to do with the retroactive effect of accumulated wealth and with the achievement of independence in the economy. Thus, as regards the first of these points, Weber contended that Puritanism, with its innerworldly asceticism, its encouragement of industry and frugality, produced wealth, but that the wealth once produced tended to react upon the asceticism out of which it had come and would overwhelm asceticism with temptation. The point is clarified with an extremely apt quotation from John Wesley, who had written that "religion must necessarily produce both industry and frugality, and these cannot but produce riches" and had added that "as riches increase so will pride, anger, and love of the world in all its branches."[30] Weber

---

and laymen who adopted some recognizable form of Calvinist ideology; the range of opinion extends from 'Scottish' Presbyterians to some of the more independent of the Independents, but not beyond." *The Revolution of the Saints*, p. 115, fn. 3. A generation earlier Merton had written: "It is precisely Calvinism which constitutes the 'ideal type' of that Puritanism which was confined to no single sect and which was represented in the Anglican Church almost as fully as in those groups which later broke away from it." *Science, Technology and Society*, p. 416. Merton's statement should be read in its fuller context. And there may be more agreement than appears on the surface of these statements. But if for certain significant purposes it may be adequate to regard Puritanism as a kind of Calvinism, it should be evident that there are traps for the unwary in these premises.

[30] *The Protestant Ethic*, pp. 174–175. Very queerly, Samuelsson (*op. cit.*, p. 29) seems to believe that Weber thought Wesley was "applauding riches as such." A glance at *The Protestant Ethic*, pp. 174–175 will quickly show that this was not Weber's view.

remarked that even among the Quakers there could be discerned tendencies to repudiate the old ascetic ideals, on the foundation suggested. Since
Weber did write, "even the Quakers," particular stress may be put on
this group. An historian of the Quaker merchants of colonial Philadelphia
from the late seventeenth century to past the middle of the eighteenth
comments that "on the one hand, Friends were encouraged to be indus-
trious in their callings by the promise that God would add his blessing
in the form of prosperity," but that they also were warned "against allowing the fruits of their honest labors to accumulate lest they be tempted
into luxury and pride." Clearly, the warning did not always have the desired
effect. Tolles reports, thus, that the wives and daughters of the opulent
Quaker merchants would have garments made of the finest materials to
compensate for their self-denial in ornaments and their not keeping pace
with non-Quaker style.[31]

In summarizing Weber's work in the sociology of religion, his widow,
Marianne Weber, remarks that, for Weber, "in its earthly course the idea,
in the end, always and everywhere works against its original meaning
and thus destroys itself." At least some of the purport of this statement

---

[31] Frederick B. Tolles, *Meeting House and Counting House,* Chapel Hill: University of North Carolina Press, 1948, pp. 57, 127. McClelland, too, remarks
pertinently that "the famous ascetic 'Quaker gray' could be, and was, converted
into a luxurious dress of costly material to be worn by the wife of a wealthy
Quaker merchant." David C. McClelland, *The Achieving Society,* Princeton:
Van Nostrand, 1961, p. 313. (Long ago, Lord Kames wrote: "The Quakers exclude . . . . vanity by simplicity and uniformity of dress. Thus, by humility and
temperance, they have preserved their institutions alive. But these passions cannot
always be kept in subjection: vanity is creeping in, especially among the females,
who indulge in silks, fine linen, bonelace, etc. Vanity and pride will reach the
males; and the edifice will totter and fall." *Sketches of the History of Man,* London
and Edinburgh, 1813, Vol. 3, p. 394. And well before Kames, Bernard Mandeville
had suggested that Quaker women wore garments having "three time the quantity
of silk" that they had had twenty years before. *Free Thoughts on Religion,
the Church, and National Happiness,* 2nd ed., London, printed for John Brotherton,
1729 p. 56.) It is of interest incidentally that among the colonial Quakers business
success could be taken as a sign that one was "living in the Light" and was favored
by God. Tolles, *op. cit.,* p. 56. The importance of time reference is again suggested
when we find Barbour writing, evidently in reference to the *earliest* period of
Quakerism: "Friends at this time were scornful of the growing puritan idea that
prosperity showed God's favor: Men claim as God's gift what they have 'stolen
. . . in usury and oppression and deceit' " and then find the same Barbour asserting
that "some later Friends came to identify wealth with virtue and poverty with
laziness." Hugh Barbour, *The Quakers in Puritan England,* New Haven: Yale
University Press, 1964, pp. 171–172, 250. Westfall suggests that it was "after 1660"
that the Calvinist social ideal became "crass" enough to allow worldly success to
signify divine blessing. Richard S. Westfall, *Science and Religion in Seventeenth
Century England,* New Haven: Yale University Press, 1958, p. 8.

is indicated when in the course of description of the specific work on the Protestant ethic Marianne Weber notes the conception of Protestant obligation or duty in relation to one's possessions. Here, she observes, "begins the tragedy of the idea," for "even Puritanism cannot resist the temptations of *acquired* wealth, any more than the medieval communities of monks. The remarkable religious structuring of life gets destroyed in virtue of its own consequences."[32]

Finally, Weber contended, the modern economic order no longer has need of the motivation he thought had once been supplied for it by ascetic Protestantism. "Victorious capitalism" now rests on other foundations. This conception of the achievement of autonomy for the economic order—autonomy, that is, in relation to what were thought by Weber to be significant originating religious factors—is a matter that must engage us again.[33]

A second sphere in which the influence of ascetic Protestantism has been thought by some scholars to be very important is, as the reader will have inferred, that of modern science. The outstandingly influential

[32] Marianne Weber, *Max Weber: Ein Lebensbild,* pp. 385, 390. If we confine ourselves to wealth and its reverse influence on the "virtues" out of which it can arise, this, however, does not mean that the tragedy of the idea is not more widely understood by Weber. See the interesting and provocative paper by Werner Stark, "Max Weber and the Heterogony of Purposes," *Social Research,* Vol. 34, 1967, p. 249–264.

[33] Aside from historical and comparative studies, Weber's work on the Protestant ethic has given rise to an increasing literature directed to statistical inquiry about differences between Protestant and Catholic outlooks and behavior in regard to such things as kinds of education gone in for (Protestants, according to the traditional expectation basing itself on Weber, going in more for scientific education than Catholics), attitudes toward economic success, and actual achievement of economic success. Weber did propose a "disengagement" when he set out the view that the modern economic order had achieved independence of Protestantism. But assuming that he had a sound point in the first place it does not seem unreasonable at least to look for some residual connections in the present-day world between Protestantism and economic activity, occupational choices, attitudes toward science and so on. Such connections are now asserted and also stoutly denied. They are defended and sustained, it should be noted, to a large extent by way of the results of survey questionnaires, which yield data on the attitudes and dispositions of individuals. There is certainly a strong current of opinion, basing itself on available evidence, against the presumption of such connections. (See, for example, Andrew Greeley, "The Protestant Ethic: Time for a Moratorium," *Sociological Analysis,* Vol. 25, Spring, 1964, pp. 20–33, and, for a very recent piece of representative research, Norval Glenn and Ruth Hyland, "Religious Preference and Worldly Success," *American Sociological Review,* Vol. 32, Feb., 1967, pp. 73–85.) All this is a matter for continuing incoming evidence, and it is far from being unimportant, but for the purposes we have in view such evidence bearing on the contemporary world and gathered through survey research need not be reviewed.

work in this area has been that of Robert K. Merton previously referred to: *Science, Technology and Society in Seventeenth Century England.* Merton's thesis is much like Weber's. He suggests that perhaps more important for encouraging scientific activity in the Puritan ethos than any other element was the persuasion that the study of nature leads to appreciation of God's works and of His power, His goodness and His wisdom. Ideas about the importance of work in a useful calling, about election as proved by good works (which are outward signs of an inward state of grace), about the need for diligence and labor, and others also played roles. None of this means that the reformers had to have a love for science any more than in Weber's view they had to have a love for capitalism. Rather, the case of Calvin, as in the following statement by Merton, provides the model for what Merton regards as the appropriate mode of analysis: "Calvin frowned upon the acceptance of numerous scientific discoveries of his day, whereas the religious ethic which stemmed from him inevitably inspired the pursuit of natural science."[34]

Here, too, there is much controversy. If we review a few representative items, we soon see that there is considerable resemblance between the issues here raised and those raised in the case of ascetic Protestantism and the economy. One writer skeptical of the notion of genetic connection between Puritanism and science, not unexpectedly, finds the *term* or concept, Puritanism, ambiguous.[35] But Christopher Hill maintains stoutly that there is something to the thesis of connection of Puritanism and science and suggests that Kearney and others are at fault either in wavering in their understanding of what Puritanism consists in or in defining it in such a way that there could not be a connection between it and science.[36] Another skeptic (Rabb) finds *time* a crucial issue. He sees a definite linkage between reformed religion and science after the 1640's. But what is in question in the contemporary debate on the whole matter is the relation of religion to the *rise* of science, and hereby the period before 1640 becomes vitally important. The *later* (post-1640's) close relationship of Protestantism and science Rabb considers to indicate the effect of science on Protestantism rather than the reverse.[37]

But we have to notice something of what is emphasized in the con-

[34] *Op. cit.,* p. 459. No more than Weber in the case of the economy does Merton argue in the case of science that ascetic Protestantism was the only factor in its rise. See, for example, *op. cit.,* p. 495.

[35] H. F. Kearney, "Puritanism, Capitalism and the Scientific Revolution," *Past and Present,* No. 28, July, 1964, pp. 81–101.

[36] Christopher Hill, "Debate: Puritanism, Capitalism and the Scientific Revolution," *Past and Present,* No. 29, December, 1964, pp. 88–97.

[37] Theodore K. Rabb, "Religion and the Rise of Modern Science," *Past and Present,* No. 31, July, 1965, pp. 111–126.

temporary debate on this matter with regard to the *specific character* of the imputed influence of ascetic Protestantism. Hill, for one, seems not to have taken a thoroughly consistent position with regard to this. Thus, in one place he regards the relationship between Protestantism and science as well established but suggests need for care in determining the precise mode of connection between the two and goes on to argue that in the development of science Protestant doctrine (although that, in his words, might "contribute something") was less important than the breaking of repressive clerical influences on science.[38] In a later article already cited he asserts that science is not a product of Protestantism or of Puritanism but that both science and Puritanism "sprang from the shift by which urban and industrial values replaced those appropriate to a mainly agrarian society."[39] The place of religious doctrine, which is of course crucial, as it was for Weber and Merton, becomes somewhat uncertain in all this.[40]

Nevertheless, in the words that have just been quoted, Hill is at any rate concerned with values. The importance of this remaining accent will be seen in due course. Ben-David, another student of European science, and specifically of the establishment of the scientific role, contends that all relevant computations, even those of writers who wish to negate the notion of a relationship between Protestantism and science, show that "Protestants were disproportionately highly represented among scientists from the sixteenth to the end of the eighteenth century."[41] However, Ben-David is clearly, explicitly skeptical of the view that Protestant doctrine played a significant role in this even if he includes "Protestantism" in a list of explanatory factors. The list allows the importance of numerous other phenomena.

We must arbitrarily cut the story of controversy short here also.[42] But

[38] Hill, "William Harvey and the Idea of Monarchy," *Past and Present,* No. 27, April, 1964, pp. 54–72.

[39] Hill, "Debate . . . ," p. 89.

[40] Note: "At the very end of his article on Harvey Mr. Hill suddenly seems to deny the importance of the very feature of Protestantism that the four authorities he cites considered so essential: religious doctrine. He emphasizes the social political and institutional changes . . . at the expense of doctrine. . . ." Rabb, *loc. cit.,* p. 124.

[41] Joseph Ben-David, "The Scientific Role: The Conditions of its Establishment in Europe," *Minerva,* Vol. 4, Autumn, 1965, pp. 15–54, at pp. 42, 44, 46.

[42] One of the intriguing questions that we cannot consider has to do with the particular *kind* of science Puritanism may be supposed to have encouraged or generated. It has been contended that a Puritan pragmatic and utilitarian stress, not concerned with understanding or theory for itself, merely nourished one element of emerging modern science, while a more determinedly theoretical and mathematical stress (associated with non-Puritan sympathies) nourished another element. See Kearney, "Puritanism, Capitalism and the Scientific Revolution," *loc. cit.*

a final point must be noted. In the field of ascetic Protestantism and science, too, Merton follows Weber in advancing, in effect, the notion of the tragedy of the idea. Once more, in Merton's view, then, modern science drew nourishment from religious roots, but this happened without religious intention: it was an unanticipated consequence, and, additionally, a consequence that in its way and in time returned upon its sources. A developed science came to challenge some of the very religious-doctrinal bases that had initially given it nourishment. "This," comments Merton, "is the essential paradox of social action—the 'realization' of values may lead to their renunciation."[43] The similarity to Weber's work is clear.

Since this point has now been noted twice, it is as well at this juncture to indicate one additional field in which the point is again suggested. Although the point is made more by implication than by outright statement, it is plain enough.

The field we refer to is literature, and in this case it is useful to turn to an older work: Schöffler's study of Protestantism and English literature.[44] Schöffler notes that there was initial Protestant opposition to literary-asthetic or belletristic reading and writing. This smacked of the worldly and the sinful and was to be avoided in favor of the Bible, particularly. "It is from the first impossible that one of the elect should write a book full of lies simply for the purpose of robbing himself and his fellowmen of time, every hour of which they would have to expend in God's work."[45] But in time there was a marked Protestant turn toward belles lettres, *based, however, on motives of moral and religious edification,* so that early English fiction in the eighteenth century had an appreciable foundation in Protestant desire to point religious and moral teachings by means of story-telling.

We must omit much of the detail of Schöffler's fascinating thesis and concentrate on the point that has occasioned interest in Protestantism and literature in the first place. Schöffler notes of John Bunyan (1628–1688), Daniel Defoe (1659?–1731) and Samuel Richardson (1689–1761)[46] that none of these three, in principle, wanted to create anything new. The transition, in their work, from the older edification-literature was half unconscious, Schöffler avers, and to be comprehended only on the

---

[43] *Science, Technology and Society,* p. 460.

[44] Herbert Schöffler, *Protestantismus and Literatur,* Leipzig: Verlag von Bernhard Tauchnitz, 1922.

[45] *Ibid.,* p. 19.

[46] Bunyan's earlier dates will be noted. He might well be considered apart from the other two with whom Schöffler associates him, not only on the ground of dates. A penetrating argument as to why Defoe, rather than Bunyan, "is often considered to be our first novelist" is presented by Ian Watt, *The Rise of the Novel,* Berkeley and Los Angeles: University of California Press, 1965, pp. 80–83.

foundation of their religious bias or that of the Puritan lower middle class. All three men defended themselves on the ground that they had written in the truth—or at least what was "inwardly true." They had written moral, and, accordingly, useful things. Defoe and Richardson even long represented themselves as mere "editors."[47] The modern novel, then, had a substantial basis in notions and values deriving from ascetic Protestantism, according to this thesis.[48] But it can certainly be reasonably contended that the novel in time came to be an art form that often put "religion" and "asceticism" on the defensive. Here, too, the thesis has in effect been suggested that the Puritans might have contemplated a (cultural) world they had never made with astonishment that it should ever in any sense have emerged from any doctrines or values which they espoused. The point need not be strained. There does appear to be a portion of truth in it.[49]

[47] Schöffler, *ibid.,* pp. 168–169. Compare Watt, *op cit.,* p. 50.

[48] The thesis is given considerable support by Watt, who writes, *op. cit.,* pp. 84–85: "The positive contributions of Puritanism . . . to the rise of the novel, and to later tradition in England, must not be underestimated. It was through Puritanism that Defoe brought into the novel a [superior] treatment of the individual's psychological concerns. . . . Nor does the fact that, in the words of Rudolph Stamm, who has given the most complete account of Defoe's religious position, Defoe's writings show that 'his own experience of reality had nothing in common with that of a believing Calvinist' disprove the positive importance of Defoe's dissenting background. For we can say of him, as of later novelists in the same tradition, such as Samuel Richardson, George Eliot or D. H. Lawrence, that they have inherited of Puritanism everything except its religious faith. They all have an intensely active conception of life as a continuous moral and social struggle; they all see every event in ordinary life as proposing an inrtinsically moral issue on which reason and conscience must be exerted to the full before right action is possible; they all seek by introspection and observation to build their own personal scheme of moral certainty; and in different ways they all manifest the self-righteous and somewhat angular individualism of the earlier Puritan character."

[49] One more statement from Watt may be noted to suggest the kind of material that the sociologically sensitive may find. The statement from Watt that follows consists of three sentences, the second of which suggests something of an analogy to Weber's conception of the achievement of autonomy for the economic order and the third of which suggests how an important ascetic-Protestant value may have carried over into the field of literature: "*Robinson Crusoe* is certainly the first novel in the sense that it is the first fictional narrative in which an ordinary person's daily activities are the centre of continuous literary attention. These activities, it is true, are not seen in a wholly secular light; but later novelists could continue Defoe's serious concern with man's worldly doings without placing them in a religious framework. It is therefore likely that the Puritan conception of the dignity of labor helped to bring into being the novel's general premise that the individual's daily life is of sufficient importance and interest to be the proper subject of literature." *Op. cit.,* p. 74.

We turn to a last selected area of concern, that of politics, and confine ourselves strictly to a few matters suggested by Walzer's recent aforementioned *Revolution of the Saints*. It is a very important part of Walzer's thesis that the Calvinist theory of worldly activity involved what he calls a new integration of private men ("or rather, of *chosen* groups of private men, of proven holiness and virtue") into the political order—"an integration based upon a novel view of politics as a kind of conscientious and continuous labor." The effects of Calvinism on these lines Walzer even believes occurred before "any infusion of religious worldliness into the economic order."[50] He adds: "The diligent activism of the saints— Genevan, Huguenot, Dutch, Scottish, and Puritan—marked the transformation of politics into work and revealed for the first time the extraordinary conscience that directed the work."[51]

Further, Walzer finds that Puritanism was preoccupied with human control. A later liberalism could be less preoccupied with it because it had already been implanted in men. Puritan repression had played an important role in this implantation, in Walzer's view, and later liberalism could profit from and rest upon this.[52] A parallel to the economic sphere is clearly suggested when Walzer writes that rural laborers, vagabonds and beggers of the sixteenth and seventeenth centuries were "not yet ready to become the subjects of a systematic self-control." They were "brutally repressed, but they were not yet integrated into a modern economic system." Walzer adds that the making of the English working class occurred much later and that "along with it came ideologies parallel to that of the saints, similarly inculcating self-discipline and teaching a religious or political activism."[53] To this we shall soon recur. Meanwhile, it is clear enough that for Walzer ideas and values sourcing in the Protestant ethic profoundly affected the political arena. Walzer makes a respectable case for his view. Even in the military sphere, discipline, organization and drill seemed congenial to those of ascetic Protestant persuasion.[54]

HERITAGE FROM WEBER: FOUR AREAS OF INQUIRY

Weber presents no very simple, sharp thesis. One can indeed easily become annoyed with him about this. It is possible and would appear

---

[50] In contrast to Weber's stress on hard work and success as signs of grace, Walzer argues that the Puritan preachers were concerned with "the social and moral effects of hard work," not so much with its spiritual significance. The problem of social order and control was crucial for the Puritans. See the remarks that follow in the text; cf. Walzer, *ibid.,* p. 211, fn. 32.

[51] *Op. cit.,* p. 2.

[52] *Ibid.,* p. 303.

[53] *Ibid.,* p. 230.

[54] *Ibid. pp.,* 276–277.

likely that he thought a certain amount of precision and rigor—and no more—were feasible in dealing with the issues raised by consideration of the Protestant ethic and that it would be foolish to press for more. He ends his essay on the famous note that it is not his aim to substitute a (one-sided) spiritualistic causal interpretation of culture and history for a materialistic (equally one-sided) one that would investigate the effect of economic conditions, particularly, on Protestant asceticism. He makes it clear that he does not think that the spirit of capitalism could have come about solely as the result of certain effects of the Reformation "or even that capitalism as an economic system is a creation of the Reformation itself." "On the contrary," he then adds, "we only wish to ascertain whether and to what extent religious forces have taken part in the qualitative formation and the quantitative expansion of [the] spirit [of capitalism] over the world."[55]

It is scarcely surprising that there has not even been complete agreement about Weber's meaning. Nor is it invariably excessive caution that will make a scholar wary of stating a plain, forthright position on many of the matters that have been gone over. It is often true, rather, that adequate knowledge is lacking. But it remains certain that Weber saw the Protestant ethic as a very important element in the genesis of modern "rational bourgeois capitalism." This, right or wrong, cannot be interpreted away. To seek to do so would create real puzzles about such of Weber's studies as those of India and China and indeed about the study of the Protestant ethic itself. It is unlikely that someone of Weber's attainments would have made central to his work on the sociology of religion a perfectly trivial phenomenon. And after about two-thirds of a century of controversy and merciless scrutiny of his themes, it is clear that Weber was indeed on the track of significant things, no matter how fumbling, in detail, his understanding of them may have been. Out of Weber's work on the ethic, at least four important lines of inquiry come. Before turning to these, let us be wholly clear on the point that we take Weber's concern with the Protestant ethic as a concern with a complex of religious ideas, values and interests. The idea-background in Calvinism needs no further explanation. "Doctrine" is a central thing in regard to the Protestant ethic and for *our* purposes, various distinctions bearing on points of doctrine fade into the background: religious ideas, generally, are important here. Religious values in this context have to do with such notions as the one that the world is for God's greater glory. "Interests" here has reference to interest(s) in salvation. Where a student of Protestantism in relation to economy or science or polity moves away from the complex just designated he may be doing something very impor-

[55] *The Protestant Ethic,* p. 91.

tant. His work might even show the complex we are concerned with to be of slight significance. But if there is any substance to Weber's thesis we should be certain that it is that thesis to which we refer, not some other, perhaps more defensible one which Weber's suggested.

Of the four lines of inquiry coming out of Weber's work that are to be indicated, the first is most important here in that it bears most directly on the matter of interchanges. (Our foregoing review of course constantly touched upon *relations* of religious and nonreligious spheres.) First, then, there are *indications* of a significant dialectic at work in the sphere, particularly, of Protestantism and the economy. The dialectic involved will recall the notion of the tragedy of the idea. Protestant asceticism, featuring industry, thrift and frugality, works for the "good," for the greater glory of God, but then it produces the "bad" in the form of temptation to abandon asceticism. The temptation is created by the wealth that asceticism itself brings about. It is a characteristic dialectical element in this that the very emergence of the "good" by way of economic productivity based on asceticism contains within itself, as it were, its opposite, the emergence of the "bad," lapse of asceticism: a phenomenon harbors its own "contradiction."[56]

The idea does readily suggest itself that we may here be coming close to some important interchanges, in a wide, generic sense, between religion and other spheres (although we are not utilizing the terms that figure in Parsons' discussions of interchange). One form of expectable religious reaction to the situation just described would be on the line of stiffening or renewed resistance. Thus, when some of the faithful succumb to blandishments of wealth, acquired through exercise of diligence in a calling, and allow themselves previously abhorred luxuries, others of the faithful, being profoundly shocked by this, reaffirm powerfully the virtues of asceticism—and thereby, paradoxically, other things being equal, assure future accumulations of wealth that will recreate the same problems. There are undoubtedly sources of schism in this and schism has repeatedly had foundations in it. But a different form of interchange would occur if—again to focus on religion and economy—the succumbing to the flesh induced by a wealth that broke down consumption-resistance, let us say, worked in due course to change the religious-doctrinal orientation, which might then in its changed character have a reciprocal effect on the economy, and so on. Cumulative change would thus be set going and in time a new "system" would be achieved. This is also a realistic conception.

This affords us a useful cue in regard to *autonomization* of the economy.

---

[56] We could use somewhat different language to describe the things pointed to in this paragraph. But the use of the word, dialectic, seems to us to be quite apt and justified in the light of what is involved.

It will be recalled that Weber contended that "victorious capitalism" is now no longer sustained by Protestant asceticism. In the process of cumulative change we have just referred to, interchanges between economy and religion would take place, as indicated, and each would be increasingly transformed over time (within definite limits as long as we refer only to the autonomization of the economy, although evidently change could go beyond this). If the economy then still depended on religious resources, perhaps for some of the motivation of economically engaged personnel, it would in any case no longer be dependent on the original Protestant asceticism, which would have been considerably changed. The process of autonomization is analogous to achievement of "functional autonomy" at the psychological level. A man may be motivated to high intellectual achievement by a disliked father who depreciates him. But then intellectual achievement comes to be valued for its own sake, in time. Whatever started it, it can become independently fascinating and be reinforced, when one is mature, by factors other than those involved in the original father-relationship—for instance, by the need to make a living by such (intellectual) skills as one has.

The above sets out elements of what we designate as a dialectical view of interchange. We may expand it slightly by reference to what may be called *culture-level coordination*. Here Parsons (among others) can be of help. He has hardly been the first to advance such an argument, but he does argue cogently that cultural spheres ("subsystems") are "integrated with each other at broadly comparable levels of generality." Thus, he asserts that "modern science cannot be conceived as part of the same cultural system as a primitive religion, but is definitely linked with Western Christianity, especially ascetic Protestantism and its later cultural derivatives."[57] (In the light of our argument the specific reference to "later cultural derivatives" is of interest.) The short outline of autonomization that has been given suggests a process in which religion and economy, in reciprocally influencing each other, as it were keep each other at similar cultural levels, so that culture-level coordination is achieved. Also, aside from the matter of autonomization, one might conceivably argue that ascetic Protestantism had a profound impact on the general lines propounded by Weber and that this was bound to express itself in the activities of Protestants, no matter what the particular sphere of activity into which they entered. It might be contended that any respectable evidence for the extrareligious effect of the Protestant ethic in any one sphere, such as the economic, would argue for the likelihood of its effect in others.

[57] *Theories of Society,* Vol. 2, p. 987, fn. 21. Cf. the subsection in which the footnote appears, *ibid.,* pp. 984–988.

Thereby, again, culture-level coordination would have been effected and here the accent would fall of course on a presumed initial cultural pervasion by the Protestant ethic.

The dialectical view of interchange proposed gets some nourishment from the evidence on the Protestant ethic. Just how much, it is extremely difficult to say. We must again stress the uncertainties with respect to the ethic itself, simply because the relevant material leaves us no choice except to do so. It would be desirable to have a precise marshalling of evidence relating specific points in the theology of the various Protestant groups Weber included in his study—from Calvinists to sectarians coming out from Baptism—to the dialectic whereby acquired wealth modifies asceticism. There is a scattering of such evidence in the relevant literature, but so far as the writer is aware, it has not been systematically searched for and collated with an eye to point for point correspondences or non-correspondences between particulars of theology and particulars on the dialectical "side." The Quakers served Weber as a group exemplifying Protestant asceticism, and undoubtedly there were numerous Quakers who worked hard and achieved success and whose success enfeebled an original asceticism. But one must at least note that the Quakers rejected the doctrine of predestination.

If we move away from the economic sphere, the case of science is inevitably recalled, where the tragedy of the idea—or a dialectic whereby science nourished by religious sources returned to those sources, in time, to question important religious notions—was stressed but where present evidence makes us uncertain about the factual grounding of the dialectical view. The field of literature seems to afford a better, more positive case. The polity was not so treated, by Walzer, as to make it relevant in this particular context beyond the rudimentary point that the saints produced something they had never intended. (Yet the–quite possibly generalized–"activism" Walzer noted could be relevant in a slightly larger context.)

But it should be clear that a dialectical view of interchange may be stimulated by someone like Weber without having to depend, in principle, on what is available in the particular field Weber covered. The view of interchange that has been sketched might, incidentally, be reconciled with Parsons on the subject of interchange, but the emphases here given are different, even if, as we have seen, Parsons' perspectives can be helpful in developing them.

A second line of inquiry suggested by Weber's work has to do with personality types. Weber sought to portray a distinctive, religiously stamped character or personality type (definitely not a Confucian gentleman!)—ascetic and dour, characterized by what one could almost call a ruthless devotion to duty in a variety of spheres, dedicated to what he conceived as divinely required, and perhaps considerably less loving than certain Christian ideals might suggest it was desirable for a man to be. Or the "personality" or character accent may be held to fall somewhat differently. Now one may think of a distinctively self-made man, newly independent of various religious routines established within the Catholic church, released in particular from the Catholic confessional, required and resolved to solve a large variety of problems "on his own." Such a "new man" might well operate in different spheres of cultural and social life in such a way as to support similar values in the different spheres—and the relevant values would thereby have a personality-mediation that takes us back to the principle of culture-level coordination. Some such type as Weber sketched undoubtedly existed. But much subtle work remains to be done in the area of personality or character types connected with religion. Weber was in his way, perhaps half without intending to be, an early player in modern sociology and social psychology of the "game" of making out distinctive character types. The game has been enriched since his time by psychoanalytical ideas. It can be carried beyond his relevant achievements. History and anthropology and comparative sociology should enable us to build (but not for aesthetic purposes) a large gallery of portraits of types that are in fact importantly influenced by religion, thus serving to enrich an appropriately nonprovincial sociology of religion.

A third line of inquiry has to do with a theory of "signs."[58] The signs referred to are signs of salvation or reprobation. Weber was concerned with profitableness and prosperity as these were historically interpreted to have symbolic religious significance, in the sense that a man's prosperity might argue that he was a man who was going to be saved. Weber stated that Calvin himself was of the view that "the elect differ externally in this life in no way from the damned."[59] But there is ground for thinking that, in time, this view of Calvin's was modified. McNeill writes:

"Certainly the bourgeois heresy of wealth as a mark of divine approval entered into late Calvinism, though always under the restraints of insistence upon charity and service. It may have broken in during the era of Puritan individualism, with the triumph of the Independents and the growth of foreign trading interests. Cromwell saw in his military victories the manifest favor of God. . . ."[60]

Similar notions on the line that prosperity indicates divine approval or election (and with a hint or more than a hint that poverty indicates disapproval or damnation) have been ascribed to the Puritan creed by

[58] The following draws on Louis Schneider, "Problems in the Sociology of Religion," in Robert E. L. Faris, ed., *Handbook of Modern Sociology,* Chicago: Rand McNally, 1964, pp. 789–792.
[59] *The Protestant Ethic,* p. 110.
[60] *The History and Character of Calvinism,* p. 419.

other historians.[61] There is not unanimity on the subject, but there is apparently agreement on the notion that, especially after the earlier decades of the Reformation, there was a *tendency* in Protestant thought to take up a kind of religious theory of signs—again on the line that worldly conditions such as prosperity and poverty symbolize or prefigure supernatural states. There were variations in the theory. We have already noted Tolles' remark that business success among the colonial Philadelphia Quakers could be taken as a sign that one was indeed "living in the Light" and was favored by God.[62] Yet Quakers were powerfully committed to charitable work; for them, every man was "a vehicle of the seed of God" and deserved sympathetic help should he have need; "nothing," Tolles writes, "could have been further removed from the Puritan view of poverty as a crime and a disgrace, a visible sign of God's displeasure."[63] In terms of a theory of signs, there are four possibilities to be noted: (a) prosperity could be taken to argue or imply a state of salvation; (b) a state of salvation could be taken to argue or imply a condition of prosperity; (c) poverty or economic failure could be taken to argue or imply a state of salvation; (d) a state of salvation could be taken to argue or imply a condition of poverty. (Any one or all of these possibilities could of course also be denied.) The Quakers described by Tolles represented one religious variant that had a bias toward accepting *a* and *b* but not toward accepting *c* and *d*.

Here, too, to the writer's knowledge, there has never been a systematic amassing of evidence to set out such historical representatives of various possible combinations as there may be and to check carefully for all these representatives how much hesitation and ambiguity existed about the combinations they espoused and to trace the decline of theories of signs. The interest of the matter comes partly from indications that it has been significant into the present-day world. Bates and Dittemore write very suggestively of Augusta Stetson, Mary Baker Eddy's follower:

"From the fundamental principles of Christian Science she boldly drew certain inferences. . . . Evil being error, and poverty being an indubitable form of evil, Mrs. Stetson argued, it followed that poverty must be error and indicated a wrong state of mind in its victims. Prosperity was a result of spirituality, its symbol and unerring accompaniment. 'To demonstrate prosperity' was an important part of the Christian Scientist's duty."[64]

[61] Hauser, *Les Débuts du Capitalisme,* ch. 2; R. H. Tawney, *Religion and the Rise of Capitalism,* New York: Penguin Books, 1947, ch. 4.

[62] *Meeting House and Counting House,* p. 56.

[63] *Ibid.,* p. 65.

[64] E. S. Bates and J. V. Dittemore, *Mary Baker Eddy: The Truth and the Tradition,* New York: Knopf, 1932.

It is of interest that in American cultist thought there is a very conspicuous psychologizing of signs whereby prosperity argues no more than "right thinking" and poverty no more than "wrong thinking" or "negative thinking."[65]

Assuming that this kind of psychologizing (or "mentalizing") has antecedents in older Protestant sign theory, we refer to it as *attenuation.* This is distinct from *extinguishment,* which would of course mean the wiping out or coming to an end of sign theory. It would be an interesting enterprise to inquire whether attenuation and extinguishment can possibly be interpreted in the light of a dialectic of interchange between religion and economy. Weber did not penetrate into this line of thought but it is clearly related to some of his central argument.

A fourth and last line of inquiry bears on the Protestant ethic as a starting mechanism. Weber's work on both the ethic and on comparative religion suggests that he thought of the ethic as such a mechanism. It will be recalled that Hill contended that the besetting problem of seventeenth-century England was that of a backward economy and that an ideology supporting regular, systematic work would be found to be helpful in such a situation. Weber was clearly probing for extra-economic sources for such an "ideology." (Of course, no idea-value-interest complex supporting regular, systematic work would result in economic success if objective conditions—such as absence of critical resources—imposed sufficient limitations.)[66]

We noted above some comment made by Walzer on the making of the English working class and Walzer's reference to ideologies inculcating self-discipline and activism. It is instructive in this connection to turn to Thompson's ambitious study of English workers in the late eighteenth and nineteenth centuries.[67] Thompson is prone to depict the life-denying, joy-killing side of Methodism. Yet he indicates that there were working-class ways which might be criticized, indeed, from certain humane standpoints, but which—and this is more important here—also stood in the way of an industrialization ultimately due to bring considerable benefits to the whole English community (although one need hardly contend that it was unaccompanied by suffering). Thompson asserts that the passing of such things as "orgiastic drunkenness, animal sexuality, and mortal combat for prize-money in iron-studded clogs calls for no lament." And to this he adds the interesting assertion: "However repressive and disabling

[65] See below, Part 4, Ch. 7.

[66] Cf. the context of Johnson's observation that religious belief will make no people rich, given unfavorable circumstances. Harry M. Johnson, *Sociology,* p. 447.

[67] Edward P. Thompson, *The Making of the English Working Class,* New York: Pantheon Books, 1964.

the work-discipline of Methodism, the Industrial Revolution could not have taken place without *some* work-discipline, and, in whatever form, the conflict between old and new ways must inevitably have been painful."[68]

The echoes of the Protestant ethic that this sounds can be said to resound elsewhere also. Underdeveloped countries, as in Asia, interest contemporary scholars partly on the foundation of a concern with starting mechanisms that would operate to get relatively primitive or backward economies "off the ground." One of the better known relevant pieces of work in this area is McClelland's previously referred to book on *The Achieving Society*. McClelland's primary focus is psychological. He is interested precisely in achievement motivation. Yet his work points back to historically grounded religious values and it suggests that conventional oppositions, as between "Protestant" and "Catholic" may conceal too much. Refinement and breakdown of such categories are indicated. If "Protestantism" has some distinctive connection with need for achievement, with activism and methodical devotion to work, what is there *in* Protestantism that gives support to such phenomena, and is the significant element stronger in some Protestant groups than others? (Can we go beyond Weber in this matter?) And, without the particular Protestant label, does it occur in quite different religious groups, as among the Jains and Parsis of India?[69]

McClelland inclines to the view that a bridge from religion to such things as business success is built not so much by asceticism as by a "reverence for life" that induces a strong sense of responsibility and active striving to push one's deeds in the direction of the "good." McClelland also assigns importance in this connection to what he calls individual rather than ritual contact with the divine (the latter featuring precise memorizing of ritual formulas) and to relative readiness to dispense with the services of religious experts in religious matters. We do not necessarily have in this some definitive restructuring of the Protestant ethic thesis (with particular reference to motivation), but it is noteworthy how wide McClelland's range becomes as he seeks to extract from both Western and Asiatic

---

[68] *Ibid.*, p. 41. It is of some interest that even when Thompson avers at a later point (p. 427) that "we cannot accept the thesis that sobriety was the consequence only, or even mainly, of the Evangelical propaganda" and even if he is more amiably disposed toward Primitive Methodists than toward Methodists, one senses in his struggles with the evaluation of the effects of ascetic Protestantism on the working class an ultimate inability to deny religion some significant "functions" for that class—valuable in the interests of the class itself. Our point is certainly not to "defend" any religion. It is to come closer to proper assessment of functions.

[69] Cf. *The Achieving Society*, pp. 367–373.

religions shared features that might explain distinctive economic performance.[70] It is relevant that another recent discussion within the same general complex of problems and questions analyzes the case of the Parsis quite deliberately in terms of values that may run across, or be found in, ostensibly quite different religious traditions.[71] If "religion" is important in all this, an obvious question is whether there are functional alternatives to religion.

But there is no design here of reviewing relevant literature on underdeveloped or recently underdeveloped countries, or of updating Weber's views on India, or the like.[72] Weber's ideas unquestionably need revision and are obviously being revised. The search for extra-economic starting mechanisms for the economy, with a special eye for the religious sphere, remains a strategic sociological enterprise, most interestingly so when the focus on the religious sphere is precisely on the idea-value-religious interest complex, not on some accidental or indirect connection with "the religious factor."

Our main interest in this last section has been in interchanges. A consideration of interchanges could not possibly be omitted from any approach (including a structural-functional one) to a sociology of religion. We cannot be sure of the form that analysis of interchange may take in the near future. But one of the things that recommends a dialectical view is that it is not less alert than any other to change itself (in the course of interchange), whether the change be within, or beyond, various limits; and it covers points of a type that must sooner or later be contended with by any reasonably "complete" theory of interchange.

[70] For a view divergent from McClelland's, see Swanson, *Religion and Regime,* pp. 251–252.

[71] See Robert E. Kennedy, "The Protestant Ethic and the Parsis," *American Journal of Sociology,* Vol. 68, 1962, pp. 11–20.

[72] Some useful material is made available in Shmuel N. Eisenstadt, ed., *The Prostestant Ethic and Modernization,* New York: Basic Books, 1968.

PART IV

Aspects of Religion as Culture

CHAPTER 7

Religious Culture, Practical Religion, and Instrumentalization[1]

We know that not all elements even of a particular religious culture, more or less closely associated historically with a particular society or community, are necessarily equally relevant to religion as a going concern—to religion in its institutionalized form in a given social context. There are elements of a religious heritage that may be idle for greater or lesser periods of time. These idle elements, however, may "break through," becoming socially important and in that sense no longer constituting an otiose portion of culture. We have already argued that it is justifiable for the sociologist to be particularly attentive to those portions of religious culture that are, as it were, socially operative. It is well now to argue also that while keeping an eye on socially operative religious culture in particular, the sociologist would be foolish not to avail himself of some general insights and knowledge in the field of religious culture proper. Such insights and knowledge could become most useful at any time. Rigid demarcations of interest in this whole area will hardly do. A certain sense for the special character of distinctively sociological tasks is useful and even indispensable, but those very tasks can often be helped forward by some ease about what one is supposed to be doing—and it may be urged that this is particularly true in the sociology of religion.

In the present chapter, some effort is expended on the content of religious culture in a broad sense. But then there is very quick movement to the matter of "levels" of such culture—in the sense that a religious elite in a particular country may be religious at one "level" while the great mass of professants in the country are religious at another "level." This, of course, is still relevant in regard to religious culture. It is often

[1] The term, practical religion, in this title is borrowed from the title of the volume edited by Edmund R. Leach, *Dialectic in Practical Religion*, Cambridge: The University Press, 1968. The term is explained in due course.

123

important, precisely, to recognize the sheer variety of religious culture. American religious culture, for example, is not exhausted by the categories of Protestantism, Catholicism, and Judaism, not only because there is some slight representation of more or less conventional faiths outside the Judeo-Christian tradition but also because there are traces of yet different religious cultural resources, as in the case of the civil religion that Bellah, among others, has pointed to—a religion that draws on the tradition just referred to but also has a distinctive character and bears particularly on America as a nation. In this chapter, however, our concern with the variety or differentiation of religious culture will in the first place be with a variety that is associated with levels in stratification systems. An inevitable concomitant is concern for "practical" religion—which term we use in the sense of Leach to mean an everyday kind of religion practiced by "ordinary" people with interests centered on this world. Practical religion shades at one end into what is loosely called popular or mass religion, in which there is a heavy magical component and a tremendous stress on attainment of the putatively good things of this world.

No account of religion should omit all reference to its practical side. Religion as it appears among men in action is not always arrayed in its most heavenly garments, so to put it, and the sociology of religion cannot ignore this circumstance. The meaning of the circumstance itself should become clearer in the course of this chapter. It is, sociologically speaking and to say no more, utterly pointless to be cynical about the existence of practical religion, and it is not necessary to tie discussion of it to controversial views about so-called mass culture. Part (though only a part) of the purpose of our chapter is simply ethnographic, and we shall present a brief description of practical religion as it appears in the form of the new Japanese religions, first, however giving some attention to a kind of American analogue to much that can be found in the Japanese phenomena. This American analogue will be allowed to motivate the discussion of manifest and latent functions and instrumentalization of religion that will complete the chapter. There is good reason to say that instrumentalization—a term about which we shall have to exercise due caution, certainly—is itself a cultural phenomenon of considerable significance.

Indications of the cultural content of religion tend to fall short of what the sociologist would like them to be. This does not deny the subtlety of various theological perspectives on religion and it is not intended to suggest that efforts by anthropologists, historians and others to probe religion in sophisticated ways are useless. It is meant only to assert that it may be doubted that we have as yet come upon units of analysis in the sphere of religious culture that are in some significant sense analogous to, say, units employed in the natural sciences. If we were to be strictly

Table 1.   *Agreements and Disagreements Among Selected Religions*[2]

	Hinduism	Buddhism	Confucianism	Taoism	Catholicism	Protestantism	Islam
1. Belief in an eternal personal God	+	−	−	−	+	+	+
2. Many supernatural helpers in need	+	+	+	+	+	−	+
3. A cult of images	+	+	+	+	+	−	−
4. Belief that creation and judgment occur but once	−	−	−	−	+	+	+
5. Belief in heaven and hell	+	+	−	+	+	+	+
6. Belief in reincarnation	+	+	−	∓	−	−	−
7. Laws relating to food	+	+	−	−	−	−	+
8. Prohibition of alcohol	+	+	−	−	−	−	+
9. Claim to exclusive validity	−	−	−	−	+	+	+

[2] Adapted from Glasenapp, *Die Fünf Weltreligionen*, p. 399. The table selects nine of fourteen units or categories given by Glasenapp, who assigns a plus or minus on the basis of what he takes to be the disposition of the majority of confessants in each case.

demanding about the units which we do select, we would ask that the selection be very clearly related to specific purposes in analysis and that the units selected throw a good deal of light on *other* units not initially chosen as fundamental. Analysts of the content of religious culture often afford indications of that content that make an intuitive appeal to a reader as "important." This, if somewhat disappointing, is nevertheless not to be despised. Some simple but significant-seeming units may be set down and their status or fortune traced, say, across a number of religions. In Table 1, "units" are numbered 1 to 9 and the presence of a unit is marked by a plus sign $(+)$, its absence by a minus sign $(−)$. (Not every item in Table I should be assumed to be unqualifiedly "correct.")

The limitations of this kind of presentation are evident enough. The plus-minus scheme of course allows no grading or nuancing beyond the evident criterion of presence or absence. The units or categories are of an obvious, common-sense character. We are still very far from a penetrating cultural morphology of religion. But there are some advantages in a mode of presentation that affords a quick overview, even if the advantages are no more than those that attach to a particular way of laying out data. The tabular form of arrangement can still be helpful where we do no more than merely use it for presenting some of the substance of religious culture by way of pertinent statements of belief. Table 2 is a case in point.

The matter of grading or nuancing has just been mentioned. Tabulations such as those in Tables 1 and 2 could in principle be modified and extended considerably, to allow for gradations and qualitative differences. The advantages of the tabular form, to be sure, would soon be gone with too extensive a tabulation. Our particular concern here, however, is that Tables 1 and 2 and like tabulations yield no information about "levels" of religion. By levels are meant different ranges of approximation to, or conformity with, let us say, "pure ideals" and metaphysically elevated beliefs in such a religion as Christianity. It is easy, in various cases, to exaggerate differences in levels, and we shall soon see reason to entertain skepticism about theories that claim sweepingly that masses "degenerate" so-called high religions. The whole matter is one that must be handled carefully. Nevertheless, and when due qualifications have been made, it is often to the point to notice (to put the matter in simplest, starkest terms) that, for example, the Christianity of learned and devout priests is not the same as the Christianity of ignorant and faithful peasants.[a]

Table 2 sets out some of the terms of several variant forms of Christianity, but the masses in various countries who have some kind of formal affiliation with Christianity will not necessarily dwell, religiously speaking, at the levels suggested by these terms. A number of the terms will not even concern them. The lack of concern may come from the circumstance that certain historical conditions are no longer so pressing as they once were, and preoccupation with certain beliefs may have gone into a kind of general abeyance, not for the masses alone. But the lack of concern may also come from something else, more peculiar to masses of believers. Thus, the matter of the respective natures of the Father and the Son and the Holy Ghost (Table 2, item 3) is a rather recondite business, the proper understanding of which requires a kind of metaphysical aptitude. The question of whether the Holy Ghost proceeds from the Father and the Son or from the Father alone clearly calls for a like aptitude. A certain fullness of comprehension of the issues involved in these matters

[a] Relevant points of view and data will be found in the discussions bearing on religion and social stratification in Paul Schmitt-Eglin, *Le Mécanisme de la Déchristianisation*, Paris: Editions Alsatia, 1952, and in Emile Pin, *Pratique Religieuse et Classes Sociales*, Paris: Editions Spes, 1956.

is not likely to be attained unless in addition to such aptitude one has some historical knowledge of controversy in the early church and of schism between Catholicism and Greek Christianity some nine hundred years ago. Masses professing a religion such as Christianity are more or less likely to drop out of active concern a variety of beliefs that relate to recondite matters (if ever they were in any sense concerned with them) or else to understand these beliefs in a popularized way. With the setting in of what might be called metaphysical mitigation we have an element in the inducement of different levels of religious culture.

"Practical," everyday, so-called ordinary people have practical, everyday needs, and their practical religion is very likely to reflect those needs. Practical religion is, indeed, eminently responsive to what we may call *soteriological pressure*—the pressure to extend salvation. The salvation in question may be salvation in another life. Item 9 in Table 2 is significant in this connection.[4] A number of religious virtuosos or athletes may not have found it especially difficult to believe in some of the "hard" doctrines of Calvinist origin, but many ordinary men did. The dogma of predestination asserted that God had decreed that some men would be saved and some not, as we have previously noted, as we have also noted that one could not in principle know whether he had been chosen for everlasting glory or for reprobation. This (in an age when the issue of salvation was a tremendously urgent one) occasioned pressure to allow some outlet for ordinary men to attain conviction of their own salvation.

The salvation that men seek may, as in Buddhism, be in a special state well known as Nirvana, involving release from the cycle of reincarnation. But, in Buddhism too, more ordinary men may desire salvation by way of a rebirth in paradise. Or soteriological pressure will bear particularly hard on *this* world and Buddhist men and women will then wish via ritual means to secure what they regard as a good life in the here and now.

Calvinism was modified by soteriological pressure, as has been indicated. So was Buddhism, in its own fashion. Tambiah, in a brilliant study of Buddhism in a Thai village which has significance far beyond that village itself, points to the "dualities" or "paradoxes" (the language is his) that arise in connection with soteriological pressure. The Buddha himself has attained Nirvana and no longer lives, *but* he (or some facsimile or relic

---

[4] There is need for care about this item. Earlier and later stages of Calvinism should be distinguished. Predestination was not an insignificant dogma in the thought of Calvin himself, but it was not developed by him until the last edition of his *Institutes of the Christian Religion,* in response to controversy. (See André Biéler, *La Pensée Economique et Sociale de Calvin,* pp. 494–495.) But, technical considerations such as these aside, the broad statement that follows in the text is justified.

Table 2. Brief Overview of Differences and Agreements Among Some Major Christian Confessions.*

	Roman Catholicism	Greek Orthodoxy	Lutheranism	Calvinism
1.	Christianity is a divine revelation that comes to man through both Bible and tradition.		Christianity is a divine revelation that comes to man through the Bible alone.	
2.	The interpretation of the Bible belongs appropriately to the church, which is continuously guided by the Holy Spirit.		There is no tribunal of interpretation for the Bible. Its divine content declares itself to every Christian.	
3.	God is triune. This means that the divine essence consists of three persons, who by nature and by inherent value are fully equal to one another.			
4.	The Holy Ghost proceeds from the Father and the Son.	The Holy Ghost proceeds from the Father alone.	The Holy Ghost proceeds from the Father and the Son.	
5.	Man is born in a corruption which he did not manifest at the origins of the human species.			
6.	Man in his natural state is sinful before God even prior to his committing actual sins.			
7.	Jesus Christ, the Son of God who became man, consisting of two natures which are inseparably bound together, obtained for man, according to God's eternal decree, reconciliation with God and salvation, for by His death He gave satisfaction to God for the sins of the world.			
8.	The precondition for reconciliation and salvation is spiritual rebirth, which man achieves with the inspiration and support of the Holy Ghost.		The precondition for reconciliation and salvation is spiritual rebirth, which man, in the absence of any power of his own to turn him to the good, can start and complete only by the action of the Holy Ghost.	

	Roman Catholicism	Greek Orthodoxy	Lutheranism	Calvinism
9.	This divine assistance is offered to all men without discrimination.			This divine assistance is offered only to those men whom God has chosen for salvation according to his eternal decree, made independently of all human influence; and the chosen can do nothing to oppose this decree.
10.	The church of Christ is the united society of all (pious or not pious) who confess Christ—united under Christ and his earthly deputy, the pope.	The church is the united community of those who under their leader, Christ, accept all the articles of belief transmitted by the apostles and approved by the general synods.	The church is the united society of saints under Christ its invisible head, in which the gospel is preached in its purity and the sacraments are properly administered. The impious among the baptized belong to the church solely in an external way.	
11.	Outside this (visible) church there is no salvation.		Outside this true (invisible) church there is no salvation.	
12.	Images and altars are an essential resource for worship.		Images and altars may only in small measure (the altar as a table for the sacrament) be used for church adornment.	Images and altars are not to be tolerated.

* Selected and slightly adapted from the tabulation afforded by Glasenapp, *op. cit.*, pp. 278–287. (Glasenapp himself follows G. B. Winer's material in the fourth edition of a book giving a comparative representation of the teachings of Christian churches, published at Leipzig in 1882 and entitled *Comparative Darstellung des Lehrbegriffs der christlichen Kirchenparteien.*) The English of the statements in the table generally follows Glasenapp's German fairly closely.

of him) possesses magical power. (The practical, popular thrust is evident.) The Dhamma (or sacred text) has to do with the overcoming of death, desire and so on to the attainment of Nirvana (and its release from the cycle of reincarnation), *but,* notes Tambiah, "the sacred texts have the power to confer the blessings of a good life on ordinary mortals." The community of Buddhist monks stands for renunciation of the world and of life, *but* the monks can tap mystical powers which (although certainly connected with life-renunciation) are adaptable to the life-enhancing needs of laymen. It is not surprising that Tambiah should say that it would be a distortion of fact to see in Buddhism only an otherworldly emphasis and to conceive the monk's role as simply one of opposition to this world. Tambiah further suggests that in both Ceylon and Thailand, in more "sophisticated" circles, "there is a tension between the actual doctrinal positon taken by monks and the lay orientation (which in turn may show divergent views between the religious virtuosi and the untutored peasant.)" The notion of levels of religious culture is thus clearly supported, for there is no doubt that there is a significant lay orientation active and effective in the direction of the "but's" suggested and that monks get involved in the lay efforts to make Buddhist religion solve problems of this life and this world.[5]

It has been suggested above that it is easy to exaggerate differences of levels. Obeyesekere, writing against a background of knowledge of Buddhism in Ceylon, emphasizes that there is "*some* acceptance of the higher theology . . . even at village level."[6] He adds significantly: "At the present day when the literacy rate of the peasantry is rising, orthodox doctrine is also coming to be spread around through the mass media and the school system."[7] But still discrepancies remain between the formal orthodox tradition or doctrine and the belief and conduct sustained by certain soteriological pressures. Obeyesekere thus remarks that "everywhere in the villages of southern Asia, lay belief presumes the existence of deities who have at least limited power to combat and overcome the vicissitudes of individual fortune." He then adds very cogently:

"The usual way of explaining this discrepancy between the formal doctrine and the practical belief is to postulate a time lag. The magic and

[5] S. J. Tambiah, "The Ideology of Merit and the Social Correlates of Buddhism in a Thai Village," in Edmund R. Leach, ed., *Dialectic in Practical Religion,* pp. 41–121, at p. 104.

[6] Gananath Obeyesekere, "Theodicy, Sin and Salvation in a Sociology of Buddhism" in Leach, *op. cit.,* pp. 7–40, at p. 31. For the point that even sacred scriptures set out different expectations for monks and laity (although this does not eliminate tension between "ideal" or "doctrinal" and "practical" religion), see *ibid.,* pp. 28–29.

[7] *Ibid.,* p. 31.

the deity propitiation are treated as a survival from a primitive form of religion which existed prior to the introduction of Buddhism. Even if this were true as historical fact it would still not explain the continued popularity of unorthodox belief in the face of the universally expressed approval of orthodox doctrine. The heresy cannot simply be a survival—it satisfies some functional need in the present situation."[8]

Even if we allow reservations that have not yet been noted, discrepancies of the kind that have just been briefly reviewed will hold. Conze, in a general treatment of Buddhism, insists that "in order to live, in order to keep its feet on the earth, a religion must to some extent serve the material preoccupations of the average man." He goes on to say that, historically, with whatever absence of consistency, men expected that same Buddhism which renounced the things of this world to afford a control "over . . . unseen magical forces . . . which would guarantee or at least assist the secure possession of the things of the world." There is nothing surprising in this, but Conze further attempts to show that a combination of high spirituality *and* preoccupation with attainment of the goods of this world can occur at what one might think to be entirely "pure" levels without worldly admixture.[9] To *some* degree, if the argument may be generalized in rough form, nearly all of religion has a "practical" tinge (particularly on the side of concern with the worldly and with the cares of man himself, even if we leave outright magic aside.) This is an argument for which, as our subsequent discussion should make plain,[10] we think there is considerable justification. Differences of degree are still important and one may well distinguish levels of religious culture where the differences are not "absolute." Conze is far from establishing that there are no religio-cultural levels in Buddhism and that there is no warrant for serious use of such phrases as "practical Buddhism" and "popular Buddhism."[11]

---

[8] *Ibid.*, p. 22. The above omits much detail. Thus, it does not indicate, à la Obeyesekere, that the traditional sacred texts do not deny the sheer existence of the dieties but deny their power. See Obeyesekere, *ibid.*, pp. 22–23.

[9] See Edward Conze, *Buddhism,* New York: Harper and Row, pp. 82–85. See also p. 142, below.

[10] See below, pp. 142 ff.

[11] The magical and mechanical extremes to which such Buddhism can go are suggested by Rosenkranz in the course of a discussion of Amida worship: "Ancient word-magic had led to the circumstance that, instead of the Buddha, his name had emerged as an object of thought. In the name the essence of the one who bears it becomes revealed. The one who knows his name and turns his thought thereto, and above all he who pronounces that name—preferably repeatedly—attains power over the one named. In place of 'thinking of the Buddha' there came the invocation of his name. Now the cry resounded: 'Adoration to Buddha Amitabha!" The name did not escape the fate of becoming a magical formula. Millions among the peoples of East Asia use the name every single day as a magical motto which they

We may finally attend at least cursorily to Islam, in the present connection. The urge to obtain everday goods and the corresponding soteriological pressure have of course been present in this religion also. Goldziher writes:

"Allah stands far apart from men. But close to their spirits are the local saints (weli), who are the worthy objects of their religious veneration and to whom their fear, their hope, their reverence and their devotion attach. The graves of saints and other places of consecration connected with this cultus are their places of worship, occasionally tied to a crassly fetishistic cherishing of relics and concrete cult objects. There are varieties of this veneration of saints as regards substance and form, according to geographic and ethnographic circumstances and differentiated by way of the pre-Islamic pasts of peoples become Islamic. In the cult of saints, actually, vestiges of cults displaced by Islam come into their own, more or less richly and in more or less powerful and direct form. The saint-cult with its provincial peculiarities confers on the unitary catholic framework of Islam in general a popular stamp determined by local circumstances.

" . . . The masses recognize and fear the exalted Allah as the power of the worlds, who rules great events in the cosmos, and do not expect Him to concern Himself about the insignificant needs of a small group or, indeed, of an individual. Rather, it is the familiar local saint who concerns himself that the fields in the area of a specific place and the herds of a tribe should prosper, that a man should recover from an illness or have joy of a rich blessing of children. To this saint one brings consecrated offerings, and to him one makes vows in his favor, in order to obtain his good will, or—if we still wish to stay close to Islamic language and outlook—'in order to effect his intercession with Allah.' "[12]

Goldziher will be referred to again very shortly. But we must further

---

prattle mechanically, their hands on their prayer-cords or a prayer-mill. Or they have the name flutter on prayer-pennants in the wind or carry it as a talisman with them without thinking with undivided heart of Amitabha and a birth beyond; indeed, without even a single thought on such lines." *Der Weg des Buddha,* p. 268. See also Max Weber, *The Sociology of Religion,* p. 78, where Weber writes, among other similar things: "In comparison with the superior intellectual contemplativeness of ancient Buddhism, which had achieved the highest peak of sublimity, the *Mahayana* religion was essentially a popularization that increasingly tended to approach pure wizardry or sacramental ritualism." Weber made an extremely sharp contrast between Buddhism in an ancient "pure" form and a later Buddhism changed by "emotional mass religiosity" and powerful magical tendencies. See *The Religion of India,* for example, at pp. 237, 247, 295. But for Weber's sense of the generally considerable importance of the "worldly" within religion, see *From Max Weber,* New York: Oxford University Press, 1946, p. 277.

[12] *Vorlesungen uber den Islam,* pp. 263–264.

guard against oversimplifying the generally cogent thesis of the reality and importance of levels of religious culture, broadly connected with stratum levels.

Some students of religion have been inclined to take a rather extreme elitist view of religion, in which "high" or universal religion is constantly corrupted by the masses. Thus, "on the one hand," Gustav Mensching writes, "universal religion, as its name indicates, aspires to make good its universal claim through the greatest possible expansion and thereby through incorporation of the masses." But incorporation of the masses, on the other hand, "is possible only at the price of the depth and distinctiveness of the high religion."[13] There is a sense in which this is true, but it can also be misleading. Goldziher was quoted extensively above on what one could call the "vulgarization" of Islam. Yet the same Goldziher, in another connection, true, but none the less strikingly, refers to coarse, barbarous peoples affected by Islam, whose coarseness Islam lessened.[14] This at once suggests that it may at least in some cases be as valid to speak of "refinement" as it is to speak of "vulgarization," since we may focus on the elevation of the "low" as justifiably as on the corruption of the "high." The essential phenomena remain the same. It is still, and again, very much to the point to note differences in cultural level, which remain real. But there can at the same time be room for differences in interpretation of the significance of the phenomena and of the direction in which development is proceeding. Do vulgar masses degrade Islam by infusing it with pagan components? Or does Islam "lift" them in some degree above the level of their pagan backgrounds? The point involved here has often been adduced in discussions of mass culture generally.

Once more by way of caution, we have suggested that there is broad connection between levels of religious culture and social strata, such as classes; but to some extent, at least, religious culture can get loose from particular stratum moorings (as it most obviously does, in fact, even if with significant modifications, when it travels "downward" from high-position groups) and diffuse to other strata, and our adherence to the notion of levels is not intended to deny this. Moreover, it is also true that different strata, with different life-outlooks and interests, may make "positive" selections from the totality of a religious outlook or tradition—selections not necessarily traceable to metaphysical mitigation, soteriological pressure or the force of magical impulse. Thus, exhortations to cast down the mighty from their seats and exalt them of low degree are bound to appeal to

---

[13] Mensching, *Soziologie der Religion,* Bonn: Ludwig Rohrscheid, 1949, p. 155. Cf. the similar view stated by Pitirim A. Sorokin in his *Social and Cultural Dynamics,* New York: Bedminster Press, 1962, Vol. 4, p. 259.

[14] *Ibid.,* p. 15.

a downtrodden but resentful class which may well find in such words an encouragement to revolution and cull them carefully from scriptural sources, while other classes perhaps do not even "see" that they are there. With all reservations and needed explanations, the notion of levels of religious culture remains significant. It will now serve the partly ethnographic purposes of the present chapter to turn to some exemplification of practical religion in the shape of American religious-inspirational literature and of the Japanese new religions, in both of which practical religion certainly tends to shade into the more extreme "popular" forms. In these forms we surely encounter religion dressed in something of lesser quality than that possessed by what men might think of as its heavenly garments.

SOME ASPECTS OF AMERICAN AND JAPANESE PRACTICAL RELIGION

Glock has made an interesting classification of forms of deprivation that underlie religious movements.[15] Economic deprivation has to do with such things as disadvantage involved in differential income distribution within a society; social deprivation with status or prestige disadvantages; organismic deprivation with poor physical and mental health (here the reader may be reminded of integrative functions of religion); ethical and psychic deprivation with felt disappointments in relation to problems of meaning, philosophically (psychic deprivation) and in terms of operative organization of one's life (ethical deprivation). Practical religion certainly needs to be understood in the light of these modes of deprivation, with particular reference to organismic, economic and (to some extent) social deprivation. Practical religion, as it moves toward extreme popular form, tends precisely to *extreme* man-centeredness[16] in its preoccupation with (physical and mental) health and "success."

A stream of inspirational religious literature has long been flowing from the presses in the United States. Much of this literature has significance for its movement in the direction of making practical "use" of religion for cherished worldly or everyday ends.[17] The question of the *precise* extent to which the literature reflects or reinforces popular religious im-

---

[15] Charles Y. Glock, "The Role of Deprivation in the Origin and Evolution of Religious Groups," in Robert E. Lee and Martin E. Marty, eds., *Religion and Social Conflict,* New York: Oxford University Press, 1964, pp. 24–36.

[16] See the next section of this chapter, below.

[17] The writer now has various reservations about the analysis of the literature presented in Louis Schneider and Sanford M. Dornbusch, *Popular Religion: Inspirational Books in America,* but he remains persuaded that the literature merits study as a cultural phenomenon.

pulses cannot be answered. But it can be noted that the literature constitutes a kind of focussing of significant elements in such cultist or sectarian
phenomena, more especially, as New Thought.[18] It can also be noted
that the literature has enjoyed appreciable prosperity. Its practical bias
is clear, both in that it has concern for the everyday preoccupations of
ordinary men and women and in that it points to, advocates and has
undoubtedly to some extent been adhered to in, "practical" conduct not in
strict conformity with what certain ideal, formal Christian prescriptions
might be conceived to lay down. There is a kind of religion that the
literature captures and expresses and that we may here conveniently tap
precisely by way of the literature itself.

The literature features a special religious strain, which has not been
culturally trivial and which it is certainly important not to miss. Possibly
this strain is doomed in the very long run, but it has unquestionably existed
and it clearly reaches into the present. It is perhaps hardly needful to
say that to "make fun" of the literature in any way would be inept,
if for no other reason than for the reason that it shows signs of aspiration
beyond its own limitations and it would be sheer inaccuracy to miss this.
But the literature is *sometimes* so extreme in its assertions that a description
can easily give the quite unintended impression of caricature.

It has been noted that the literature has been prosperous. Joshua Liebman's *Peace of Mind* had sold over a million copies by 1956. Books
by Emmet Fox, who writes with a strong emphasis that "proper" mental
attitudes generate "proper" conditions of the emotions or the body, and
even of the external world, have done extremely well. Fox's *Sermon on
the Mount* alone has, to date, sold over 600,000 copies. Norman Vincent
Peale's *The Power of Positive Thinking* (originally, 1952), perhaps the
catchiest title one can refer to in the long listing one could make of books
of this type, has sold over two and a half million copies;[19] and Hackett
reports that with Peale's ninth book, *Stay Alive All Your Life,* his book
sales had gone beyond the four million mark.[20] We assume that all this

[18] See Charles S. Braden, *Spirits in Rebellion,* Dallas: Southern Methodist Uni-
versity Press, 1963; and for a literate, revealing older treatment, Horatio W.
Dresser, *Handbook of the New Thought,* New York: Putnam's, 1917. New
Thought has a powerful "positive thinking" component.

[19] See Alice P. Hackett, *Seventy Years of Best Sellers,* 1895–1965, N.Y.: R. R.
Bowker Co., 1967, *passim.* It is possibly indicative of new trends that, while, among
Peale's recent books *Stay Alive All Your Life* made the nonfiction best seller list for
1957 (being third on the list of ten highest-selling non-fiction items for that year),
his books since that year, through 1966, have not done so. It should be said that
the description of the literature given in these pages is based mainly on information
extending through the late 1950's.

[20] *Ibid.,* p. 114.

(even in a time of generally high book sales) is not without important social and psychological correlates, although we cannot assess these with the accuracy we would like.

What is more significant for present purposes in the literature may be summed up by saying that the contemporary or near-contemporary writers of it tend to show strong organismic (or integrative) and economic preoccupations, in particular, and that this is accompanied by a very powerful instrumental bias. It is so well known that the writers are concerned to point to ways to obtain "peace of mind" and emotional health that it hardly seems needful to give the point considerable documentation. The works of Peale, Fox, and Liebman, among numerous others, make the point utterly clear, as did the work of other writers in the same vein in earlier years. The physical health preoccupation of the literature, which is also very marked, may be allowed to be adequately exemplified by the title of Glenn Clark's book, *How to Find Health through Prayer*.[21] Clark may be cited again in connection with economic concerns to give some slight sense of the depth in time, or long history, of this kind of literature, although Clark is far from being one of the most unrestrained advocates of the notion that a man's religion will bring him worldly prosperity. Clark inquires what would happen if we should "ask, seek, and knock for spiritual ideas, and not for material things." His answer is that "a veritable downpour of ideas," nearly "a hurricane or blizzard of ideas, if you please" would come down upon us; and "as soon as these ideas struck the atmosphere of this earth they would—many of them, at least—be converted into good round hard practical dollars."[22]

The instrumental bias goes along with the preoccupations noted. "Practical needs," "results," the formula "it works"—all these receive emphasis. And there is stress that there is close affinity between religion on the one hand and science and technology on the other. Sometimes this presumed

---

[21] New York: Harper and Brothers, 1940.

[22] *The Soul's Sincere Desire*, Boston: Little, Brown, 1925, pp. 37–38. Clark's reference to "good round hard practical dollars" may serve to set off a long-time strain of association in popular American thought between business and religion. A half century before Clark wrote, the *Congregationalist* for June 21, 1876, had commented that "men who have tried it have confidently declared that there is no sleeping partner in any business who can begin to compare with the Almighty." (As quoted by Henry F. May, *Protestant Churches and Industrial America*, New York: Harper and Bros., 1949, p. 51). And a generation after Clark, Peale strongly encourages the notion of the affinity of business and religion, as in the assertion (in its context very significant) that "it is well to study prayer from an efficiency point of view." *The Power of Positive Thinking*, New York: Prentice-Hall, 1952, p. 53. This, however, also already adumbrates the matter of instrumental use.

affinity is asserted in highly dramatic fashion. In what is actually a rather restrained statement, taking the literature in more recent years as a whole, Peale and the psychiatrist Smiley Blanton argue that the church is "a scientific laboratory dedicated to the reshaping of men's daily lives" and that "its great principles are formulas and techniques designed to meet every human need."[23] Peale and Blanton go on to say that the New Testament is a textbook of laws, "spiritual laws as specific as the laws of physics and chemistry." Further, they aver that the church encourages people to have faith "but does not give them specific techniques for attaining it," and that it urges the practice of love but affords "no detailed methodology" for its practice in daily life.

The entire language of science, technique, methodology is not a matter of accidental metaphors in this literature. Its writers are on the whole far too insistently and single-mindedly concerned to employ religious resources, or what they regard as such, instrumentally and "rationally" for the deliberate achievement of health, wealth and happiness for the accidental metaphor notion to be persuasive. The practical and eudaemonistic and at the same time "scientific-technical" orientation of the literature could be virtually endlessly illustrated. A generation before Peale's most successful writing Clark could say that "a man who learns and practices the laws of prayer correctly should be able to play golf better, do business better, work better, love better, serve better." Clark could also recommend that one "pray if possible out of loyalty to God, for the joy of it, not for practical results," and this strikes quite a different note, but again he could aver that "the trouble with most of our praying, as with our breathing, is that it is too negative," and the suggestion of "technique" that this may convey is reinforced by the advocacy of "scientific" prayer.[24] The above is not intended to suggest that the inspirational religious literature contains *nothing but* the elements that have been presented. Nevertheless, when all significant reservations have been made, the biases indicated remain powerful, and this is what is crucial.

In a very different part of the world, religious phenomena have emerged that show striking resemblances to the kind of religion involved in the literature just reviewed. We turn to Japan's so-called "new religions." Drummond writes that the popular designation of the new Japanese religions is "religions of personal advantage." That is, he amplifies, "they are seen as essentially spiritual techniques to get what one wants out of life." Such material on the new religions as is available in Western languages would seem to give good warrant to such a characterization. Drummond

---

[23] See Peale and Blanton's *The Art of Real Happiness,* New York: Prentice-Hall, 1950, pp. 12–13.

[24] *The Soul's Sincere Desire,* pp. 12, 17, 34, 49.

indicates that the characterization is apt enough, but he adds that "it applies almost equally to the whole of the popular side of the Japanese religious tradition, including both Buddhism and Shinto." "Empirical Christianity," too, Drummond avers, has at different times and places shown much of the bias toward being a "religion of personal advantage."[25] This is correct and it is important. It is also important to recognize the presence of other than purely "crass" and materialistic impulses in these religions themselves. After all qualifications, however, a distinctive picture emerges.[26]

The new religions are "popular," if indeed one wishes to distinguish popular from practical on the ground that the former is more extreme. But even popular religion is *not* altogether lacking in "spiritual" elements. *Nor* must more "spiritual" religious complexes lack *all* of the elements of practical or popular religion. Tentatively, we may specify popular religion in this fashion: It exhibits a relatively *very heavy* stress on this-worldly goods, especially on the line of physical and emotional health and economic prosperity. It has a considerable "technological" or magical-instrumental component. Its concerns on the lines of metaphysics, cosmology, eschatology and the like are likely to be lacking in intellectual profundity and to appear exceedingly simple. It has widespread appeal.

---

[25] Richard H. Drummond, "Japan's 'New Religious' and the Christian Community," *The Christian Century*, 81, Dec. 9, 1964, pp. 1521–1523.

[26] Maurice Bairy sees in the success of the new religions in Japan a confused but genuine popular striving to attain to a personal experience and individual contact with the divine. If not with entire clarity, then dimly but again genuinely one may discern in the new religions an element of awakening of both a sense of personal identity and of conscience. This does not prevent Bairy from writing with respect to P L Kyodan, the new religion he came to know best, that "prayer for earthly goods is the true essence of this religion" and that the religion belongs among those naturalistic faiths in which "prayer serves to avert misfortune and to attain good fortune in this earthly world." Bairy later avers that this religion "does not rise above the realm of a magical religion with prayers for earthly goods." It is clear that he would take this as a fair characterization of the new religions in general. Maurice A. Bairy, *Japans Neue Religionen in der Nachkriegszeit*, Bonn: L. Röhrscheid Verlag, 1959, pp. 68–69, 110, 111. One may note more recently numerous similar characterizations, as by McFarland, who remarks that "anticipation of concrete results—which is fairly common among all religions, particulary at the folk or mass level—has been especially prominent throughout the religious history of Japan. It is now one of the most conspicuous characteristics of the New Religions." It is of interest that McFarland employs Yinger's term, "bridging" sects, to suggest that the new religions "have at least the potentiality of helping to carry their members over into a new life." See H. Neill McFarland, *The Rush Hour of the Gods*, New York: Macmillan, 1967, pp. 78–79, 229. We need not deny the bridging function, any more than we need to deny the less crass elements Bairy finds.

We cannot attend in detail to all of these things in the case of the new Japanese religions, but the following statement may help to clarify our specification.

According to Thomsen, some of the so-called new religions in Japan are actually not so new, in that they began in the nineteenth century, while others that came into formal being in the aftermath of World War II hark back to earlier Shinto and Buddhist beginnings.[27] The new religions numbered 171 in 1963, of which approximately a third were registered under Buddhism, a larger number under Shinto, while some thirty were listed as "miscellaneous." These religions claimed one of every five Japanese as a member when Thomsen wrote.[28] They are obviously of some importance on the Japanese scene. The new religions are evidently easy to enter, comprehend and follow. They are optimistic. If it is well attested that they are this-worldly and strongly preoccupied with organismic and economic ends, it would also seem that a case can be made for the view that "for a large number of the adherents of the New Religions, religion is nothing more than a tool utilized for the purpose of attaining completely selfish aims."[29]

It is a constant emphasis of one of the religions, known as Seicho no Ie, with a membership of about a million and a half when Offner and van Straehlen wrote, that such a thing as sickness does not exist. "It is merely a dream, a figment of the imagination. Thinking on sickness, aches and pains results in the body experiencing them." Indeed, for this religion "health or sickness, wealth or poverty depends upon the thoughts which pass through our minds;" and phenomenal existence itself is shadow, the mind's mere reflection. Offner and van Straehlen quote from Taniguchi, the founder of this religion, drawing from his "Revise Fate through the Power of Thought." It is impossible not to think of Western inspirational analogues to this title. (The mentalism suggested, together with emphasis on thinking positively, is definitely not confined to this particular one among the new religions.) Referring to Seicho no Ie again, Offner and van Straehlen write: "One must make his mind receptive and repeat over and over again such thoughts as 'God fills the universe. Everything in

---

[27] But Drummond, *loc. cit.,* p. 1521, suggests that while this is true the emergence of the new religions as "highly significant sociological phenomena" has been subsequent to the second World War.

[28] Harry Thomsen, *The New Religions of Japan,* Rutland: C. E. Tuttle Co., 1963, pp. 15–17.

[29] Clark B. Offner and Henry van Straehlen, *Modern Japanese Religions,* New York: Twayne Publishers, 1963, p. 273. Cf. also Ichiro Hori, *Folk Religion in Japan,* Chicago: University of Chicago Press, 1968, ch. 6, which deals with the new religions and old shamanic tendencies.

the universe loves me. There is nothing that is hostile to me.' "[30] Physical as well as mental health is a great concern. Taniguchi, for one, averred that cancer, too, is an embodiment of a mental condition.

Very pertinent to the new religions is Sōka Gakkai, a much discussed movement that already claimed a membership amounting to some ten percent of the population of Japan a few years ago. It is especially interesting that Offner and van Straehlen[31] observe that, although this huge organization receives much criticism from both Buddhist and non-Buddhist sources, it is simply an "outward and unashamed expression of an attitude which views religion as a means to attain present, immediate benefits which is implicit in the teaching and propaganda of many other New Religions as well." We once more put our stress on religion as an instrumentality or means here and may profitably turn to some further material on Sōka Gakkai.

Sōka Gakkai is not itself, technically, a religion. But it has regarded itself as the "advertising arm" of Nichiren Shoshū and therefore as affiliated with the latter, whose religious affinities are in turn with the Nichiren religious complex and go back to the thirteenth century. A figure in the founding of Sōka Gakkai, who may be referred to here simply as Makiguchi (born in 1871), held the view that a religion must justify itself by its ability to "work" and bring happiness. Accordingly the loyalty one may have to a religion can be a qualified one, contingent on the receipt of worldly benefits. Toda Jōsei (born in 1900), the second president of Sōka Gakkai, was at one time a Christian but, according to one writer, gave up Christianity "because it did not enable him to pay off his debts."[32]

---

[30] *Ibid.*, pp. 163, 164, 204. The resemblance of some of the conceptions of the new religions to elements in Western thought is noted also by these authors, who write of "the metaphysical world of Christian Science, Unity and New Thought" in discussing Seicho no Ie (*ibid.*, p. 127). One cannot help suspecting actual contacts, and McFarland (*op. cit.*, p. 249) writes of Seicho no Ie that "it is quite possible that its essential message would appeal to many people in this country, as we may assume from the persistence here of various other 'peace of mind' and 'divine science' cults, from some of which indeed Taniguchi initially appropriated some of his initial teachings." Braden explicitly takes Seicho no Ie as a "branch" of New Thought. He writes: "It would not do . . . to say that Seicho no Ie is identical with any Western New Thought system. It is clearly oriental in many respects. . . . But the characteristic ideas and techniques of New Thought are there." See *Spirits in Rebellion*, pp. 494, 497.

[31] *Ibid.*, p. 108.

[32] Robert L. Ramseyer, "The Sōka Gakkai: Militant Religion on the March," in *Studies in Japanese Culture*, ed. R. K. Beardsley, Ann Arbor: The University of Michigan Press, 1965, pp. 141–192, at p. 187. Ramseyer comments (p. 160) that "this element of personal gain is found to some degree in all of the great religions of the world, but only in perversions of them does it achieve the dominance that it is given" in Makiguchi's views. This is clearly in accord with our interpretation, although we might put the matter somewhat differently.

Makiguchi wanted to "apply the scientific method to religion." Science and religion, for him, were both concerned with ultimate truth, but also with how to make men happy in their daily lives, and thereby religion became comparable to applied science, whose affinity with religion he and other Gakkai leaders have stressed.[33]

Several years ago a Sunday newspaper magazine carried an article on Sōka Gakkai with the interesting title, "Sōka Gakkai Brings 'Absolute Happiness.' "[34] The title is cited here for obvious reasons. But it must also be said that the concerns of the new religions are already in some flux. They may be making some important accommodations in the interest of presenting an appearance of greater "respectability" in the face of higher-status conversion prospects. Indeed, according to Thomsen, Sōka Gakkai, which initially advised followers against consulting doctors, now advises them in case of disease to consult doctors first and come to Sōka Gakkai later; and Tenrikiyo (another of the new religions) has shifted its stress away from faith healing, once a major preoccupation: "Tenrikiyo and a few others have even built hospitals whose doctors more often than not are unbelievers."[35]

Babbie, in a very thoughtful article on Sōka Gakkai, has noted how that organization has mitigated its stress on organismic and economic deprivation and concentrated more on other kinds of deprivation as it has sought to expand its appeal.[36] But we have not sought to sustain any thesis to the effect that popular religion is unchanging. It is of interest, finally, that there appears to be a measure of agreement that the new religions have gotten much support from Japan's lower classes. Thus, Offner and van Straehlen contrast them in this respect with the Christian Church in Japan and observe that they have demonstrated "a definite ability" to reach the lower strata. Thomsen observes that "the vast majority of new religions seem to concentrate on the farmers and workers in the first stage of development." Ramseyer noted that Sōka Gakkai political candidates got strong support from wards with high percentages of very poor people. Morris has emphasized the appeal of the same organization to the lower levels off the working class in the cities.[37] But a definitive

[33] Ramseyer, *ibid.,* pp. 160, 162.

[34] *New York Times Magazine,* July 18, 1965, pp. 8, 9, 36–39.

[35] Thomsen, *ibid.,* pp. 23–24.

[36] Earl R. Babbie, "The Third Civilization," *Review of Religious Research,* 7, 1966, pp. 101–121. In the light of our references to Makiguchi, above, it is of interest that Babbie contends with regard to the Gakkai movement (*loc. cit.,* p. 105) that "justification for present activities is found in the life of Nichiren, and Makiguchi has greatly faded into the background as an historical figure for the religion."

[37] Offner and van Straehlem, *op. cit.,* p. 269; Thomsen, *op. cit.,* p. 17; Ramseyer, *loc. cit.,* p. 179; Ivan Morris, "The Challenge of Sōka Gakkai." *Encounter,* 26, May, 1966, pp. 78–83, at p. 82.

study of this matter is not yet available. The statements of individual writers are not always clear nor do all writers seem quite consistent with one another so far as one can tell. Kitagawa asserts that for the most part the new religions draw their followers from the "lower middle" class.[38]

INSTRUMENTALIZATION

Much of religious history has been informed by a tension between a "for God" or (more broadly) "spiritual" principle and a "for man" principle. On the one hand we have a principle that asserts that God's existence is for God's "benefit" regardless of men or that concentrates on and advocates exclusively the intrinsic spiritual merit of things spiritual, and on the other hand a principle whereby God's existence, or the spiritual realm, is presumed to be for men's benefit regardless of God or the spiritual. Broadly, men have "wanted" things from their religions, beyond a doubt—health, serenity, wealth, and much else. "Some of the Quietists," Knox notes, "seem to have spent their whole lives under the conviction that they were destined to be lost." This is at least a conviction that men ordinarily want to get away from. They want to be saved. Knox observes, too, that "perhaps we must not quarrel with the eccentric legacy by which a disciple of Père Piny endowed a series of Masses, not for the welfare of her soul, but in thanksgiving to God for having decreed her salvation or damnation, as the case might be." But this features a rather remarkable neutrality about one's self, a kind of heroic devotion to the "for God" principle.

Knox also refers, finally, to "a young priest who asked God in set terms to send him to hell, so that the Divine justice and the Divine glory might be more fully manifested."[39] This takes the "for God" principle to great lengths and exhibits a downright "enthusiastic" abnegation of one's own interest in salvation. It is unusual, to say the least. Ordinarily the two principles are in tension within religion. Conze observed that the message of the Prajnaparamita books in Buddhism was that "perfect wisdom can be attained only by the complete and total extinction of all self-interest" and yet noted that side by side with this "extreme spiritual teaching" there was stress on "the tangible and visible advantages which perfect wisdom confers in this very life here and now."[40] The two principles we refer to are thus clearly suggested, and it may be added that, as the present writer has expressed the matter elsewhere, "either

---

[38] Joseph M. Kitagawa, *Religion in Japanese History,* New York: Columbia University Press, 1966, p. 333.

[39] Ronald Knox, *Enthusiasm,* New York: Oxford University Press, 1961, pp. 272, 273.

[40] Conze, *op. cit.,* pp. 84–85.

principle alone (insofar as either has ever been adhered to alone) has constantly generated difficulties for the religious or religiously interested, and the blending of the two principles constantly threatens to be unstable."[41]

The blending is threatened in popular religion in the direction of a very powerful "for man" emphasis—and this has been one of the central matters in our conception of this kind of religion. Once more, it is not that it contains *no* "spirituality," nothing "for God." It is not that generally different, more "spiritual" religious phenomena are quite without "for man" components. One may well doubt whether in utterly extreme form in either direction any "religion" (if that term could still be retained) could endure for any length of time. One of the principles seems constantly to hover in the background even when the other is to the fore, and too strong a movement toward either pole appears to generate a countermovement to the other.[42]

It is well to recall now our earlier reference to Merton's distinction of manifest and latent functions, in connection with which he raised the question, "What are the effects of the transformation of a previously latent function into a manifest function (involving the problem of the role of knowledge in human behavior and the problems of 'manipulation' of

[41] See Robert E. L. Faris, ed., *Handbook of Modern Sociology,* Chicago: Rand McNally, 1964, p. 785. The above paragraph draws on the article by Louis Schneider, "Problems in the Sociology of Religion," in Faris, pp. 770–807, from which these words are quoted, and the article is further drawn upon, with what now appear to be suitable modifications, in what follows.

[42] Alexis de Tocqueville long ago perceived how religion is constrained to blend ingredients of the "material" and the "spiritual," the "selfish," and the "unselfish," that which is "for God" and that which is "for man." Tocqueville wrote: "We shall see that of all the passions which originate in or are fostered by equality, there is one which it renders peculiarly intense, and which it also infuses into the heart of every man; I mean the love of well-being. The taste for well-being is the prominent and indelible feature of democratic times." To this Tocqueville added at once: "It may be believed that a religion which should undertake to destroy so deep-seated a passion would in the end be destroyed by it; and if it attempted to wean men entirely from the contemplation of the good things of this world in order to devote their faculties exclusively to the thought of another, it may be foreseen that the minds of men would at length escape its grasp to plunge into the exclusive enjoyment of present and material pleasures." And finally one kind of "blending" or compromise: "The chief concern of religion is to purify, to regulate, and to restrain the excessive and exclusive taste for well-being that men feel in periods of equality; but it would be an error to attempt to overcome it completely or to eradicate it. Men cannot be cured of the love of riches, but they may be persuaded to enrich themselves by none but honest means." *Democracy in America* (ed. Phillips Bradley), New York: A. A. Knopf, 1945, Vol. 2, p. 26. Tocqueville is close enough to what interests us here.

human behavior?)"[43] This is a most pregnant query for the type of religion that is more particularly set out in the inspirational religious literature, as will be indicated. Historically, in a broad, general way, there has undoubtedly been considerable awareness, especially on the part of persons in certain social positions, of various functions of religion. To that extent, as a mere matter of definition, functions of religion have been manifest. But there also has been such a thing as becoming aware of functions previously unsuspected or only dimly known.

Pratt argued very plausibly that in human history after long periods of a kind of "innocent" worship unconscious of human effects, "more reflective worshipers discovered that the cult in its various forms exerted an influence not only upon the gods but upon their own spirits." This suggests an important event of the kind to which Merton's basic query points. Not only did religion "originally" (a dubious though useful word in this context) actually work in certain ways, without the knowledge of worshipers that it did so; but there followed a time when some knowledge of its effects came at least to "more reflective worshipers." Information not previously available became available to some; and causal reinforcement could be added to original effect as men were consciously motivated to engage in religious exercises *because of knowledge of* their social and psychological consequences. Pratt adds that "the leaders of religion" were presumably the first to find out that religion influenced men, and the next stage in the relevant development was for those leaders "to conduct the cult in such fashion as not only to influence the gods but also to affect their fellow worshipers." Pratt also observes that the whole history of religion might be written in the light of the process reviewed, in its course "from the naive attempt to influence the deity to the sophisticated and deliberate effort to bring about a psychological effect on the worshiper."[44] It may be added that it is not necessary to confine this kind of "model" strictly to "psychological effect on the worshiper" but that it may be extended to include "social" functions. The two kinds of phenomena are of course closely connected. A death ceremony that allays the sorrow of any individual ("psychological effect") also helps to return him to the circle of the living and enables him to resume his ordinary routines and associations (thereby exercising "integrative" social function).

Where there is awareness of psychological effects and social functions of religion and where those effects and functions are regarded as good or useful, it is not by any means a fantastic notion that some men should seek to "help along" the "natural" workings of religion. If religion brings

[43] *Social Theory and Social Structure*, p. 51.
[44] James B. Pratt, *Eternal Values in Religion*, New York: Macmillan, 1950, p. 27.

peace of mind (as it *sometimes* does), for example, why not help it out a bit and use it to bring peace of mind? One may even wish to "talk one's self" into faith because one has pressing emotional difficulties and believes that faith may afford a way out of them, on the line of a kind of desperate "will to believe." The content and tone of the American inspirational literature strongly suggest a process whereby there has come to some persons, at least, an awareness of effects and social functions of religion that are taken to be desirable; whereby, further, these persons have sought to utilize religion instrumentally so that it becomes something on the order of a set of devices to attain peace of mind, prosperity, and the like; and whereby, finally, these persons have sought to make the instrumentalized religion available to others. There is a kind of reversal of spiritual principle in all this. The principles adhered to in inspirationalism do *not* seem to follow the line suggested by "Seek ye first the kingdom of God and all these things will be added unto you." One interesting question is whether inspirational devices actually "work" or are perhaps selfdefeating, in that the "good things" of this world that religious activity may possibly bring and has sometimes brought come most surely as by-products and not when they are directly pursued.[45]

But we must not understand what is involved here too crudely and unqualifiedly. If there is indeed something like a movement from latent to manifest functions (which is after all a matter of the emergence or spread of awareness or knowledge), we must, for one thing, specify *for whom* the new awareness or knowledge supervenes. If new knowledge of psychological effects and social functions of religion is employed in a kind of reconstruction of religious activity, *who* does the reconstructing? Is it merely inspirational "leaders" or is it followers also, and in what degree does it occur for members of each category? Instrumentalization need not be "absolute." Thus, there may be some measure of instrumental utilization of religion on a person's part while the same person also

[45] Also involved here is the question of how much intrinsic "truth" or presumption of religious verity one retains in an inspirational outlook. Pratt comments that "it is interesting to note the fervor with which certain psychological writers extol the value of prayer and in the same breath either state or imply that its value is due entirely to subjective conditions." He continues, observing that "since the subjective value of prayer is chiefly due to the belief that prayer has values which are *not* subjective, it will with most persons evaporate altogether once they learn that it is *all* subjective. Hence if it be true both that the subjective value of prayer is very great and also that it is the only value which prayer possesses, this latter fact should assiduously be kept secret." Pratt concludes his reflections on this line with the remark that if the subjective value of prayer is all the value it has, then "we wise psychologists of religion had better keep the fact to ourselves," on pain of soon having no religion left about which to psychologize. Pratt, *The Religious Consciousness,* p. 336.

adheres to religious ways that have nothing particularly instrumental about them. Granted that there must be an element of the deliberate in instrumentalization there is no suggestion here, say, of a very purposeful, perhaps even cynical, plan on the part of "leaders" to instrumentalize religion and dilute or even destroy the high spirituality of a spotless Christian tradition. Instrumentalization in the sense in which we have been employing the term is a more subtle phenomenon than this.

It should by now be entirely plain that we do not in the case of inspirational religious literature postulate a breakthrough of utter, wholly unprecedented coarseness and concentration on the good things of this world. It will be recalled that we cited Drummond, above, to the effect that empirical (that is, historically actual) Christianity has at various times and places shown considerable tendency toward being a "religion of personal advantage." So much of historical religious activity has in fact been pointed toward "getting" things, so decidedly "for man"—oriented, that instrumentalization as here understood might well often have been superfluous. But if we think of instrumentalization as a significant *strain* in various concrete religious manifestations and do not seek to set off the strain in absolute terms, the category would appear to have considerable utility. Possibly instrumentalization is decidedly more important in the American religious situation than in the Japanese. The new religions of Japan clearly rest on a very old folk base of phenomena like popular magic and there is need for caution in imputing to them an instrumentalizing, de-spiritualizing process, considering the large magical and homocentric component that is present in them as it were "naturally." Yet there is the suggestion of instrumentalization that comes to us via the description of the outlook of someone like Makiguchi. It may be proposed that each of the two popular religious manifestations we have touched upon is a "mix" of the naively popular and of instrumentalization, while the Japanese, by comparison with the American case, has a relatively smaller instrumentalization component. Clearly, we should know more about all this. But it is worthwhile, in considering phenomena on the line of instrumentalization, to keep in view a simple paradigm (into which various subtleties and qualifications may be introduced as needed) which involves these elements:

1. Latent functions of religion become manifest.
2. They are then recast as goals.
3. Old ceremonial or other religious activity (such as prayer) becomes new technological device.

(Instrumentalization can be *self*-referring, in accordance with resolve to find for one's self health, wealth, peace of mind, through prayer; or *other*-referring, as in elite machinations to exploit the sincere religious beliefs of a nonelite. Obviously, the "meaning" of the paradigm will differ for these two kinds of cases.)

The above discussion may be allowed to give occasion to a wider consideration of the whole matter of instrumental use of religion. We may note first the bias toward use of religion for what are regarded as desirable psychological results. One of its most distinguished representatives was William James. James cites James H. Leuba's view that "so long as men can *use* their God, they care very little who he is, or even whether he is at all." He quotes Leuba further: *"God is not known, he is used*—sometimes as meat-purveyor, sometimes as moral support, sometimes as friend, sometimes as an object of love. If he proves himself useful, the religious consciousness asks for no more than that." It would seem, too, that "not God, but life, more life, a larger, richer, more satisfying life, is, in the last analysis, the end of religion."[46] James himself did not hesitate in making use of deity or religion. His *Varieties* is in a sense a very "practical" book. He was most alert to the psychotherapeutic potential of religion and was concerned to develop a psychology and philosophy of religion that would exploit that potential. James made the potential itself entirely plain. He had clearly come to think of it as something that could be formulated as a goal for "seekers." Problems of instrumentalization are thus once more suggested, obviously long before Peale wrote and against a background of far greater sophistication. Once again, questions of "amount" and of "blend" arise. In particular, the query always remains whether, given a certain amount of instrumental emphasis, the "religious" enterprise does not become self-defeating. If religion can at times produce tranquillity, to put the matter bluntly, will a rather deliberate search for tranquillity via a religion relatively unblended with different ("spiritual," "for-God," "unselfish") components have prospects of success?

Instrumental thought has not been lacking with regard to broader social functions of religion. In an interesting essay on the antirevolutionary Joseph de Maistre (1753–1821), Lord Morley once wrote that in the eighteenth century, prior to the French Revolution, men were wont to ask of Christianity whether it was true or not, whereas after the Revolution their question was likely to be whether and how it might contribute to the rebuilding of society. People had come to ask "less how true it was than how strong it was." They had come to be concerned less about Christianity's "unquestioned dogmas" than about "how much social weight it had, or could develop." They inquired "less as to the precise amount and form of belief that would save a soul" than as to the way in which

[46] See William James, *The Varieties of Religious Experience,* New York: Modern Library, 1936, p. 497.

Christianity might specifically "be expected to assist the European community."[47] Whether the before-the-Revolution-after-the-Revolution contrast is overstated or not, there certainly was considerable post-Revolutionary interest in the social functions of religion.[48] Particularly prominent in this connection is the philosopher and sociologist Auguste Comte. In his early work Comte had already revealed a considerable understanding of various social aspects of religion. When in his later work he conceived that some kind of religion was indispensable to social order, he unquestionably drew on his knowledge of social functions of religion and tailored a new religion ("the Religion of Humanity") to the "uses" he derived from that knowledge. In a popular book on religion, Comte's follower, the English thinker Frederic Harrison, suggested that Comte had seen "deeply" to the foundations of all religion and had "apprehended what religion *really has to do.*"[49] The emphasis is Harrison's own and the suggestion of an instrumental orientation to religion, of thinking in terms of the "uses" to which it must be devoted, is very far from alien to Comte's work.[50]

Comte's outline of the Religion of Humanity is a very detailed affair. We confine ourselves to noting a few pertinent matters. Comte was convinced that man must be subordinated to some larger existence than his own in order to perpetuate his life, which otherwise must be transitory. This larger existence for man is a Great Being, a Grand Etre, roughly a kind of essence of the "best" in deceased humanity. Man is a selfishly inclined creature who must be made more altruistic, and this can be effected through worship of women, which will ultimately be transferred to the Great Being. Religion will perform an indispensable function in "combining" and in "regulating" individuals. A new priesthood will guide mankind religiously. In all this, the Great Being is a species of invented divine or quasidivine substance or essence, and religion is deliberately enlisted in the performance of important social functions, although it is certainly also supposed to afford "spiritual" satisfactions. An interesting speculative set of questions is suggested by all this. Just *who* was to be enlightened as to what religion "really has to do," to use Harrison's words? How much popular enlightenment was there to be? Would enlightenment on the uses of religion be compatible with authentic belief in and devotion

---

[47] John Viscount Morley, "The Champion of Social Regress," in *The Works of Lord Morley*, vol. 12, London: Macmillan, 1921, p. 177.

[48] See D. G. Charlton, *Secular Religions in France, 1815–1870*, London: Oxford University Press, 1963.

[49] *The Positive Evolution of Religion*, London: Heinman, 1913, p. 233.

[50] See particularly Comte's *System of Positive Polity*, Vol. 4, London: Longmans, Green, 1877.

to the Great Being? A number of commentators on Comte have been much concerned with the last of these questions in particular. It is important to note their skepticism about instrumentalization à la Comte. The general tone of these commentators is suggested by the philosopher, Edward Caird:

"In Comte's reconstruction of religion there seems to be something artificial and factitious, something 'subjective' in the bad sense. It is religion made, so to speak, out of *malice prepense.* 'We have derived,' he seems to say, 'from the experience of our own past and of the past of humanity a clear idea of what religion should be: and we also know from the same experience that, without a religion, we cannot have that fulness of spiritual life of which we are capable. Go to, let us make a religion, as nearly corresponding to the definition of religion as modern science will permit. . . .' "[51]

Caird's last sentence, "Go to, let us make a religion. . . ." is exceedingly apt. It fits the Comtean case quite precisely. Another commentator, Hawkins, evidently paraphrasing a much earlier critic of Comte, asks: "What can produce a more profound sense of unreality than the consciousness that we are worshiping a deity who is nothing but our own memory of the dead, who is avowedly a mere doll-providence, made and dressed for us by the priest, and handed to us to be worshiped in order to satisfy our craving for the Infinitely Lovely and Great?"[52] And near the end of his illuminating review of nineteenth-century "secular religions" in France, Charlton comments that "it is surely doubtful whether we can for long feel awe, experience 'the sense of the holy,' in contemplating what we have ourselves invented."[53] In Comte's work there was unquestionably a strain toward instrumentalization within the context of latent-becoming-manifest (for to the eye of Comte much had become manifest that would not have been so to dimmer sociological sight), and it is at least entirely plain that critics of Comte were dubious about the feasibility of an invented, instrumentalized religion or deity or similar entities. It may be suggested that the doubt had some justification.

Comte's particular efforts are of special interest for a number of reasons, not least because they present the speculative religious endeavors of a very gifted (if in a number of respects quite rigid) man. But the problems Comte suggests in this particular context go well beyond him and his

[51] See Caird's *The Social Philosophy and Religion of Comte,* Glasgow: Maclehose and Sons, 1885, pp. 163–64.

[52] Richmond L. Hawkins, *Positivism in the United States,* Cambridge: Harvard University Press, 1938, p. 85.

[53] *Secular Religions in France,* pp. 214–215.

followers and the religion he invented. The question of *who* (or what social strata, or other significant portions of a societal community) knows what, of the distribution of knowledge, is important in the sociology of religion beyond what Comte brings up—as is the allied question of whether religion can continue to exercise a variety of social functions when people are merely aware of those functions but have lost faith in the professions and exercises that constitute religion itself. It is worth quoting two pertinent statements, one by a sociologist and the other by a church historian. Ronald Dore writes in his study of a ward in Tokyo, Japan:

"For socially useful fictions to be maintained it is, perhaps, necessary that only a small minority should be aware that they are fictions and should keep the knowledge to themselves. It is difficult to imagine a society in which everyone performs rites towards supernatural beings which they (*sic*) believe not to exist *as if* they did exist, solely because they consider that the sentiments which they are thereby inducing *in themselves* are necessary to that society. In ancient China, Mo-tzu, whose rationalistic approach led him to assert that 'to hold that there are no spirits and learn sacrificial ceremonies is like learning the ceremonies of hospitality when there is no guest, or making fishnets when there are no fish,' explicitly attacked the skepticism of the Confucians because, diffused among the common people, it led to an abandonment of moral standards and the disintegration of society in unfilial conduct, wickedness and rebellion. For the common people to hold a skeptical Confucian outlook and yet train their moral responses by performance of the rites he clearly held to be impossible."[54]

This plainly suggests certain difficulties likely to arise if social functions of religion are projected as goals and an effort is made to achieve them by a process of self-manipulation (and also suggests difficulties about manipulating others). We are inevitably reminded of Pratt's view that, since the psychological value of prayer rests on the presumption that it has more than psychological value, prayer is likely to disappear when the persuasion arises that its value is all, or merely, psychological. Félicité de Lamennais (1782–1854), a most significant figure in Catholicism who sought in a parlous time to combine firm adherence to Catholicism with a liberal outlook in social, political and economic matters, lived well over two millemia after Mo-tzu. But the following statement by the church historian Vidler shows that Lammennais held views reminiscent of Mo-tzu:

"[Lammennais] pointed out that *les philosophes* admitted that the people needed religion to persuade them to those duties without the performance of which society would not hold together. Indeed their theory was that

[54] *City Life in Japan*, p. 328.

God and morality had been invented by governments for this very reason. Lammennais naturally made play with this fantasy, and also pressed the point that religion must be believed to be true if it is to provide the required sanction for order and morality. But *les philosophes,* while they admitted the necessity of religion, were engaged in disseminating proofs of its falsehood. They were therefore involved in a hopeless contradiction and they should think again."[55]

This has evident enough implications for our present themes and at this point it is no longer needful to elaborate them. Let us here simply remark some scattered historical instances in which the ancient insight that religion exercises significant social functions is accompanied by the disposition to exploit those functions in some sense and in which we are consequently close to an instrumental orientation toward religion. Dansette quotes Voltaire's cynical comment, "I like my attorney, my tailor, my servants and my wife to believe in God because I can then expect to find myself less often robbed and less often cuckolded."[56] Dansette also notes that Napoleon held the view that religion must be reckoned along with money, honors, and fear of punishment or death as something close to the springs of human action. The people needed religion, Buonaparte was persuaded, and he was persuaded as well that their religion had to be governmentally controlled. In this conception, religion was an instrumentality of the law. The state had at its disposal the force represented by religion, "which bridled men's instincts and influenced their intentions," and the force represented by the police, which punished where religion did not effectively restrain.[57] Cross reports that Mark Hanna was supposed to have viewed the Supreme Court and the Roman Catholic Church as the sole safeguards against American anarchy, as he remarks that William Howard Taft in a similar spirit averred that Catholicism was "one of the bulwarks against socialism and anarchy in this country, and I welcome its presence here."[58] And Baltzell observes that the railroad baron, James Hill, a Protestant who donated a large sum to establish a Catholic theological seminary, answered a query as to why he did this with the words, "Look at the millions of foreigners pouring into this country for whom the Catholic Church represents the only authority they fear or respect."[59] In these views of Hanna's, Taft's and Hill's, we are close

---

[55] Alec R. Vidler, *Prophecy and Papacy,* New York: Scribner's 1954, p. 75.

[56] Adrien Dansette, *Religious History of Modern France,* New York: Herder and Herder, 1961, Vol. 1, p. 265.

[57] *Ibid.,* p. 142.

[58] R. D. Cross, *The Emergence of Liberal Catholicism in America,* Cambridge: Harvard University Press, 1958, p. 35.

[59] E. Digby Baltzell, *Philadelphia Gentlemen,* Glencoe: The Free Press, 1958, p. 224.

indeed to instrumental outlooks on religion. (Of course, the mere *observation* that religion can exercise control functions is in itself "innocent" and does not necessarily imply an instrumental orientation.)

There are three points we would indicate terminally, having to do with relations of religion, magic and instrumentalization; with ambiguities in the term, instrumentalization; with the "future" of instrumentalization.

First, then, we may note what we regard as a fruitful way in which religion, magic and instrumentalization can be conceived to relate to one another, giving a special turn to things already said. There is more than one way in which magic can be defined, or, alternatively, there are various types of magic. The "for God"—"for man" tension, however, obviously suggests that religion and magic may be considered to blend into one another. When the "for God" element in religion recedes into the background and men's own needs are clamorously to the fore and when various manipulative techniques come into play (such as using the name of a spiritually exalted figure to obtain power over that figure for one's own practical purposes), we shall, accordingly, now say that we have to do with magic. Magic as here understood, however, arises in a cultural situation where there is at least some "high-level" comprehension of what a "for God" orientation means. In other words, magic, as we wish to define it, refers to a potentiality in an entire "religiomagical" complex. When the emphasis within the complex moves toward the "for God," nontechnique and nonmanipulative side, there is movement toward "religion" rather than toward "magic." Again, this is not the only possible way to define magic (or there are other types of magic) and it leaves out phenomena that might in other perspectives be legitimately labeled magical. Thus, it does not pretend to deal with "primitive" magic, or cases where there is no cultural background of a so-called high religion. Instrumentalization (in a *self*-referring sense, as when one seeks to utilize prayer to attain peace of mind) is an enterprise in magic that of course (since it is "magic" in our sense to which we refer) comes within a high-religion cultural context and that very strongly seeks to exploit "religious" resources (such as belief in high, ethically elevated divinities).

Second, we may reaffirm the utility of the term, instrumentalization. But to recognize that utility it is not necessary to overlook the point that the term suggests certain ambiguities. Given the use that has been made of the term here, it is easy—perhaps too easy—to associate it with what may strike many as undesirable phenomena in the field of religion. But this could be a misleading association. One might conceivably argue that there is an element of instrumentalization in giving movements of social reform a religious backing, as it could be contended that ministers and rabbis who publicly support the civil rights movement and engage in certain demonstrations "use" their religion to further reform. No doubt, quite a few who would be content to let pass what might appear to be a hint of the pejorative in the application of the term, instrumentalization, to inspirational religious literature would resist any such hint in relation to the "application" of religion to the uses of enhancement of Negro rights. On the other hand, the men of religion committed to furthering reform and their followers might for their part argue that they were merely "realizing" or "acting out" their religion and that the employment of the term instrumentalization in relation to their activity was completely inept. Once again, to complicate matters, some persons might take the position that it is indeed a "use" of religion to employ it to further reform, that this is a decidely better and more justifiable use than some others, but that it is still a use and therefore subject to criticism in the light of ultimate religious values. We need not go further into the problems hereby suggested. It suffices to suggest them, but they are unavoidable and they are important.

Finally: it may be that a growing skepticism and an increasing secularization—understood in the sense of releasing more and more of the "world" from the presumption that one has to do with the sacred, as when problems of sickness once within the sacred orbit come to be handled in nonreligious and nonmagical ways—it may be that skepticism and secularization will ultimately make some of the religious phenomena touched upon in this chapter effectively obsolete. But as long as something on the order of "religion" continues to exist at all, it will inevitably continue to have psychological effects and social functions of some sort. If these appear desirable to particular persons and groups, the impulse to *make* religion bring them about, to make religion "useful" will presumably be hard to eliminate altogether. Whatever ambiguities the term instrumentalization conceals, the substantial sociological and psychological issues the term suggests, which we have sought to delineate, will remain, and sociologists of religion, if any there be, will be constrained to try to understand them.

PART **V**

Religion and Society

CHAPTER 8

Some Features of Religious Organizations

Culture and society interact in particularly interesting ways in organizations. Religious ideas and values do often inevitably find organizational loci and, as they do so, afford some of the most important problems considered in the sociology of religion. The present chapter will then be particularly concentrated upon religion *in* society (although this concentration involves a carrying on of interests that have of course been evident previously). The chapter will first offer a general perspective on religion and organization, then will examine particular forms of organization—church, sect, denomination (about which there is currently much controversy but which have nevertheless been of central interest up to now). Finally, I shall devote considerable attention to a mode of functioning in sects in particular that is likely to occur where there is an environment of some toleration for them.

Social organization, on the one hand, and the holy or sacred, on the other, do not always easily blend or fit with one another. Relevant phenomena may be noted in the most distant places. Obeyesekere discusses a forest hermitage in Ceylon where virtuous monks had come to live in caves and meditate. Their fame spread and they were soon no longer isolated. Laymen from all Ceylon wished to come to give them alms. A local committee finally had to be formed to coordinate arrangements for the alms; and, increasingly, "the world intruded into the isolation of the hermitage." Nor could those monks escaping to a renewed greater solitude hope for more than temporary respite.[1] They would again be accorded fame and be unable quite to escape laymen. Being available to laymen, they transmit a holiness supposed to be very useful to the latter. But their very state of availability reduces their holiness. Their contact with laymen will make them "profane."

[1] Obeyesekere, in Leach, ed., *Dialectic in Practical Religion*, p. 37.

Numerous sociologists have noted rather similar things. Thus, Sorokin observes: "As soon as . . . Asectic imitators attract the attention of other men, they begin to acquire followers. As the number of followers increases, an organization appears; and with it the pure ascetic attitude—the attitude of complete indifference toward, and non-interference in, the affairs of the empirical world—becomes impossible."[2] *Whom* does the fact of organization "corrupt"—the asectics or monks or those who would follow them or profit from their religious virtue, or both? *How* does organization "corrupt?" Does it make administration or involvement in worldly things too attractive in itself or does it bring rewards that constitute temptations to the reduction of religious virtue? Such questions merely point to some of the interesting problems that arise in this context. But the context itself is important.

Men constantly try to build some kind of organizational "home" for religious messages and impulses. They try to come to terms with what they conceive of as the sacred in ways such that they can interact around and about it and understand and accept it and make it in some fashion operative among them. But the very effort to do this will constantly generate dissatisfactions. One sociologist, O'Dea, has set out a number of dilemmas for religious organizations as religion in fact finds its place in organization and is accepted and carried on by men—dilemmas in the "institutionalization" of religion. As religion becomes organized, specific statuses and offices and roles are set up which bring a variety of rewards, including worldly ones, which tend to become very important for some. An original "purity" of motive tends to be less prevalent after an initial so-called charismatic or extraordinary period.[3] Organization harnesses a variety of men's interests and reinforces their motivations just because it makes it "worth while" *both* spiritually and otherwise to carry out their assigned tasks. But this carries with it a danger that the "material" and "worldly" will come to prevail. In Christian history, the higher clergy in particular became powerful in virtue of their church offices and outside the church itself and were natural allies of those who were wealthy and ruled within the larger society.[4] Once again social organization somehow appears to threaten the religion it in a sense harnesses and organizes.

O'Dea presents a number of additional dilemmas in the institutionaliza-

---

[2] Pitirim A. Sorokin, *Social and Cultural Dynamics*, Vol. 1, p. 135.

[3] The reader may be reminded of Weber's statement that charisma refers to "supernatural, superhuman, or at least specifically exceptional powers or qualities" of an individual—powers or qualities "regarded as of divine origin or as exemplary." Weber, *The Theory of Social and Economic Organization*, New York: Oxford University Press, 1947, pp. 358–359.

[4] Cf. O'Dea, *Sociology of Religion*, p. 91.

tion of religion. Something, at least, of what he and others have suggested within this field may be put as follows. Once a religion such as, say, the Christian religion is organized or institutionalized, critical reactions to it are very apt to arise. Critics will say that the charismatic founder of the religion, extraordinarily endowed as he was and possessed as he was of a special, quickening sense of the divine, would never have tolerated the rigidity now observable, on the lines of such things as mechanical worship of images and refusal to turn to the fresh springs of scriptures and even red tape or a blasphemous bureaucratization. The founder would surely have wanted less formal leadership. He would have wanted more democracy. The Molokans, religious kin of the Doukhobors (who are better known because of the intransigence of that important group among them referred to as the Sons of Freedom) dissented from Greek Orthodoxy nearly three centuries ago, and some thousands of them came to California early in the present century. There they were studied over a generation ago by Pauline Young, who reported that Molokans would say: "The only prelate in our midst is Jesus; all others are brothers. Our only teacher is the scriptures, and our guide is God." The founder, again, would have been open to all, including the weary and the heavy-laden and the lowly. Did he not say that it would be harder for a camel to pass through the eye of a needle than for a rich man to enter into the kingdom of heaven? Clearly, the organized church is now too much dedicated to the exalted and proud. Molokan elders, according to Young, would aver: "When Christ needed help, he called neither for the merchants, traders, nor professional men. He called for the humble people—the farmers, the fishermen, and all those unpolluted by commerce."[5]

Where there is indeed a critical sentiment that conventionally established churches have abandoned original ideals, elaborated unnecessary and inept organizational forms, fixed and celebrated injustice, reared proud princes of the church and exalted an existing society and its dominant groups and persons, it is not easy to adopt a "rational" attitude toward a variety of organizational problems. One may be critical and feel that the religious spirit does in some sense resist a social organization of statuses and offices and roles and yet contend that this produces a tension with which men must live and which they must mitigate as best they can by way of a constant readiness to reform and reconsider. It may further be felt that it is of no special use to make officers and administrative functionaries objects of scorn and hostility, since they perform tasks that have to be performed on pain of anarchy and organizational failure to achieve any-

---

[5] The Molokan statements are taken from Pauline Young, *The Pilgrims of Russian Town*, Chicago: University of Chicago Press, 1932, pp. 37, 83.

thing, even if the officers and functionaries admittedly do not always manifest high morality or unexceptionable piety. It may even be recognized that the problems of religious organization are not entirely unique; that in the educational enterprise, too, for example, analogous problems arise, as when intellectual endeavor and aspiration must seek a home in an environment of academic organization, where administrators also can readily become objects of negative affect. (Here is one of numerous and important points of contact between the sociology of religion and the wider field of sociology at large.) But powerful sentiments often sweep away reservations that all this may suggest.

Organizational problems and dilemmas, in any case, are always with or upon organizations.[6] It is one of the consistent emphases of the sociological literature on sects that schismatic sects are likely in time to face many of the same problems to which they originally reacted by separation, because of the development of their own organizational forms—which may occasion new separations.

The above represent some necessary sociological observations. They do not blunt the incontrovertible facts that if terms such as injustice and subservience-to-the-powers-that-be mean anything whatever in human discourse, religions and churches have repeatedly engaged in conduct that warrants the use of such terms. Thus, in Tsarist Russia there prevailed for a long time great subservience of the orthodox priesthood to the state. The clergy often performed the functions of police inspectors. This was, we may note not incidentally, a factor of importance in the rise of the dissent or schism, the Raskol, in the seventeenth century, the adherents of which in 1917, it has been suggested, must have approached at least twenty-five million.[7] But it is important to note now that interest in organizational forms in the sociology of religion has not only been directed to broad organizational problems but also to efforts to distinguish types of organizations. The work on organizational problems, to be sure, has afforded nourishment to these latter efforts, as these efforts in turn have affected the sense of organizational problems.

The distinction between church and sect has been much to the fore in the sociological literature. One of the most influential statements of the distinction has been that of Ernst Troeltsch.[8] Troeltsch's work has sustained a view of the sect as an organization that maintains a radical

---

[6] See the Study of Paul M. Harrison, *Authority and Power in the Free Church Tradition,* Princeton: Princeton University Press, 1959.

[7] See F. C. Conybeare, *Russian Dissenters,* passim; for the numbers of the Raskol, p. 249.

[8] See Troeltsch, *The Social Teaching of the Christian Churches,* vol. 1, pp. 331–343.

Christian ideal, insisting on the rigorous ethic of the Sermon on the Mount; that is disposed not to compromise with worldly and ecclesiastical authorities and is frequently hostile to them; that relies on an individualized form of access to the divine and of attainment of good standing with the divine rather than on formalized means of grace safely consolidated in, and in the keeping of, an established ecclesiastical organization; that makes a point of having a membership that is voluntary rather than by birth. The contrast-conception of the church is one of an organization that considerably abates the rigors of the Sermon on the Mount in its expectations of ordinary men, makes compromises with the world, and so on. It has become usual to employ the term, denomination, in close connection with these two, and it usually refers, briefly, to a sect that has made its compromises with the world and taken its place with other similar entities as an "accommodated" organization, in a situation where the exclusive dominance of one overall religion is not feasible. Numerous sects turn quickly into denominations; others develop into "established" sectarians forms, whose sectarian traits persist.[9]

There have been interesting endeavors to distinguish types of sects, as when militant-oppositionist sects active in antagonism to the world are contrasted with passive sects that withdraw from the world; or as when rigoristic sects that require strictly correct morality are contrasted with antinomian sects that encourage moral laxness;[10] or indeed as when established, enduring sects are contrasted, as above indicated, with impermanent ones that soon become denominations. One of the best known classifications is that of Bryan Wilson who proposes that we may usefully distinguish conversionist sects, with an evangelistic bias, typically fundamentalist or pentecostalist; adventist sects, typified by stress on the Bible and on

---

[9] See J. Milton Yinger, *Religion, Society and the Individual*, New York: Macmillan, 1957, pp. 150–151. Yinger suggests that the sects that turn into denominations are those that have an original preoccupation with individual anxiety and sin, whereas those turn into established sects that have an original preoccupation with social justice.

[10] Cf. Stark, *Sociology of Religion*, Vol. 2, p. 184 *ff.* and *ibid.*, Ch. 2, for other distinctions. The phenomenon of antinomianism (which may be briefly defined as the doctrine that faith frees one from obligation to moral law), incidentally, has been of considerable importance in religion and has great psychological and sociological interest. It may be found in historical and comparative contexts that are far removed from one another. For American Christianity, relevant material may be found, for example, in Edwin A. Gaustad's *The Great Awakening in New England*, New York: Harper's, 1957 and Wilbur R. Cross's *The Burned-Over District*, Ithaca: Cornell University Press, 1950. For an interesting instance of the kind of theological dispute to which concern about antinomianism can give rise, see John Cunningham, *The Church History of Scotland*, Edinburgh: James Thin, 1882, **2**, pp. 247–256.

Christ's second coming; introversionist sects, tending to rely on inner illumination of the spirit; gnostic sects, which offer a special knowledge adaptable to the attainment of conventionally valued worldly goods.[11] Wilson indicates that the basis of his classification is a characterization of types of missions that sects exhibit. There are clearly other possible bases of classification. The distinction between church and sect as it has come from Troeltsch and as it has been modified by others and the efforts to set out schemes of types of sects have met with considerable dissatisfaction. There are unquestionably difficulties here. The field is marked by less than ideal clarity and rigor.[12]

One of the more interesting recent criticisms of the dichotomy of church and sect is made by Werner Stark, whose work will serve as an instance of dissatisfaction with the state of typological work in the field. Stark wishes to abandon the simple church-sect dichotomy and introduce a threefold scheme of what he calls established religion, sectarianism and the universal church. An established religion he thinks of as absorbed in and fused with a social system. Within such a religion sacred and secular become one; established religion moves toward deification of ruler or nation or mission. Much of Stark's sense both of established religion and of sectarianism is rendered by his statement that the sectarian is opposed to the official establishment because he is "appalled . . . that the mantle of religion should have been thrown over the sores of society, that a supposedly godly church should have allied herself with an unmistakably devilish world."[13] The sect, as might be inferred, is seen by Stark as an organization in revolt against an existing social system which downgrades the sectarian, as it may for instance downgrade his social status. Finally, the universal church does not identify with or divinize any particular state or society. It aims to take in the whole human world, beyond the boundaries of any state or country, and might accordingly be said to be horizontally universal; and since it also aspires to take in all classes of people it might be said to be vertically universal. It does not confine

---

[11] Bryan R. Wilson, "An Analysis of Sect Development," *American Sociological Review*, Vol. 24, February 1959, pp. 3–15. (Another well known classification is presented by Yinger, *op. cit.*, pp. 150–151.) One might quarrel with Wilson's placement of gnostic "groups" within the sect category. But, in any case, New Thought, as Wilson is quite aware, affords a good example of the gnostic mode. Charles S. Braden's *Spirits in Rebellion*, again, is helpful on New Thought.

[12] See the several papers on reappraisal of the church-sect typology in *Journal for the Scientific Study of Religion*, Vol. 6, Spring, 1967, pp. 64–90. (The valuable paper on "Church-Sect Typology and Organizational Precarciousness," by John A. Coleman, in *Sociological Analysis* **29**, Summer, 1968, pp. 55–66, became available too late to allow the full utilization it merits.)

[13] Stark, *The Sociology of Religion*, Vol. 2, pp. 68–69.

itself to the comfortably accommodated, sleek and well to do, à la establishment religion, and it does not confine itself to the lowly and humiliated, à la sectarian religion.[14]

Catholicism and Calvinism, the former in particular, have authentically pursued the ideal of the universal church, for Stark, who thinks they have been notably different from other churchly or ecclesiastical forms. But there have clearly been important strains *away* from the universal bias within the Catholic church; and we believe that Stark exaggerates the degree of worship of actual rulers or nations or missions that he has found in some of the cases that he characterizes as cases of establishment. There is still some point in distinguishing establishment *tendency* from universal *tendency*. But it is clear in any event that Stark does not quarrel with the distinction of sect from church. The second volume of his *Sociology of Religion* is on sectarian religion and draws on a number of authorities usually drawn upon in sociological studies of the sect phenomenon.

We continue to need *some such* terms as church, sect and denomination, whatever revisions may have to be made of them. Sect stands in rough contrast with church (or, à la Stark, with established religion and with universal church). The denomination can still be regarded as a halfway house, a sect on its way to becoming "accommodated" to existing social circumstances, or established, in Stark's sense. The sect itself is a religious group apart, conceived by itself as apart and so conceived by others, marked either by active hostility to the society in which it finds itself and to the central political establishment of that society—the state—or at least by indifference to these phenomena;[15] and it has no love for what Stark calls established religion.

These indications of the meanings of essential terms are certainly not conclusive. We may soon be struggling toward much more sensitive typologies in this field, involving analytical and empirical work at a level not yet reached. There is considerable awareness that no scientifically ambitious formulation in the field will ultimately be able to avoid close comparison of sect phenomena in the Western world with what appear to be rather cognate phenomena in such religions as Buddhism and Islam.

[14] See Stark, *The Sociology of Religion,* Vol. 3, p. 27. Note also Yinger, *op. cit.,* p. 148, on the universal church.

[15] See Wilson, *loc. cit.,* p. 4. Wilson writes that the sect is "hostile or indifferent to the secular society and to the state." Stark, *op. cit.,* Vol. 2, *passim,* strongly emphasizes sectarian hostility. Wilson affords a concise, representative listing of sect characteristics, including, among others, the voluntary nature of the sect association, emphasis on exclusiveness, self-conception as an elite, some presumption of the priesthood of all believers, a high level of lay participation, and the aforementioned hostility or indifference.

Schism among the Jains of India may prove as important for purposes of analysis as schism among groups much closer to home.[16] Sects as they have been more or less ordinarily understood in the West also need comparison with various modern messianic cults, such as those covered in Lanternari's wide-ranging popular survey.[17] In what follows, we shall be concerned with certain features of selected sectarian phenomena and our limited enterprise does not depend heavily upon the logic of the discriminations in the field we have been discussing.[18] But it is well to note the eminently "unfinished" character that the field exhibits.

Sects perform a variety of functions. We are especially concerned, however, with their functions in the way of effecting upward social mobility for their members and incorporating those members into a larger society, thereby "civil-izing" them or "including" them (to use a term that T. H. Marshall and Talcott Parsons have made familiar). Not all sects perform such functions. The best reading of the evidence is that such functions are more readily performed where sects exist in a relatively tolerant environment. Thus, it is to be expected that sects would perform such functions in a country like the United States, where pressure toward conformity is at a minimum and an official church establishment is lacking.[19] On

[16] Cf. Helmuth von Glasenapp, *Der Jainismus*, Georg Olds: Hildesheim, 1964, particularly pp. 346–357.

[17] Victorio Lanternari, *The Religions of the Oppressed*, New York: Alfred A. Knopf, 1963.

[18] Our enterprise also cannot give adequate consideration to other matters not touched upon in the text that may be allowed a word here. Thus, there are problems as to why sects in particular will develop under given circumstances. Stark suggests that the rejection of the social environment and spirit of revolt that he believes the sect exhibits will sometimes express themselves in specifically "metaphysical-religious" and sometimes in "physical-practical-political" terms, in the form of a religious sect proper or in the form of a political party. He further suggests that where reform is a distinct possibility a political party will emerge and that where reform is not feasible a sect will emerge. *Op. cit.*, Vol. 2, p. 51 *ff*. There seems to be some warrant for associating political and religious extremism. Lipset has suggested an affinity between the two. See Seymour M. Lipset, *Political Man*, Garden City, N.Y.: Doubleday, 1960, pp. 107–108. Clark notes that the sects of the poor who feel alienated from other elements in the community may have affinity with various non-religious movements engaged in by monetary cranks, political rebels, vigilante leaders and medical quacks. See S. D. Clark, *Church and Sect in Canada*, Toronto: University of Toronto Press, 1948, pp. 433–434. One may think in terms of a kind of logic of narrowing determination, in which, within a given sociocultural context, there is increasing likelihood that a certain particular sort of social movement will come into being. (For an exposition of this kind of logic, see Neil J. Smelser, *Theory of Collective Behavior*.) In this framework, some delicate questions may well arise as to whether at particular conjunctures religious-sectarian movements or more secular, more "political" movements will emerge. That we must turn away from these problems clearly does not make them unimportant.

[19] For appropriate background argument, see Stark, *op. cit.*, Vol. 2.

the other hand, where sects emerge in a country such as Tsarist Russia, sect functions would have to do more especially with things achieved through membership in the sect itself—on the line of emphatic repudiation of official church and society and of exaltation of the "lowly" members of the sect. If in what follows the representation of sectarianism should seem "optimistic," it must be remembered that the representation is deliberately a limited one. We concentrate on sect functions of the first type and there is a sufficiency of challenging problems in the material to which we confine ourselves.

The Methodist movement in England exhibits features that have a special interest for us. Sociologists have definitely tended to regard Methodism as a sectarian movement or at least as a movement showing marked sectarian features.[20] The historian, Lecky, remarks in his history of eighteenth-century England that early in that century "a large proportion of the poor lay almost wholly beyond the range of religious ordinances."[21] Methodism reached out to these people beyond the range Lecky writes of. According to Lecky, it was the Methodist leader, George Whitefield, who instituted field-preaching—preaching where the people were in their own haunts, not in the church. Field-preaching brought the evangelical Methodist doctrines (again in words of Lecky's that virtually repeat what he had already said) "before vast multitudes who had scarcely before come into contact with religion." With the establishment of lay preaching (in 1741), Lecky notes, "Methodism became in a great degree independent of the Established Church." And Methodist chapels were created in 1739, these being "intended not to oppose or replace, but to be supplemental and ancillary to, the churches, and to secure that the doctrine of the new birth should be faithfully taught to the people."[22] The "democratic" or "people-reaching" thrust of all this seems evident.

[20] Note, e.g., Stark, *op. cit.*, Vol. 2, p. 24, who writes of Wesleyanism, the major element within Methodism, that it "attracted and embraced the indigent and is thus the sectarian movement of the eighteenth century par excellence." Cf. also Earl D. C. Brewer, "Sect and Church in Methodism," *Social Forces,* Vol. 30, 1952, pp. 400–408.

[21] On the sheer circumstance that the Church of England at the end of the eighteenth century provided inadequate seating accommodations for the population, see Robert F. Wearmouth, *Methodism and the Common People of the Eighteenth Century,* London: Epworth, 1945, pp. 184–185.

[22] The quoted matter is from W. E. H. Lecky, *A History of England in the Eighteenth Century,* New York: D. Appleton and Co., 1879, Vol. 2, pp. 579, 611, 627. It is pertinent again that Lecky writes of Whitefield (and with reference to the colliers of Kingswood) that "he was filled with horror and compassion at finding in the heart of a Christian country, and in the immediate neighborhood of a great city [the reference is to Bristol—L.S.] a population of many thousands, sunk in the most brutal ignorance and vice, and entirely excluded from the ordinances of religion." *Ibid.*, p. 711.

Methodism soon enough dropped sectarian traits and became more of a denomination than a sect. Lecky could already write that it had "long since taken its position as pre-eminently and almost exclusively the religion of the *middle* and lower classes of society."[23] Its reaching into lower strata outside "the ordinances of religion" lasted but a relatively short time. And this could be amply and widely documented. Clark notes of the Wesleyan Methodist Church in Canada that "in becoming increasingly the church of the successful classes in the community it had ceased to serve the needs of the unsuccessful." Newer Methodist sects became "movements of the dispossessed."[24] And a new outreach was thereby effected.[25]

But let us now mark in some detail how the functions of civil-izing or imbuing with the norms of middle-class society, incorporation or including or "taking into" the middle-class society, and effecting upward mobility were carried out. Robert Wearmouth is one of the writers on Methodism who has in effect given considerable stress to the functions suggested. Like a good many others, Wearmouth noted that "Methodism gained its greatest successes amongst the socially distressed and ostracized, among the laboring masses."[26] Again we are reminded that Methodism travelled well down into the strata of the society of its time. Wearmouth writes that in response to Wesley and his preachers "thousands of poor folk pledged themselves to a life of abstinence from every form of evil and dedicated themselves to good works." Many persons in the Methodist societies had apparently been won away from "drunken and criminal ways."[27] One of the rules of the Strangers' Friend Society, established by the Methodists at Hull before the end of the eighteenth century, required visitors "to recommend to the poor attendance on divine worship;

[23] *Ibid.,* p. 696; italics supplied.

[24] S. D. Clark, *Church and Sect in Canada,* p. 317.

[25] A new outreach in Canada was also effected not long ago by the Salvation Army, the first Canadian branch of which was organized in London, Ontario, in 1883. The Army developed as "the poor man's church." It ministered to outcasts, drunkards, ex-criminals and prostitutes and offered a simple gospel message. It grew, Clark notes, with all the enthusiasm of a new religious sect. But by 1914, within a single generation, it had changed considerably. It had ceased to be a movement of the urban social masses. "Where the typical salvationist had been a reformed drunkard, ex-criminal, or ex-prostitute, he now became a person of some social standing with a particular competence as a religious teacher and social welfare worker." See Clark, *op. cit.,* pp. 378, 421, 429. The Army in Canada, then, also ran quickly through something like a sect-to-denomination change, and this is important, but we stress its initial thrust toward taking in elements of Canadian society previously excluded from the "ordinances of religion."

[26] Robert F. Wearmouth, *op. cit.,* p. 263.

[27] *Ibid.,* p. 166.

industry, economy, cleanliness, white-washing the walls of their homes, and the admission of fresh air."[28] Methodist travelling preachers were "commanded," Wearmouth observes, to preach against "Sabbath-breaking, dram-drinking, evil speaking, unprofitable conversation, lightness, expensiveness or gaiety of apparel and contracting debts without due care to discharge them."[29] Methodism brought a measure of education to miners in England. It gave their children some schooling, and the miners themselves at times accompanied the children. Indeed, there were miners who went to chapel, found it "necessary to appear decent there" and obtained new clothes and "became what is termed respectable." Guns and dogs and fighting cocks were discouraged by the Methodists, but not such things as hymns rather than public house ditties or prayer-meetings rather than "pay-night frolics." Methodists even "drove into the minds of the naturally improvident race that extravagance was in itself a sin."[30]

Sobriety, refraining from violence, responsibility in economic matters, industry, frugality, restraint, cleanliness—these "bourgeois" virtues, these attributes which, once possessed, would help to civil-ize or incorporate into the larger society and aid in upward social mobility were strongly encouraged by the Methodists. Moreover, Methodism extended to many of the poor and socially inexperienced a chance to learn something about organizational realities on the line of relating themselves to others under formal religious auspices.[31] Laymen could and did become class leaders, stewards, trustees, and local preachers, and had positions of some responsibility. The "bourgeois" training thus provided was apparently not negligible. "Poverty was no bar, no ban, to membership and to office."[32]

Wearmouth writes of "captains of industry" who grew up among the Methodists. Some of the things just reviewed might indeed have been

[28] *Ibid.,* p. 216. Wearmouth quotes the *Report of the Hull Strangers' Friend Society.*

[29] *Ibid.,* p. 246.

[30] See Wearmouth, *Methodism and the Working-Class Movements of England: 1800–1850,* London: Epworth Press, 1937, p. 226, and note the matter there quoted from studies of the miners of Northumberland and Durham. Trade union leaders apparently also learned from the Methodists something of "earnestness, sobriety, industry and regularity of conduct." Wearmouth, *ibid.,* apparently quoting from Sidney Webb's *The Story of the Durham Miners,* London, 1921. (Very likely there was in all this an element of principled anti-hedonism and repression. Its presence does not by any means eliminate the phenomena we note.) See also Horace F. Mathews, *Methodism and the Education of the People,* London: Epworth Press, 1949, p. 75 *ff.*

[31] Wearmouth makes the interesting suggestion that the Methodist organization may have had some significant effect on modern organizational forms in industry, commerce and finance. *Methodism and the Common People,* p. 178.

[32] *Ibid.,* p. 189.

expected to produce such men among them. It was hardly "Job and John Ridgway of Hanley" alone who "owed their business achievements to the training they got in the Methodist Society," as Wearmouth writes.[33] (We are inevitably reminded, broadly, of Max Weber on Protestantism.) John Wesley declared that it was legitimate for a man to gain all the money he could, although he must not do this to his own harm or to that of others and although Christian people must be in their guard against the use of money for self-indulgence.[34] If there can be little doubt that Methodism inculcated certain economic virtues, served to civil-ize or bourgeosify, to incorporate or include low-stratum elements into the larger community, to effect some measure of social mobility, it is somewhat ironic in this connection to reflect on the Marxian view that religion is the opium of the people. Much of the effect of movements such as Methodism is a this-worldly effect that helps to bring "the people" into enhanced participation in a larger community, raises their status, and improves their economic situation. Such a movement seems, in other words, to afford them this-worldly goods (whether this is intended or not) and, to put the matter conservatively, it is not obvious that it provides only an illusory distraction in ostensible compensation for lack of such goods.

It should not be inferred that Methodism originally represented a straightforward, powerful pro-working-class bias. That has not been the thesis of the above at all. Methodism was not a movement pointed toward a revolutionary reorganization of the social system. It was greatly concerned with the individual soul. John Wesley's own Toryism has been endlessly commented upon. There was a profoundly conservative strain in the movement which could and did take the form of antagonism to labor when the latter sought to redress grievances. On the other hand, non-Wesleyan Methodism (like that of the Primitive Methodists) could and did often show sympathy with and provide leadership for working class movements. The story is a complex, ambiguous one and one, moreover, that changes over time. But the functions of incorporation, civil-izing and mobility that we have noted remain. We must leave the matter at this, mentioning only as a last point that the mobilization of working-class motivation for the uses of a new industrial era that was aided by Methodism may well have been, as has been suggested for example by Walzer and Thompson, in a number of ways a most uncomfortable thing."[35]

Aside from the material we have reviewed, there is much more to support the thesis that it has been a crucial function of numerous sects

[33] *Ibid.,* p. 237.

[34] Cf. also Kathleen W. MacArthur, *The Economic Ethics of John Wesley,* New York: The Abingdon Press, 1935, pp. 78–79.

[35] Very interesting problems with regard to motivation and the psychology of the early industrial worker and his family, in the context of a major process of

in relatively tolerant environments to civil-ize and escalate their followers. Indeed, there is an embarrassment of riches on the point. The Holiness sects have been described in relevant terms by Benton Johnson in a seminal article with the significant title, "Do Holiness Sects Socialize in Dominant Values?"[36] But we must narrow our range. Sects feature many paradoxes. They can present opposition to an existing society and at the same time can subtly inculcate its values. They can ostensibly repudiate bourgeoisdom and at the same time at least in some measure sustain it. They can liquidate themselves via the consequences of some of their distinctive attributes—as, in line with Weberian thought, sects disposed to industry and frugality will often produce a wealth that reacts disintegratingly on those very things. Interesting paradoxes are presented by some of the American Negro sects, and we turn to these in an effort to understand certain of their distinctive features.

A generation ago, Arthur H. Fauset made a short but capable study of Negro religious cults of the urban north of the United States (specifically, in Philadelphia) which we may regard as sects with very little violence to Fauset's objects.[37] Fauset studied five sects (or cults) in particular. His findings are fascinating in detail. We wish to concentrate on only one feature of them, however. Near the conclusion of his study Fauset wrote: "The American Negro religious cult exercises rigid taboos over certain features of the private lives of its members, frequently reaching into the most intimate details of their lives. *Sex inhibitions are of paramount importance in most of the cult groups.*"[38] In describing a typical service of the Mt. Sinai Holy Church, Fauset noted that the preacher, a woman, made "constant reference to adultery, to the sin of looking upon one another with a lustful eye." Divorce, Fauset reported, was not allowed by this church. The marital status and sex relationships of prospective members had to be "rigidly scrutinized." And Fauset referred to "the rigidity of the sex rules." In the case of the Church of God (Black Jews) Fauset noted that "the usual holiness sins, fornication, adultery . . . are very much taboo." In the Father Divine Movement, in order to live "evangelically," one had to refrain from "lust after the oppo-

---

structural differentiation in which economic work was separated from the household, are intimated by Thompson's suggestive comment that (in the early industrial revolution in England) "the family was roughly torn apart each morning by the factory bell, and the mother who was also a wage-earner often felt herself to have the worst of both the domestic and the industrial worlds." *The Making of the English Working Class,* p. 416.

[36] In *Social Forces,* Vol. 39, 1961, pp. 309–316.

[37] See Fauset's *Black Gods of the Metropolis,* Philadelphia: University of Pennsylvania Press, 1944.

[38] *Ibid.,* p. 108; italics supplied.

site sex." Marriage was disallowed and hence there could be no divorce, and married couples entering the Movement automatically separated. Even dancing with members of the opposite sex was firmly forbidden.[39]

It may be suggested that this kind of attitude toward manifestations of interest in members of the opposite sex has profound sociological significance. Studies of sexual behavior in classes in the Negro community have repeatedly shown that by comparison with higher-stratum groups the Negro lower classes have definitely been "easy" in the area of sexual morality. Of the many documents that could be extensively drawn upon in this connection let us cite only Drake and Cayton's work on Negro Chicago. "Lower-class women don't expect much from their husbands in terms of . . . sexual fidelity." "The lower class, unlike the middle and upper, not only tolerates illegitimacy, but actually seems almost indifferent toward it." "The pursuit of 'pleasure'—direct and exciting—is a dominating feature of lower-class life"; and "pleasure" definitely includes a sexual dimension.[40] Closer to the present day, the Moynihan report has vividly documented the condition of the Negro family, with its "matrifocal" or matriarchal bias separating relatively vast numbers of lower-class Negroes from the familial experience of the American middle classes. (This should not be understood to suggest a "universal" condition of the Negro family.) It must suffice on the statistical side to refer to the single datum in the Moynihan report indicating that the nonwhite illegitimacy ratio (measured by number of illegitimate births per one thousand births) is eight times the white illegitimacy ratio.[41] This is a complex matter, certainly, but sexual controls and restrictions of certain well known kinds have historically been a very important aspect of middle class status in our society.

We would interpret the rigid sexual conservatism of the Negro cults reviewed by Fauset as an "effort" (emphatically *not* a conscious "effort") to inhibit Negro sexuality in conformity with the requirements for the achievement of social status. This construes the requirement of sexual restraint as cognate with historically rather common requirements of industry, frugality and the like, which, other things being equal, will help the sect member achieve a certain economic and social standing. These things

[39] *Ibid.*, pp. 17, 19, 39, 64, 66. Stark, *op. cit.*, Vol. 2, p. 197, deals briefly with repression of sex in the Father Divine movement, but, although he refers to the movement as "ascetic," does not give the interpretation that we do in the following.

[40] See St. Clair Drake and Horace R. Cayton, *Black Metropolis*, New York: Harcourt, Brace, 1945, pp. 586, 590, 608.

[41] From the Moynihan report as reproduced in Lee Rainwater and William Z. Yancey, *The Moynihan Report and the Politics of Controversy*, Cambridge, Mass.: The M. I. T. Press, 1967, p. 55.

together, it is suggested, fall into an *overall* pattern of gratification-defer-
ment that has been historically important in the rise of low-level social
strata.

But we cannot stop the story here. At least, relevant material from
the important sect of the Black Muslims must be added. Essien-Udom's
study of the Muslims "suggests rather strongly that upwardly mobile
lower-class Negroes join and remain" in the Muslim movement, and
Essien-Udom notes the Muslim encouragement "to practice and assimilate
habits that we associate with the middle class."[42] This is especially interesting because there can be no doubt of the powerful hostility to whites
and white American society that the Black Muslims have shown since
the time of their establishment about 1930. If we find here, too, the
seeds of a kind of "embourgeoisement," we have an impressive finding
indeed to support the notion that escalatory functions have played a very
important role in sect development (although it must be recalled that
we never claim that all sects perform such functions, nor, indeed, that
sects alone perform such functions!) It is instructive to turn to that remarkable document, the autobiography of Malcolm X, who was in his
time certainly a leading Muslim and a figure very much in the public
eye before his assassination. Malcolm shows in his autobiography that
he was most devoted to the Muslim cause. Some of the Black Muslim
hostility to American whites (and their ways toward Negroes) and toward
the religion of those whites is indicated in the following entirely typical
words that Malcolm would address to his listeners in the mid-nineteen-
fifties:

"Brothers and sisters, the white man has brainwashed us black people
to fasten our gaze upon a blond-haired, blue-eyed Jesus! We're worship-
ping a Jesus that doesn't even *look* like us! Oh, yes! Now just
bear with me, listen to the teachings of the Messenger of Allah, The
Honorable Elijah Muhammad. Now, just think of this. The blond-haired,
blue-eyed white man has taught you and me to worship a *white* Jesus,
and to shout and sing and pray to this God that's *his* God, the white
man's God. The white man has taught us to shout and sing and pray
until we *die,* to wait until death, for some dreamy heaven-in-the-here-after,
when we're *dead,* while this white man has his milk and honey in the
streets paved with golden dollars right here on this earth."[43]

Malcolm indicates that lying, cheating, gambling and smoking were very

[42] E. V. Essien-Udom, *Black Nationalism,* Chicago: University of Chicago Press,
1962, pp. 104, 105.
[43] *The Autobiography of Malcolm X,* New York: Grove Press, 1966, p. 220.
Copyright 1964 by Alex Haley and Malcolm X; copyright 1965 by Alex Haley and
Betty Shabazz.

much frowned upon by the Muslims and that the "moral crimes, such as fornication and adultery" were dealt with extremely severely. He reports: "In my twelve years as a Muslim minister, I had always taught so strongly on the moral issues that many Muslims accused me of being 'anti-woman'." If the officially strict Muslim attitude toward "moral" (meaning sexual) issues is unambiguously indicated by Malcolm, a more general middle-class aspiration is also very plainly documented. The Fruit of Islam, élite members of the Black Muslims, Malcolm asserts, expended time in lectures and discussions on such topics as "the importance of the father-male image in the strong household . . . . why honesty, and chastity, are vital in a person, a home, a community, a nation, and a civilization; why one should bathe at least once each twenty-four hours; business principles. . . ." The Black Muslim leader, Elijah Muhammed, "taught that idleness and laziness were among the black man's greatest sins against himself." It is entirely credible that Malcolm should say that in early years the Black Muslim converts were in considerable part from the "lowest" social levels, but, later, "gradually we recruited other black people—the 'good Christians' whom we fished from their churches." And once more, in the mid-nineteen-fifties, Malcolm reports, "we began . . . getting those with some education, both academic, and vocations and trades, and even with some position in the white world."[44]

Certainly something of the motivation of the Black Muslims in their "bourgeois" orientation is suggested by Malcolm's own view: "The white man *wants* black men to stay immoral, unclean and ignorant. As long as we stay in these conditions we will keep on begging him and he will control us."[45] The middle-class thrust of the Muslims is striking. For all their repudiation of whites and their ways they may be laying the foundations for an effective incorporation into general American society, and, if that society proves sufficiently willing to have large-scale Negro inclusion, the Muslims may well find themselves in a relatively advantageous

[44] *Ibid.*, pp. 288, 294, 227, 204, 262, 224.

[45] *Ibid.*, p. 221. Incidentally, the stress on *cleanliness* should be carefully remarked. Stark, *op. cit.*, Vol. 2, pp. 139–140, notices the general importance of cleanliness among sectarians. He sees it as a symbolic self-freeing by the sectarian of "the dirt of this world." Stark is much more concerned than the present writer with sects in countries with a developed state religion, where the "contracultural" features of sects are generally more marked than in a country like the United States. Given our preoccupation with sects that effect upward mobility and incorporation, the emphasis on cleanliness (as in the specific Black Muslim stress on bathing at least once every twenty-four hours) is perhaps best understood as one more manifestation of what might be caled the self-bourgeoisfying propensity of sects. Stages of sectarian development are also important, and sects will show differing degrees of hostility toward or acceptance of general cultural norms depending on what stage they are in, whether it be one of "hot" revolutionary beginnings or one of incipient "capitulation" to the larger society by way of "success."

position. Stark makes a particularly pregnant comment in this connection: "The sectarians remain tied to those whom they abhor. They are . . . different, yet not so different at the same time."[46]

In the sectarian effecting of upward social mobility, sects themselves may move upward or sectarians who have prospered can move out of their original sect homes and affiliate with more "respectable" or "better established" religious groups. In the processes of self-liquidation of sectarian groups, connected with upward social mobility, the classic paradigm, the central form, does appear to be afforded by the situation in which sect-reinforced ways of diligence and frugality create a wealth that by its temptations, irresistible to some, breaks down the sectarian opposition (or indifference) to the conventional world and its ways.

Finally, let me comment briefly on religion and stratification today, with special reference to the United States. The situation is one of considerably fluidity. Among the few apparently solid and reliable truths is the circumstance that members of lower classes are generally less likely to be church members or attend services of worship on Sundays[47] a circumstance that also holds well beyond the United States. Sects have arisen and changed. Distinctive denominational developments have occurred. Both these phenomena have been of importance in relation to stratification, as has the history of the immigration of various religious groups and as has the ethnic or national affiliation of the members of those groups. In the present day there are homogenizing forces at work (in the form, for example, of a generally diffused culture emanating from the mass media) that reduce sources of heterogeneity that were once operative. Differences in the class standings of religious groups remain, but they are shifting, and it is not at all always clear that they are exclusively due to religion. Jews enjoy a relatively very favorable situation with regard to education, occupation and income. Catholics appear to have been making gains by way of at least some catching up in these fields—of education, occupation, income—in recent years with Protestants. There are differences among Protestant denominations, with Episcopalians and Presbyterians ranking above Methodists and Lutherans and Baptists.[48] Where such groups as Negro Baptists are concerned, it is to be expected that overall ranking on education-occupation-income criteria will be very low.

---

[46] *Op. cit.,* Vol. 2, p. 137.

[47] Charles Y. Glock and Rodney Stark, *Religion and Society in Tension,* Chicago: Rand McNally, 1965, p. 187.

[48] See Bernard Lazerwitz, "Religion and Social Structure in the United States," in Louis Schneider, ed., *Religion, Culture, and Society,* pp. 426–439. See also Norval Glenn and Ruth Hyland, "Religious Preference and Worldly Success," *American Sociological Review,* February, 1967, pp. 73–85.

But, as intimated, circumstances other than religion are at least to some extent at work amid the shifting differences. A recent release of the Bureau of the Census, in a table specifying selected characteristics of persons fourteen years of age and over, by reported religion, for the United States civilian population in 1957, shows that 55.6% of white Protestants and 66.1% of nonwhite Protestants resided in urban areas, while 78.8% of Roman Catholics and 96.1% of Jews resided in such areas. Over a third of white and nearly sixty per cent of nonwhite Protestants resided in the South, while only 13.9% of Roman Catholics and 7.7% of Jews, respectively, did so.[49] These differences with respect to community and region of residence are bound to have some influence. Clearly, corrections or standardizations are needed to remove the effect of extraneous or nonreligious factors in the status or stratification situation of religious groups. (It may also be worthy of attention that as in the case of the Jews, traditional biases help to create peculiar population distributions in the first place). But it is abundantly clear that we are living amid considerable changes. It is possible that, in a relatively short time, status or stratification differences among religious groups will lose much of their current importance and that the connection of religion and class will become quite accidental. And it may even be that in a new time with new orientations, with its distinctive combination of affluence and poverty, with its continuing great problem of the relations of the white and Negro communities, sects will alter appreciably the historic functions they have performed.

[49] *Source:* Table 1 in *Tabulation of Data on the Social and Economic Characteristics of Major Religious Groups,* March, 1957, U.S. Dept. of Commerce, Bureau of the Census.

CHAPTER 9

*Drift in Religion and Society: Toward the Future**

Reference was made at the close of the previous chapter to "a new time with new orientations." It is quite evident that religion and society are today involved in significant change in much of the world and will change further in the future. The changes marked by efforts at *aggiornamento* in the Catholic Church may prove most important for Christianity and world religion as a whole—just as the very inconsistencies and hesitancies of the church on the matter of "updating" are important. Catholicism is, in any case, under tremendous strain and faced with mighty inner and outer challenges to its traditional stances at the present time. The civil rights struggle in America is important in a variety of ways for what we think of as "the three faiths" of Protestantism, Catholicism and Judaism (particularly since Herberg wrote on American religion), even if liberal clergymen are often profoundly dissatisfied with the character of the effects of the struggle upon the churches and disturbed about the opposition of conservative parishioners to reform. Winds of doctrine swirl about. Theological speculation is far from dead.

Sociologists among others inevitably speculate about the possible forms of religion in the future. Occasionally they and others believe they discern specific trends that yield clues to what at least some details of religion may be like in due course. In a recent report on changing ministries, the *New York Times* quoted one sociologist to the effect that the contemporary clergyman has great uncertainties about his role. New ministries

* This chapter was written before I encountered the suggestive article by Larry Shiner—"The Concept of Secularization in Empirical Research," *Journal for the Scientific Study of Religion* 6, Fall, 1967, pp. 207–220—and has been left in its original form. Some overlap is virtually unavoidable when writers independently touch on the same subject, but Shiner's article might well be consulted as an item that presents a number of considerations not taken up in the following pages yet pertinent to them.

may be emerging. There have been some signs in recent years that seminarians are turning away from the conventional jobs available for clergymen in serving parishioners and that the new ministries referrred to are being sought in social work, in medical services, and in the offering of clerical services in the unconventional contexts of shopping centers, coffeehouses, skiing resorts and other kinds of vacation spots.[1] These phenomena reflect social change; in a sense they constitute social change; they may well effect further change.

But it is not always easy to evaluate or interpret the change amidst which we live. It is useful in this connection to attend to some of the meanings that attach to that highly complex term, "secularization." In one meaning, secularization has reference to the loss of a certain "bewitched" quality of the world, to what is sometimes called desacralization. Those who sustain the notion that secularization in this sense has taken place as a long-time movement in human life will aver things such as the following. Entities of the type of sprites and leprechauns are more and more removed from the field of what men think they witness when they look about them.[2] The world is increasingly a "matter-of-fact," prosaic one. We go about the business of relating ourselves to nature, to work, to other men in a way that presumes that there are no special esoteric-supernatural forces operative *within* the world, at any rate, and in a way that makes very considerable use of human rationality—detachment, dispassion, clear analysis and the like. In line with this, science has become of tremendous scope and significance and reaches into human affairs in the most pervasive ways. Angels have long, long ceased to sing in the endocrines, which are securely within the province of biochemical analysis. A determinedly scientific outlook is much in evidence even in matters having to do with the emotions.

Secularization in this sense is a reality, without doubt. A long-time trend of the kind suggested is present. It is true that it does not have its own way exclusively. Various forms of magic still have their hold in the western world, as for instance Emile Pin found in his study of the working class in a parish of the city of Lyons.[3] It is difficult to tell by just how much this mitigates or qualifies the secularizing developments we have just indicated. The impact of secularization in our first sense is not the same for all strata even of western society. Possibly new forms of religion will prove significant in this whole connection. But we may nevertheless make the suggestion that secularization in the present sense represents a very potent force and will figure importantly in the pattern

[1] *New York Times,* Sunday, April 21, 1968, pp .1, 68.
[2] See Harvey Cox, *The Secular City,* p. 36.
[3] See Pin's *Pratique Religieuse et Classes Sociales,* pp. 401–402.

of the future throughout the world as well as in the West. Distinctive processes of "disenchantment" and rationalization need not sweep absolutely everything before them in order to have a powerful hold. There have been many who have seen in this a great threat to religion. Without question, there have been conflicts between religion and science and their hostile encounters have often had appreciable historical significance (although religion has also afforded some nourishment to science). But more significant in the present context is the circumstance that secularization as so far understood need not represent a threat to religion. Much of course depends upon how "religion" is understood. If a religion of sprites and leprechauns is meant, then obviously secularization represents a threat to it. But there is also a type of religion for which it has become securely established that religion is differentiated from endeavors of the kind represented by science. The two spheres or realms address themselves to different problems and the concern of religion with the sacred or ultimate involves a dimension to which science has no access. Even very sophisticated demarcations of religion and science may, it is true, still leave touchy problems but it has long been clear that there are strong trends in the direction of the differentiation indicated. There are senses of religion in which it may be conceived to "gain" from secularization in the meaning suggested.[4]

Secularization may also be understood, in the second place, in a manner which is bound up with social differentiation as that has been expounded by Parsons in particular. In Parsons' view of the social differentiation of the church, most especially as the "church" has developed on denominational lines in Protestantism in the United States, the church has become precisely a much more differentiated organization over a period of time covering some four centuries since the Reformation. Just as the family has done, the church in the Protestant denominational case, distinctively, has lost a variety of functions. It does not have the political power possessed by state-established churches. In the areas of industrial production, education and family relations it has also come to have decreasing formal influence. Again just as the family has done, the church, as Parsons sees matters, has "tended to come to exert influence increasingly through its 'moral' hold on individuals rather than through the more 'massive' societal means of exerting influence."[5]

All this raises a question about the possible "decline" of religion in contemporary society. Parsons has answered this substantially with the contention that there has been no decline. Treating the family and the

---

[4] See, for example, Cox, *op. cit.*

[5] Parsons, *Social Structure and Personality,* New York: The Free Press, 1964, p. 311.

church together as organizations that have undergone the differentiation indicated, he writes, again in the source from which we have just quoted:

"This differentiation does not, as is often contended, imply that either or both have lost most of their 'importance' in modern society. It means that the influence they do exert is not through organizational jurisdiction over certain aspects of life now structurally differentiated from them, but through the value-commitments and motivational commitments of individuals. In spheres outside their families and their churches, then, individuals have come to be by and large free of organizational control and in this sense to act *autonomously,* on their own responsibility. But this is by no means to say that their behavior in these "external" spheres is uninfluenced by their participation in the family and the church respectively."[6]

Parsons' view is based on a carefully reasoned theoretical position and it merits serious consideration. It does *not,* however, present evidence on a number of significant matters. There is a current of sociological opinion that suggests that, in a way, even if men were influenced in "external" spheres by church-derived religious standards this would be of doubtful importance. Thus, Wilson contends flatly that early in the era of industrialization businessmen depended on religion for social control to discipline and order the work force, and that, associated with this, there was a certain relevance or place for testimonials to a man's solid, industrially relevant qualities (punctuality, sobriety, thrift, and so on); whereas today such control is wholly irrelevant in a situation where the conveyer-belt effects whatever discipline is needed—and industry has thus "passed from internalized 'character' values to mechanical manipulation."[7] We would like to have more evidence than we do on points like these, and the evidence should be cross-national: numerous writers remark, for example, that there are differences in the way religion fares in the United States by comparison with European countries.[8]

[6] *Ibid.,* p. 307.

[7] Bryan R. Wilson, *Religion in Secular Society,* London: C. A. Watts and Company, 1966, pp. 47–48.

[8] See, e.g., Wilson, *op. cit.,* pp. 98, 223. It is true that many of the writers who point to pertinent differences between the United States and Europe will incline to contend that basically *both* the United States and Europe are still involved in "secularization." The United States is supposed to continue to have a kind of non-marginal, middle class adherence to the churches because it has accommodated church religion to the values of the "world and thereby secularized the churches. See, e.g., Wilson again, *op. cit.,* p. 98; Peter L. Berger, *The Sacred Canopy,* New York: Doubleday, 1967, p. 108; Thomas Luckmann, *The Invisible Religion,* New York: Macmillian, 1967, p. 36. See the remarks below on secularization in the third sense we give to the term.

It should be evident that secularization in the second sense carries no necessary implication of decline. The sheer differentiation Parsons points to is precisely differentiation. The question of decline remains open. If secularization in the first sense disenchants the world and in the second sense features a socio-structural differentiation, secularization in a third sense would cover phenomena previously suggested in our references to the tragedy of ideas. Where economic profit comes out of the traits grounded in religious values but then retroactively changes those values so that they become directly congenial to and in the end actually favor profits *as such* and thereby become "worldly" values—there we have an instance of secularization in our third sense, for religion gets transformed precisely in the direction of worldliness.

This third sense comprehends a decidedly different set of things from those comprehended in the first two senses. But once again the matter of evidence is important. We definitely do not doubt that there are significant phenomena of secularization in the third sense abroad in the religious world today. But there are also phenomena that point in quite different directions that suggest refreshment and renovation of relevant values (and, for the matter of that, they do not always stem from what are conventionally taken to be religious resources, although books of sermons alone will often yield pertinent evidence on them.) An overall assembling of evidence and assessment of its meaning, in this area, would be a great task even for decidedly less ambitious fields than are afforded by such entities as entire nations. We can only say that even achievements on a relatively modest scale might well be highly illuminating here.

A fourth sense of secularization has to do with a "process whereby religious thinking, practice and institutions lose social significance."[9] In the third sense, religion changes and becomes "denatured" as its values are transformed. But in the fourth sense, religion simply lapses or fails of social effect. We may remark that Parsons suggests that "in a whole variety of respects modern society is more in accord with Christian values than its forebears have been—this is, let it be noted, a relative difference; the millenium has not arrived."[10] There might conceivably be a considerable measure of truth in this assertion, while at the same time, the relevant role of Christianity might have become largely historical, or the "moralization" that Parsons notes might be compatible with loss of religious influence in other respects.[11] These are possibilities. The suggestions they carry

---

[9] Wilson, *op. cit.*, p. XIV.

[10] Parsons, in Edward Tiryakian, ed., *Sociological Theory, Values, and Sociocultural Change,* Glencoe: The Free Press, 1963, p. 65. Pitirim A. Sorokin's paper, "The Western Religion and Morality of Today," in *International Yearbook for the Sociology of Religion,* Vol. 2, Koln and Opladen: Westdeustcher Verlag, 1966, pp. 9–43, may be read as an interesting response to Parsons' view.

may be wrong. But emphatically they should not be lost from sight.

The uncertainties we confront in this whole area are well summarized by two sociologists who note that there are those who contend that we are already in a post-Christian age, involved in "the death throes of a doomed religion," while on the other hand there are those who profess to see in prospect a reinvigoration of religion and a renewal of its pertinence to the modern word.[12] The picture is surely not entirely clear. It would be foolishness to give up all reliance on relevant statistics. An array of important statistical evidence intended to suggest secularization in the fourth sense is presented by Wilson for England[13] (although the question of interpretation of the evidence remains an urgent one). Yet Wilson, although he clearly does not regard his concession as definitive, nevertheless concedes that "the ways in which men express their religiosity may be changing, and church attendance and ritual may be felt by some quite religiously disposed people to be outworn patterns unadapted to the modern world."[14] If we turn to America, it is of much interest that another sociologist has recently set side by side a number of selected findings bearing on religion and on politics, in a provocative comparison. Swanson, who does this, reminds us usefully that "in the absence of good longitudinal information we cannot be certain of the meaning of the statistics on religion," but he adds that "in the presence of comparable information from contemporary politics I believe that the religious data require our being cautious indeed concerning assertions of the present irrelevance of religion for the personal lives or institutional commitments of most Americans."[15]

This caution seems not wholly unreasonable. Swanson's collation of statistical data on such things as participation in and knowledge of religious and political life in America suggests that religion might possibly be in as good a state of "vitality" as the political system. Again we should ideally have better and finer data than we do. Stark and Glock note that Gallup interviewers recently found that "Americans overwhelmingly believe that religion is losing its influence in American life." But only a short time ago

---

[11] Also most interesting in relation to the view expressed by Parsons is the work of Stark and Glock suggesting a newer theological emphasis on social justice and the creation of a humane society—which emphasis, however, seems *not* to encourage the giving of money to the church or participation in its life: this being true for both Protestants and Catholics. See Rodney Stark and Charles Y. Glock, "Will Ethics be the Death of Christianity?" *Trans-action*, June, 1968, pp. 7–14.

[12] Stark and Glock, *loc. cit.*, p. 7.

[13] *Ibid.*, Ch. 2.

[14] *Ibid.*, p. 2.

[15] Compare Guy E. Swanson, "Modern Secularity," in Donald R. Cutler, ed., *The Religious Situation*, Boston: Beacon Press, 1968, at pp. 813–814

a heavy majority of Americans evidently believed that the churches were doing "a good or excellent job."[16] Changes may well be occurring with tremendous rapidity. Perhaps we should stress the need for caution anew when we make the obvious but pertinent observation that "what Americans believe" to be happening in religion is a significant datum and itself involved in what is happening but nevertheless a datum that may be in some indeterminate degree misleading with regard to what is in fact happening. The category of "Americans" is scarcely even equivalent to that of "sociologists," who are known to be capable of mistakes in matters of the kind under discussion.

It is insisted upon by some that secularism and secularization are different phenomena.[17] The insistence can be justified. But it need occasion no confusion if we suggest that, in a fifth sense of the term secularization, it refers to a development such that *secularism increases*. It is convenient again to quote Swanson:

"Secularism is the denial that a sacred order exists, the conviction that the universe is in no meaningful sense an expression or embodiment of purpose, the belief that it is unreasonable, other than anthropomorphically, to have toward the universe or its 'ground' a relationship mediated by communication or by any other interchange of meanings—to have toward it a relationship in any sense interpersonal. The clearest example is atheism. The more common approximation to secularism is intellectual agnosticism."[18]

Swanson observes that authentic secularism is rare in history generally and "probably uncommon today" and presents supporting data. He sees no evidence of an upward trend in secularism in America (and "regrets the absence of comparable data from other countries"). Indeed, the several studies he cites, done on college students in America, and yielding data from 1929 to 1958, suggest rather a downward trend in this regard.[19] Swanson notes that on the basis of studies done by James H. Leuba in 1914 and 1933 it appeared a majority of American scientists were unbelievers. But Leuba's questions were evidently defective, and in 1931, for over 1300 students at Syracuse University, Daniel Katz and Floyd Allport found that "only 21% exhibited a belief in God as that belief was defined by Leuba, despite the fact that at least 78% of these students

---

[16] Stark and Glock, *loc. cit.*, p. 8; Swanson, *loc. cit.*, p. 812, citing Hazel G. Erskine, "The Polls: Organized Religion," *Public Opinion Quarterly*, vol. 29, Summer, 1965, pp. 326–327.

[17] See Swanson, *loc. cit.*, pp. 801–804.

[18] *Ibid.*, pp. 803–804.

[19] *Loc. cit.*, p. 808.

had some meaningful belief in God."[20] In a recent study of over 600 American natural scientists based on data published in *American Men of Science* and on mailed questionnaires, Vaughan, Sjoberg and Smith found that few scientists could legitimately be labeled as traditional or orthodox in their religious orientations, but that still fewer could be considered outright nonreligious. Most showed a liberal or neo-orthodox kind of religious commitment. These numbered 52.4% of the sample and were one or two (but not all three) of the following: church members, regular attenders at church (at least twice monthly), believers in life after death.[21] Not all relevant studies are precisely comparable, and measures have not reached the highest degree of refinement.

The study just noted, by Vaughan and his associates, has a particular interest in that it indicates that some 60.9% of the questionnaire respondents in the sample studied conceived that science and religion were not in conflict but were separate realms, while 17.3% saw them as complementary. Only 13.6% viewed them as being in conflict. This has obvious pertinence to our previous statement that there is a type of religion for which it has become securely established that religion is differentiated from endeavors of the kind represented by science. Moreover, it again suggests the importance of the whole matter of "level" of belief. Stark and Glock, it may be recalled, note that only a minority of church members at present reject or doubt "the existence of some kind of personal God or the divinity of Jesus."[22] They note this, it is true, with the significant preface of the word "although" and go on to stress rejections of various items of faith. Yet the tenor of their article is such as to allow the possibility that abstract, "high-level" belief may still be quite important. It should be noted how high-level the definition above given of secularism is—secularism, in brief, is "the denial that a sacred order exists." Granted that some portion of high-level belief may be nearly empty or meaningless, we must still reaffirm a need for wariness with respect to secularism and its trends also.

It is of course to be hoped that studies yet to come will reveal less crudity than those now available, will rest on better methods and subtler theories than we presently have. But it is notable for now that, with respect to the future of religion, even such a student as Wilson, who seeks to convey a conviction of the reality of secularization in the fourth sense, remarks that "secular society has little direct regard for religion"

[20] *Loc. cit.*, p. 808.

[21] Ted R. Vaughan, Gideon Sjoberg and Douglas H. Smith, "The Religious Orientations of American Natural Scientists," *Social Forces*, Vol. 33, June, 1966, pp. 519–526.

[22] *Loc. cit.*, p. 8.

but immediately adds that "it would be too early to say that it functioned without it, or that it could ever do so." Stark and Glock, whose conviction that widespread doubt of various conventional Christian doctrines is a recent development has been remarked, say that they do not suggest that religion itself is due to perish. They aver that "as long as questions of ultimate meaning persist, and as long as the human spirit strives to transcend itself, the religious quest will continue," although they wonder whether forms in any sense specifically Christian will persist.[23] In this same connection it is of interest that Sabino Acquaviva put together a wide-ranging set of data on the "decline" of the holy or sacred in industrial society some few years ago. He was persuaded that the sacred was indeed in decline in industrial society, yet he was elaborately cautious in stressing that sure prognosis about man's religious destiny was impossible.[24] Whatever may happen to conventional religion and conventional religious beliefs, we have sufficiently suggested that the category of the religious has a larger scope than these, and some important developments may conceivably lie potential in unconventional forms, as well as in forms whose "religious" character has not yet been adequately explored.

We could scrutinize some of the relations to one another of the various kinds of secularization discriminated. Thus, we might expect that increase of secularism—secularization in sense five—would have a considerable effect in forwarding secularization in sense four. But some of these connections are fairly obvious and about others we are too much in the dark. It should not be thought that the five meanings that have been presented exhaust the possible senses of the term secularization. Another meaning of the term is indicated by the previously suggested process whereby in a modern society "control" comes to be exercised by *generic* religious beliefs or commitments.[25] Still another meaning is intimated by removal of an aura of the divine from human constructions or "institutions."[26] And the possibilities are not exhausted yet.

The tasks for analysis that this final chapter hints at are difficult. But

---

[23] Wilson, *op. cit.,* p. 233; Stark and Glock, *loc. cit.,* p. 14.

[24] Sabino S. Acquaviva, *Der Untergang des Heiligen in der Industriellen Gesellschaft,* Essen: Ludgerus-Verlag Hubert Wingen KG, 1964, Ch. 2 and p. 174. Something of Acquaviva's feeling about the chance that the sacred might again break through (as he thinks of the matter) is conveyed by his saying (p. 172) that "in the human psyche there remains, after all, an archetype which is always ready to bring religious feeling into consciousness again, whenever circumstances are propitious."

[25] See Ch. 4, above.

[26] Suggestive in regard to this are Eric Voegelin, Vol. 1 of *Order and History,* Baton Rouge: Louisiana State University Press, 1956; Peter Berger, *The Sacred Canopy;* and Werner Stark, *Sociology of Religion,* Vol. 1.

it seems likely that they will engage scholarly attention for an indefinite time to come. Social systems, presumably, will have to continue to perform pattern maintenance and integration functions and it seems a fair presumption also that religion will continue to make a contribution to the performance of these functions in particular. The problem of the character of "religion," however, has constantly obtruded itself upon us. "Religion," I would certainly suggest, does not necessarily have to suppose a highly elaborate supernatural order; nor need it disallow considerable variation in the inner range of "elements" that go to make it up. And any sensible conception of it must allow that it changes. It is in line with the sociologist's task to attend carefully both to what changes in it and what in it seems to have greater permanence.

Index